INSIDE THE DREAM

THE PERSONAL STORY OF

Walt Disney

Katherine and Richard Greene

Foreword by Diane Disney Miller

A ROUNDTABLE PRESS BOOK
NEW YORK

EDITIONS

We dedicate this book to our children,
Sandy and Ben.

For Disney Editions
EDITORIAL DIRECTOR: Wendy Lefkon
DESIGN DIRECTOR: Elliot Kreloff
SENIOR EDITOR: Sara Baysinger
ASSISTANT EDITOR: Jody Revenson

For Roundtable Press, Inc.
DIRECTORS: Susan E. Meyer, Marsha Melnick, Julie Merberg
DESIGN: Joel Avirom and Jason Snyder
EDITOR: John Glenn

CONTENTS

ACKNOWLEDGMENTS

WE CAN'T BEGIN TO THANK Diane Disney Miller and her family enough for their support and cooperation, not just on this book but on many projects through the years. It goes without saying that, without them, this book would not exist. Beyond that, we have come to consider Diane and her husband, Ron, as good friends; the relationship is one we treasure.

We've also worked with most of the Miller children at one time or another, and we want particularly to thank Chris, Joanna, Tamara, and Jennifer for their help. And while we know it's always hazardous to single out one sibling of many, we'd be remiss not to take special note of Walter Elias Disney Miller. Over the course of the last couple of years we have worked closely with him and have come to appreciate his wit and his generosity of spirit.

Amy Green provided invaluable assistance in coming up with many photographs for this book; her selfless dedication to bringing the story of Walt Disney to the world is inspirational. She and her husband, Howard, are the nexus of the men and women who care about preserving Walt's history; and they have been determined allies in our work. They're also among the most selfless, giving, and irresistibly fun people on the face of the earth; we are enriched for knowing them.

Our good friends at Pantheon Productions must also be recognized. Without the documentary *The Man Behind the Myth*, this book could not have existed. And without Cathie Labrador and Jean-Pierre Isbouts, there would have been no documentary. What's more, they were cheerily important in helping us to put together the illustrations for this book.

And while we're on the subject of illustrations, we should say that were it not for Ed Squair, of the Disney Photo Library, many of the pages in this book would be blank. Marty Sklar kindly made suggestions through the process. Others who helped us put together the artwork are Troy Lindquist, Kay Malins, Hugh Chitwood, and Michael Jusko.

It seems only appropriate that we properly thank the dozens of men and women whose interviews for the documentary provide the bulk of the stories in the pages that follow. In alphabetical order, they are: Paul Anderson, Ken Annakin, Xavier Atencio, Sharon Baird, Buddy Baker, Ray Bradbury, Bernice Bradley, Michael Broggie, Bob Broughton, Bobby Burgess, Harriet Burns, John Canemaker, Mickey Clark, Tim Considine, Kevin Corcoran, Mary Costa, Bill Cotter, Rolly Crump, John Culhane, Alice Davis, Marc Davis, Roy E. Disney, Karen Dotrice, Buddy Ebsen, Peter Ellenshaw, Bill Evans, Richard Fleischer, Bruce Gordon, Joe Grant, Bob Gurr, John Hench, Don Iwerks, Rush Johnson, Ollie Johnston, Chuck Jones, Dean Jones, Bill Justice, J. B. Kaufman, Betty Kimball, Ward Kimball, John Lasseter, Jack Lindquist, Art Linkletter, Bill Littlejohn, Leonard Maltin, Lucille Martin, Virginia Davis McGee, Sam McKim, Bill Melendez, Floyd Norman, Dick Nunis, Fess Parker, Don Peri, Buzz Price, Dorothy Puder, Glenn Puder, Mel Shaw, Richard Sherman, Robert Sherman, Brian Sibley, Marty Sklar, Dave Smith, Charles Solomon, Jack Spiers, Robert Stack, David Stollery, Bob Thomas, Frank Thomas, Dick Van Dyke, Card Walker, and Ilene Woods.

In addition, we'd like to show our appreciation to the men and women who weren't actually in the documentary but contributed their thoughts about Walt's legacy, including Walter Cronkite, Bruce DuMont, Frank Gehry, Paul Goldberger, Karal Ann Marling, Maurice Sendak, and Richard Weinstein.

We'd be remiss not to thank a number of men and women whose help in the past contributed information that was used throughout this book. Sadly, some of those whose names follow are no longer with us, but our gratitude is undiminished: Lillian Disney, Sharon Disney Lund, Ruth Disney Beecher, Bill Cottrell, Marjorie Davis, Marvin Davis, Carolyn Beecher, Ted Beecher, Nanette Latchford, Melinda Carfagno, Ron Dominguez, Annette Funicello, Harper Goff, Bob Moore, Hayley Mills, Fred MacMurray, Herb Ryman, and Lorraine Santoli. A series of interviews with Walt by journalist Pete Martin were particularly valuable.

We've already mentioned Dave Smith's name as one of those interviewed for this book, but he deserves mention again as head of the Walt Disney Archives, a singularly invaluable resource. In addition, we want to thank his staff: Robert Tieman, Becky Cline, Collette Espino, and Brigitte Dubin. Animation historian Charles Solomon was also very generous with his time and expertise.

We also want to acknowledge Wendy Lefkon of Disney Editions. We first mentioned doing a book for her a couple of years ago, long before we actually knew what we wanted the book to be. She was gracious and supportive then and has continued to be. Her staff, including Sara Baysinger and Jody Revenson, have also been unflaggingly helpful.

Much credit for the book goes to the great people at Roundtable Press, including Susan Meyer and our designers, Joel Avirom and Jason Snyder. Our editor on the book, John Glenn, must be noted for a problem-solving approach that often made it feel like there weren't really any problems; in putting together a book like this, that's a small miracle.

As always, we want to thank our agent, Stuart Krichevsky. We now refer to ourselves as his oldest living clients and guess that makes him our oldest living agent. We trust and appreciate him.

KATHERINE AND RICHARD GREENE

On the documentary set: Diane Miller (right) and her family, (from left to right) daughters Jennifer and Joanna, son Walter, grand-daughter Danielle, and daughter Tamara

FOREWORD

I KNOW IT IS A NATURAL THING that anyone who achieves great success and fame during his life will be the subject of continuing interest for some time after his death. My father's great success was in the field of entertainment, and he took his particular brand of entertainment to great heights by developing new concepts in animation, film, and the amusement park experience. With his older brother Roy he founded a company that continues to grow around the world. As often happens, the interest in my father—as an artist, businessman, and human being—seems to grow as the years go on. There have been several biographies written about him, and I—along with my late mother and sister—cooperated with several of the authors, always in the hope of helping to create an honest portrait of my dad.

My father loved life and he loved people. He was incredibly open and accessible. He was not ashamed of any part of his life but viewed it all as a wonderful experience. He had nothing to hide, nor did we, his family, ever attempt to portray him in any altered or enhanced manner. Far from it.

In 1956, Dad was approached by the *Saturday Evening Post*, which wanted to serialize his biography in the magazine. Pete Martin, who had done previous profiles for the *Post*, would be the author, and it would be featured as a kind of autobiography "as told to Pete Martin." But Dad wasn't interested in doing a memoir at that point in his life. And the fee they'd offered him, though generous, didn't change his mind.

At the time, my husband and I had begun our family and were the parents of an 18-month-old son and an infant daughter. We had been living with my parents since my husband's discharge from the army and were beginning to look for a home of our own. Dad told me of the proposal from the *Saturday Evening Post*. He told me that he had refused to do it himself, but that he'd suggested they change their concept and have his story told by me, his eldest daughter. My sister and I would be paid for it and, although it would be about half of what they'd offered him, it was still a lot of money. I said, "Dad, I don't want to do anything like that." I was 22 years old, the mother of two babies, and my mind and life were full of them. Dad replied, "You want to buy a house, don't you? I can't get any money to you kids, and this is a way to do it!" So we did it.

I was always uncomfortable with assuming credit for authorship of the ensuing book, because I had very little to do with it, save for attending, with great delight, all of Pete's interviews with Dad. Sharon earned her one-third share by doing some babysitting for her nephew and niece. Pete spent many days at our home that summer taping conversations with Dad. The result is hours of taped interviews, which have been a wonderful resource for subsequent researchers.

Several books have been written about my father that claim to be biography but are really not that at all. Rather, they are attempts to take advantage of the interest in my dad in a negative way. One in particular was so full of outright lies and malicious invention that I could not believe the media would give it any credibility. They did. Some newspapers and media anchors hailed this book as a "New look at Walt Disney. Maybe he's not as nice as we thought he was." I had to do something. This was not right, and it was not fair.

I cannot remember if I called Katherine and Richard Greene first, or if they called me. I had met them some years before, when they were doing a biography of Dad and interviewed Mother, Sharon, and me. I reasoned that I could not go on simply getting angry at anyone who took advantage of my father's having died to invent a new history for him. We needed to create some response to this kind of thing. We needed to find an effective way to present my father to the world in as complete a manner as possible—as a father, son, husband, friend, boss, and human being.

Richard spoke of having seen a TV presentation of the lives of Lucille Ball and Desi Arnaz done by their children, using some home movies. Dad was an ardent and enthusiastic home-movie maker, though he was behind the camera most of the time, not in front of it. Nevertheless, we did have some film of the early times of him and Mother, Roy and Edna Disney, and others, as well as endless footage of my sister and me growing up. But we felt it was very personal stuff, and were not willing to share it. Would anyone else want to see it? Richard and Katherine did. I think it was Katherine who actually watched all 19 hours of video of our family films. Richard suggested the medium for our project: a CD-ROM. At the time, I didn't know what that was.

The Greenes interviewed many software producers before recommending Pantheon Productions. It was an excellent collaboration and very good experience, and we were really pleased with the product. About a year later, the Greenes and Jean-Pierre Isbouts and Cathie Labrador of Pantheon suggested we go one giant step further and develop a documentary film about Dad.

We decided that our film should focus on those who had known my dad and had worked with him, as well as writers and historians who had done considerable work about him. Some years before his death in December 1966, Dad was interviewed on television by Fletcher Markle for the Canadian Broadcasting Company. It was an excellent interview. My husband, Ron, worked as the assistant director and marveled that he'd never seen Dad more relaxed. Ron had directed Dad in many of his TV lead-ins, in which Dad was never very comfortable. They were rather a chore for him, although he always comes across like he's having fun. The Pete Martin tapes, the interviews with his friends and co-workers (the two are often synonymous) and family, the commentary of our "experts," and the CBC interview—which brings my father into the film in an immediate and compelling way—along with our sometimes silly but much-loved family film bits—are the stuff from which the film is made.

In that context, this book, like the documentary, is about my father and every one of his friends and colleagues who came to be interviewed. They are all talented, interesting, creative people, many of whom came to work for Dad and became part of an exciting collaboration with him. Others are friends who knew him pretty well at some point in his life and shared his enthusiasm for life. It is a chronicle of a wonderful period of creativity and camaraderie. I feel very privileged to have been an onlooker and, actually, more than a little envious of some of the others.

My entire family was supportive in this project. Our oldest children—Chris, Joanna, Tam, and Jenny—found their roles difficult, as did my husband. Like me, they felt inadequate. I don't know what we expected from ourselves, but we all wanted to do our best for him. Our son Walt was barely five years old when his grandfather died and had very few substantial memories of him. In his role as executive producer of our film, he immersed himself in the details of his grandfather's life and the content of the interviews. He was also my constant support and collaborator. His performance would have earned Dad's highest esteem.

For me, this was an amazing experience, an odyssey of discovery. I thought I knew my father so well. I did, but not in the same way those who worked with him had known him. I cherished him and enjoyed him as a father and a friend, but maybe I didn't appreciate his importance as a creative genius, or even realize why that label fits him. This film, and the interviews from it that made this book possible, are probably the most important thing I have ever done for my father, besides giving him grandchildren.

DIANE DISNEY MILLER

INTRODUCTION

THE IDEA FOR THIS BOOK emerged during the creation of a documentary about Walt Disney called *The Man Behind the Myth*. Walt's family—particularly his daughter Diane and grandson Walter (who was executive producer of the film)—were deeply involved and sat in on all the interviews. If you actually view the film, you'll see us listed as co-producers and writers. But our most important contribution is missing from the credits. It was our job—our pleasure, really—to interview the 77 men and women whose comments about Walt are the heart and soul of the documentary.

As the process of these interviews moved forward, it became clear that an unacceptable amount of powerful material was going to wind up on the cutting-room floor. Just do the math. Seventy-seven interviews times an average of 30 minutes each leaves you with about 38 hours of filmed interviews. The entire American broadcast amounts to only one hour and 28 minutes.

And so the idea of a book jumped into being. At first, we thought it would simply be a book about making the documentary. But when we shared that concept with our agent, Stuart Krichevsky, he augmented our thoughts in an important way. "No," he said, "It should not be a book about a documentary. It should be a book that is a documentary." He was correct, and that's exactly what we've tried to accomplish here. We wanted the story to be told by the men and women who knew Walt best. Of course, we didn't want to limit ourselves to that material alone. One way or another, we've been in the Walt Disney business for a long time. We started work on our first biography of the man about 15 years ago. In 1997, we also co-produced a CD-ROM–based biography called *Walt Disney: An Intimate History*, and we continue to oversee a virtual online museum at www.waltdisney.org.

As a result, we've accumulated a great deal of research about Walt, including interviews with a number of people who, sadly, are no longer with us, such as Walt's wife, Lillian; his sister, Ruth; his daughter Sharon; friend and artist Herb Ryman; his brother-in-law and

Walt at ten months

long-time employee Bill Cottrell; his niece Marjorie Davis and her husband Marvin; and others. These, too, have found their way into this book. Of perhaps greatest importance, we've also relied heavily on a series of interviews with Walt done by journalist Pete Martin.

You may well ask (we certainly have) what's kept us interested in Walt Disney over such a prolonged period of time? By this point, we know more about the details of his life than those of our own parents. And we certainly can speak with authority about his major creations, from Mickey Mouse to Disneyland and beyond. What continues to fascinate us is not the endless accumulation of facts, nor a desire to know the personal history of every hippo in the Jungle Cruise. We are still fascinated by Walt Disney, the man.

For the documentary, dozens of men and women came to a Hollywood soundstage to be interviewed. Given the advanced age of many of these people, it wasn't always easy. Marc Davis, Walt's "Renaissance man," had been ill for some time, but he shared his memories with love and generosity. Only a few weeks later, he passed away. Toward the end of each interview, when talking about Walt's death was inevitable, nearly every person was moved to tears.

What kind of man could have led the world in animation, television, theme parks, city planning, and more, while continuing—more than three decades after his death—to inspire loyalty, love, and tears from dozens of people who knew him (and not just family members)? That's what we want to understand. And we think you'll find some of the answers to this question in the pages that follow.

You won't find all the answers, however. You simply can't tie Walt up with a pretty red ribbon and say, "Here he is." As Peter Ellenshaw, a brilliant artist who worked for Walt for years, told us, "You won't find anyone who can really explain the magic of Walt. People see him in black or white, but he was an extraordinary mixture. He was a common man who was endowed with a touch of magic."

Obviously, some of the keys to Walt derive from his youth. Since there are no contemporary witnesses to that period of his life, we've given those years little attention in the following pages. And the fact is, Walt's early years were not unusual. He was born in Chicago to Flora and Elias Disney, the fourth of their five children. When he was four, his family moved to a farm in Marceline, Missouri, where he formed his earliest memories of an idyllic place in which neighbors helped neighbors, children skinny-dipped in the pond, and friends and relatives abounded. In later years, Walt loved telling stories of his aunt Margaret, who gave him crayons and papers; his uncle Mike Martin, the train engineer; and a neighbor named Doc Sherwood, who paid him a few cents for a picture he had drawn of a horse.

TOP: *Aunt Margaret*

ABOVE: *Walt's work at age sixteen*

Later, after the family moved to Kansas City, Missouri, Walt's appreciation of entertainment began to emerge, even though he was a mediocre student at best. He dressed up as Abraham Lincoln and delivered the Gettysburg Address to classes in the school. He and a friend, Walt Pfeiffer, used to go to vaudeville shows, and from these Walt created skits based on Charlie Chaplin. In his one year of high school, after the family had moved back to Chicago for a while, he also became known for his artistic talents, creating artwork for the school newspaper.

It was on these twin pillars of art and acting that Walt's career was to begin in his late teens. But where did his astonishing sense of audiences come from? Bob Thomas, who wrote biographies of both Walt and his brother Roy, put it well in *The Man Behind the Myth*: "Here was a man who had scant education. His parents were not exceptional, except in their character. He was not much of an artist. But somewhere came this amazing factor of knowing what drama and comedy was."

Bob Thomas can't tell you where that knowledge originated. Neither can we. But we can tell you how it expressed itself during his long and storied career. And what it meant to others.

Date	Walt's Personal History	Walt's Professional History	Other Significant Events
1888–1900	Flora Call and Elias Disney married January 1, 1888. First child, Herbert Arthur Disney, born December 8, 1888. Family moves from Florida to Chicago, 1889. Raymond Arnold Disney born December 30, 1890. Roy Oliver Disney born June 24, 1893.		Thomas Edison builds first film studio in 1893.
1902–1906	Walter Elias Disney is born December 5, 1901. Ruth Flora Disney born December 6, 1903. Family buys 45-acre farm and moves from Chicago to Marceline, Missouri, April 1906.		Orville Wright takes first powered flight in 1903. First animated film, *The Humorous Phases of Funny Faces*, by J. Stuart Blackton, comes out in 1906.
1907–1911	Herbert and Raymond leave farm in 1908. Roy attends high school. Walt and sister, Ruth, begin first grade at Park School in 1909. Elias falls ill with typhoid. Disneys sell farm November 1910; move to Kansas City in summer 1911. In fall, Walt and Ruth enroll at Benton School, repeating second grade.		
1912–1916	Walt and Walt Pfeiffer become best friends. Walt is indifferent student but impresses teachers with talents in acting and art; attends Saturday art classes.	Walt delivers newspapers; trades drawings at local barbershop for haircuts; does amateur vaudeville routines with Pfeiffer.	First professional animation studio opens in New York City in 1913. Charlie Chaplin's first films appear in 1914. Assassination of Archduke Ferdinand and wife in Sarajevo in 1914 sets World War I in motion.
1917	Walt and Ruth graduate from seventh grade in June; Walt reads patriotic speech at graduation. Elias invests in O-Zell Company. He, Flora, and Ruth move to Chicago. Walt joins them in September, starting as freshman at McKinley High School; he draws for school magazine, *The Voice*; attends night art classes.	Walt works as news butcher on Missouri Pacific Line in summer.	United States enters war in spring 1917.
1918	During summer, Walt dates girlfriend, Beatrice; loses interest in school; tries to enlist in military but is too young. In fall 1918, after joining Ambulance Corps, Walt gets influenza and is sent home from local Red Cross camp.	Walt takes summer job at post office; bomb kills four at post office in September during Walt's shift. Walt joins Red Cross Ambulance Corps.	Influenza epidemic—nearly half a million people die in USA, 20 million worldwide.
November 1918–October 1919	Walt recovers. War ends, but cleanup operations continue, and Walt is sent to France. Letters are exchanged with girlfriend Beatrice; when Walt gets home, he finds she has gotten married.	Walt works as Red Cross ambulance driver in France; sends cartoons to magazines, but all are rejected.	World War ends November 11, 1918.
1919–1921	Walt moves in with brother Herbert, Herbert's family, and Roy in family home in Kansas City in October 1919. O-Zell Company fails, and Elias, Flora, and Ruth move back to Kansas City. Herb and family move to Portland, 1920. Walt borrows camera to experiment in "car barn" in back of home. Roy gets tuberculosis and is sent out West to Veterans Hospital. Walt's parents and sister move to Portland in 1921.	Walt is hired by Pesmen-Rubin Commercial Art Studio in fall 1919, then let go after pre-Christmas rush. Iwerks-Disney Commercial Artists is formed by Walt and other former Pesmen-Rubin artist Ub Iwerks; it lasts one month. Walt and Ub both join the Kansas City Film Ad Company in 1920 and are introduced to primitive animation.	First *Out of the Inkwell* cartoon short by Max Fleischer appears in 1919. Commercial radio debuts in November 1920. Women get right to vote.
1922–1923	Walt moves to Kansas City rooming house; struggles to support himself but can't pay rent and is kicked out; sleeps in office. Walt moves to Hollywood "to be a director" in late summer 1923; moves in with Elias's brother, Robert. At Walt's request, Roy leaves Veterans Hospital; he and Walt share small apartment.	Walt quits Film Ad. His first cartoon company, Laugh-O-gram Films, is incorporated in May 1922; files for bankruptcy in May 1923. One of last Laugh-O-gram projects is half-finished *Alice's Wonderland*. After move to California and brief unsuccessful job search, Walt sets up makeshift cartoon studio in Uncle Robert's garage. New York distributor orders twelve Alice Comedies in fall 1923. Walt and Roy launch partnership.	

Date	Walt's Personal History	Walt's Professional History	Other Significant Events
1924–1925	Lillian Bounds is hired as inker and painter by Disney Brothers in 1924. Roy asks girlfriend, Edna Francis, to move to California; they are married April 11, 1925. Walt and Lilly are married July 13, 1925, in Lewiston, Idaho.	The Disney Brothers Studio is set up on Kingswell Avenue. First Alice Comedy is shown March 1924. Ub Iwerks joins team. Disneys get contract for 18 more Alice Comedies.	
1926–1927	Walt and Roy buy adjoining lots and build prefab houses on Lyric Avenue in fall 1927. Lilly's mother moves in. Walt gives Lilly a chow puppy, Sunnee, for Christmas.	In February 1926, Disney Brothers moves to Hyperion Avenue, becomes Walt Disney Studio. Alice Comedies enjoy moderate success. *Oswald the Lucky Rabbit* series is launched in mid-1927.	Charles Lindbergh makes solo flight over Atlantic in May 1927. *The Jazz Singer*, first "talkie," premieres in October. Experiments in transmitting "television" pictures begin.
1928	Walt and Lilly enjoy home life; evenings are often spent at the studio or driving around town in Walt's Moon roadster to see competing cartoons.	A professional blow—the loss of much of Walt's staff and the rights to his cartoon rabbit—is followed by train trip during which Walt comes up with idea for cartoon mouse; Lilly nixes name Mortimer in favor of Mickey. *Plane Crazy*, first Mickey cartoon, is completed, followed by *The Gallopin' Gaucho* and *Steamboat Willie*. Walt experiments with adding synchronized sound effects and music.	
Fall 1928	Working for months in New York City, Walt writes Lilly, "I wish I was home." His beloved Moon is sold to finance his new sound cartoon.	Walt pursues sound; finds Cinephone, an independent system, and hires orchestra to record music. On November 18, 1928, *Steamboat Willie* premieres at New York's Colony Theater; it is a smash hit.	
1929		Mickey Mouse, with Walt providing voice, is great success. Walt launches Silly Symphony series—cartoons based on musical themes; *Skeleton Dance* is first.	Stock market crashes in October 1929; Great Depression begins.
1930–1931	Walt and Lilly want children, but suffer two miscarriages. Lilly's sister Hazel and niece Marjorie live with them. Roy and Edna's son, Roy Edward Disney, born January 1930. With sudden success and relentless workload, Walt has "nervous breakdown" in 1931; long vacation relieves pressure and Walt returns refreshed.	Mickey Mouse licensing takes off; a comic strip appears; Mickey Mouse clubs spring up in theaters. Ub Iwerks and musician Carl Stalling, another Kansas City friend, leave Walt Disney Studio—a personal blow to Walt.	
1932	On doctor's advice, Walt starts exercising; sport of choice is polo; he and other Disney employees match up with celebrities like Spencer Tracy and Will Rogers.	Walt signs exclusive two-year contract with Technicolor and releases *Flowers and Trees*, the first cartoon made with a three-color process. This Silly Symphony is the winner of the first Academy Award given to cartoon; Walt also gets honorary Oscar for the creation of Mickey Mouse.	Charles Lindbergh's baby son is kidnapped and killed. 12 million Americans are jobless.
1933	The Walt Disneys build a new Tudor-style home. On December 18, 1933, Diane Marie Disney is born.	*Three Little Pigs*, an eight-minute Silly Symphony, is major hit, as is signature song, "Who's Afraid of the Big Bad Wolf?"	Newly-elected President Franklin Delano Roosevelt embarks on "New Deal" to salvage economy.
1934		Donald Duck makes first appearance, in *The Wise Little Hen*. Walt acts out the story of *Snow White* to animators. The Disney staff grows to nearly 200.	
1935–1937	Walt, Roy, Lilly, and Edna take first trip to Europe in 1935. Back in California, Walt's home movies—some shot in sound and color—record Diane's every move. After Lilly's third miscarriage, Sharon Mae Disney is adopted January 1937.	*Snow White* in production. Studio adds 300 artists in 1935. *The Band Concert* is first color Mickey cartoon. Silly Symphonies allow experimentation: *The Old Mill*, released in 1937, has sense of depth provided through multiplane camera. On December 21, 1937, *Snow White and the Seven Dwarfs* premieres at Carthay Circle Theater.	
1938	In January, 50th anniversary party held for Flora and Elias, who move to California later that year into home purchased by Walt and Roy. In November, furnace malfunctions, and gas fumes fill the house; Elias recovers, but Flora succumbs.	*Snow White* is major success, bringing in $8 million in first release. Work begins on *Pinocchio*, *Fantasia*, and *Bambi*. Disney brothers buy property in Burbank for new studio.	

Date	Walt's Personal History	Walt's Professional History	Other Significant Events
1939–1940	Weekend outings with daughters to Griffith Park carousel and other local attractions get Walt thinking about need for spot where families can have fun together.	Silly Symphony series ends in 1939. Walt gets special Oscar for *Snow White*. *Pinocchio* premieres in New York in February 1940. *Fantasia* premieres there in November. The company moves to Burbank studio; loss of foreign markets strains finances.	Hitler invades Poland; Britain and France declare war on Germany in September 1939. NBC, followed by CBS and DuMont, begins first formal television broadcasting.
1941	Walt is personally devastated by strike. He and Lilly travel to South America with artists and storymen. Lilly's sister Grace, who now lives with family, watches children. Elias dies while Walt and Lilly are away.	Strike pits employees against managers at Disney studio. Company begins making training films. In heat of strike, Walt and artists are invited to tour South America. *Dumbo* is released in December. The army moves troops and equipment into Burbank studio.	Pearl Harbor is bombed on December 7. The United States enters war.
1942–1945	Weekend outings with daughters continue; Saturday visits to studio include bike riding and roller skating. Disney family vacations at Palm Springs dude ranch.	Walt receives prestigious Irving Thalberg Memorial Award. *Bambi* premieres in 1942. War period is characterized by production of multiple training, education, and propaganda films, including *The New Spirit* (1942), *Der Fuehrer's Face* (1943), and full-length *Victory Through Air Power* (1943). Two feature-length products of South America trip are released—*Saludos Amigos* in 1943 and *The Three Caballeros* in 1945. Studio begins exploring television in 1944.	Germany surrenders in May 1945; Japan surrenders in September 1945.
1946		*Song of the South*, combining live action and animation, is released, as is *Make Mine Music*, first of several cartoon package features. Studio lays off 300 workers in August.	
1947–1949	In October 1947, Walt testifies before House Un-American Activities Committee. At home, Walt buys himself electric train set in December; travels to Railroad Fair with animator Ward Kimball in 1948. Disneys purchase property on Carolwood Drive for new home, with land for miniature railroad. In summer 1949, Walt, Lilly, Diane, and Sharon take two-month trip to Europe, including five weeks in England during shooting of *Treasure Island*.	*Seal Island*, first True-Life Adventure, is booked in Crown Theater in Pasadena in December 1948, opening new market. Diversification continues with the (mostly) live-action *So Dear To My Heart*, released in January 1949. Talk of a "Mickey Mouse Park" accelerates. Work in progress includes several major animated features and the fully live-action *Treasure Island*.	Chuck Yeager breaks sound barrier, October 1947. Milton Berle becomes first major television star with "Texaco Star Theater" in 1948. ABC network begins television broadcasting. Fears of Soviet expansionism lead to "cold war."
1950	Disneys move into Carolwood house. Walt writes sister, Ruth, "I am going to take time out to play with my train."	*Cinderella* released in February, followed in July by *Treasure Island*—the first of four live-action movies shot in England. Walt enters world of television with "One Hour in Wonderland" in December.	
1951–1952	Walt enjoys building and collecting miniatures and playing with backyard "Carolwood Pacific" train. By himself, he builds "Granny Kincaid's Cabin" for traveling exhibit. Diane starts college at University of Southern California. More family trips to Europe in summers.	*Alice in Wonderland* is released; Walt begins experimenting with concepts for traveling exhibit of three-dimensional miniature scenes and figures that move. Studio continues diversification with second television special and more live action. Walt plans for family park across street from studio. WED Enterprises is started.	
1953	Walt borrows from life insurance and sells vacation home in Palm Springs to help finance Disneyland planning.	*Peter Pan* is released. *The Living Desert* (1953) is first feature-length True-Life Adventure and winner of Academy Award for Best Documentary; Walt hires Stanford Research Institute to help select site for theme park. On weekend in September, Walt works with artist Herb Ryman to create expansive Disneyland concept painting, which Roy uses for raising funds.	
1954	Diane and Ron Miller are married. Sharon starts college at University of Arizona. Walt and Lilly's first grandchild, Christopher, is born at year's end.	Construction begins on Disneyland in Anaheim. "Disneyland," the television series, premieres on ABC (wins best variety show Emmy for first season); "Davy Crockett" is smash hit. *20,000 Leagues Under the Sea* is Walt's first major American live-action film; wins Academy Award for best special effects.	

Date	Walt's Personal History	Walt's Professional History	Other Significant Events
1955	Walt and Lilly celebrate 30th anniversary at pre-opening Disneyland party.	Disneyland opens in July. "The Mickey Mouse Club" premieres on ABC in October. *Lady and the Tramp* is released.	
1956–1957	Extensive taped interviews with Walt and family are done by journalist Pete Martin, writer for the *Saturday Evening Post*. Walt's second grandchild, Joanna, is born in 1956, followed by third, Tamara, in 1957. Sharon has bit part in *Johnny Tremain* and goes to work as secretary for studio. Walt and Lilly build and move into new vacation home in Palm Springs; take two months in Europe. Ron Miller joins studio.	Disneyland expands with many new attractions. In 1956, Fess Parker is featured in three Disney movies, including a highly successful theatrical release of *Davy Crockett*. In 1957, *Johnny Tremain* and *Old Yeller* are released.	The Soviet Union launches *Sputnik* satellite in 1957.
1958–1959	Sharon marries Bob Brown in 1959.	The last major "fairy tale" animated feature of Walt's life, *Sleeping Beauty*, is released in 1959. *The Shaggy Dog* is first in line of very successful broad comedies. Walt "plusses" Disneyland with major new attractions, including country's first Monorail. Walt begins thinking about developing a new kind of city and looking for spot for "Eastern Disneyland."	
1960	Through early 1960s, Walt and Lilly continue to enjoy vacations at Smoke Tree Ranch in Palm Springs. Walt takes up lawn bowling, the sport of choice for his later years. Walt and Lilly's fourth grandchild, Jennifer, is born.	Walt is in charge of pageantry for Winter Olympics in Squaw Valley, California. A record year of movie production includes *Swiss Family Robinson* and *Pollyanna*—first of six Disney films that Hayley Mills made during Walt's lifetime.	
1961	Walt's namesake, Walter Elias Disney Miller, is born—the fifth of Diane and Ron Miller's children. Walt's oldest brother Herbert dies (the only sibling to pre-decease him).	*101 Dalmatians* and *The Absent-Minded Professor*, starring Fred MacMurray, are hits. A switch in television networks brings a new show, "Walt Disney's Wonderful World of Color," to NBC.	
1962–1963	Walt becomes personally dedicated to forming a new, multifaceted arts university, to be called the California Institute of the Arts ("CalArts"). Walt and Lilly's sixth grandchild, Ron, is born in 1963. Company's purchase of 15-passenger Grumman Gulfstream eases frequent air travel. Bob Brown becomes planner at WED.	Studio's tremendous output continues with a dozen more live-action films and an animated feature, *The Sword in the Stone*. The Tiki Room at Disneyland features the first public show of Audio-Animatronics figures. Walt works on plans for 1964 World's Fair while exploration for east-coast amusement park and city of tomorrow continues.	President John F. Kennedy is assassinated in Dallas, November 22, 1963.
1964		*Mary Poppins* is released, winning five Oscars. The New York World's Fair opens with four of its top attractions created by Disney, including It's A Small World and Great Moments with Mr. Lincoln. Walt receives Presidential Medal of Freedom.	U.S. Surgeon General issues warning about hazards of cigarette smoking.
1965	Walt and Lilly travel to Europe—one of many trips taken there in later years; they visit Disney Street in London.	At close of World's Fair, the four Disney attractions are moved to Disneyland. Walt and Roy settle on Florida as site for ambitious new project, buying 27,443 acres for about $5 million; plans for a new Disney World are announced in a November press conference.	
January–October 1966	Walt is grand marshal of Tournament of Roses parade. Sharon and Bob Brown have a daughter, Victoria, in January. In July, Walt rents boat and takes family, including seven grandchildren, on cruise through waters of British Columbia. In October, Walt and Lilly travel to Williamsburg, Virginia, with Sharon and Bob.	New Disneyland attractions include New Orleans Square. U.S. accepts Disney bid to develop Mineral King resort. Studio output includes *Lt. Robin Crusoe* (based on story by "Retlaw Yensid") and featurette *Winnie The Pooh and the Honey Tree*. Work progresses on *The Jungle Book*.	
November–December 1966	On November 2, Walt enters St. Joseph's Hospital for tests; X-ray reveals spot on left lung, which is removed November 7. Walt is released two weeks later, visits studio, and has Thanksgiving with family. He travels to Palm Springs with Lilly but stays only one night; returns to hospital November 30.	Walt visits WED and studio for last time on Monday, Tuesday, and Wednesday of Thanksgiving week.	
December 15, 1966	Walt dies.		

PART ONE

FIRST DREAMS

As a young man, Walt demonstrated talent in art and acting. In view of these dual talents, what could have been a more natural fit than a career in the infant field of animation?

By age 20, in Kansas City, Walt was president of his own cartoon company called Laugh-O-grams, which produced a number of ambitious, if crude, cartoons. The venture ended in financial failure. The last project Walt started at his little studio was called Alice's Wonderland, *featuring a little girl, in live action, frolicking in a cartoon universe. When Laugh-O-grams folded, Walt headed west with the unfinished film in his suitcase. While staying with his uncle Robert in Los Angeles, Walt talked a distributor into ordering a series of cartoons based on the same theme as* Alice's Wonderland.

Contract in hand, Walt persuaded his brother Roy to join him in forming their own cartoon studio. He hired a small staff, including a pretty young woman named Lillian Bounds. This was a serendipitous personnel choice, as Walt and Lilly soon began a romance that led to marriage and a lifelong love affair.

Walt followed up the Alice comedies with another series featuring Oswald the Lucky Rabbit. Oswald was a great success, but the character was hijacked by Walt's distributor, who also hired away most of his staff.

Never easily deterred by setbacks, Walt developed a new character, a mouse named Mickey. When Mickey didn't catch on among distributors, Walt decided to latch onto the latest innovation in live-action films, adding sound to the first Mickey Mouse shorts.

Soon Mickey Mouse was an international success, giving Walt the resources to embark on a new series, called Silly Symphonies. *These musically based cartoons allowed his artists to experiment with a variety of innovations in animation.*

And that was just the beginning.

"A GOOD HARD FAILURE"

IN 1919, WHEN WALT WAS ALMOST 18, he returned home from a year in France in the Red Cross Ambulance Corps and moved back into the family home on Bellefontaine Avenue in Kansas City. His ever-practical father, Elias, presented his youngest son with a future: Walt would go to work in the O-Zell Company. This was the Chicago jelly manufacturer of which Elias was a partial owner.

But Walt was full of fire, and he was loath to use that fire to make jelly. He wanted to be an artist. Walt resisted his father's will, and he applied for a job as an artist at the *Kansas City Star*. He was turned down. He applied for a job as an office boy. No. Truck driver? Forget about it.

Walt went to his brother Roy for advice. Roy had heard about an opening at a commercial art studio run by a fellow named Louis Pesmen. Walt applied for a job there drawing farm equipment, horses, and bags of feed for catalogues. He showed Pesmen samples of his work, which consisted of sketches of street scenes in Paris. Despite the absence of tractors on the Champs Elysées, he was hired. "I worked at this drawing board and during the day I never left it," Walt said. "If I had to go to the toilet, I just held it. Until noon. Finally, at the end of the week, this fellow came over and said, 'Well, I don't know.' I was just shaking in my boots. He stalled and said, 'Uh, $50 a month.' I could have kissed him. I thought I was going to get fired."

Here Walt got his first training in commercial art. Perhaps more important, he met an intense young man named Ub Iwerks. Iwerks was exceedingly talented and very quiet.

TOP: *Elias hoped O-Zell's new soft drink would rival Coca-Cola.*

ABOVE: *A portrait by Walt of father and son*

Dorothy Disney Puder

Dorothy Disney Puder lived this entire story. Her memories of the good times in the home on Bellefontaine are warm and vivid. She knew my dad as the youngest of three adoring uncles and participated in his early filmmaking experiments. As a high school student in Los Angeles, she worked in Ink and Paint during the making of *Snow White.* **Her best girlfriends were to marry artists Ken O'Connor and Ward Kimball. Her presence in our film is wonderful. She is a unique witness.**

DIANE DISNEY MILLER

Unfortunately, after a month, sales fell off and Pesmen had to lay Walt off. After a brief stint working at the post office to make ends meet, Walt suggested to Iwerks that they start their own company. "They were going to call it Disney-Iwerks, but that sounded like an optical company," says Dave Smith, archivist for The Walt Disney Company. "So they changed it around to Iwerks-Disney." They did a lot of commercial art projects, like advertisements for magazines and program covers for the local Newman Theatre. But they were barely making enough to get by. And then they saw an ad in the paper for the Kansas City Slide Company, which wanted artists.

So Walt applied for a job at the Kansas City Slide Company, which soon became the Kansas City Film Ad Company. He was hired at $40 a week. Eventually Ub joined him there. "They paid him $35 a week," said Walt. "It always bothered Iwerks. He was older. He'd been in the business longer."

At Kansas City Film Ad, Walt helped make cartoon commercials for local businesses. The cartoons were made using cut-out figures held in place by pins. Walt was captivated by the effort. But he was interested in trying to improve on this primitive animation technique and wanted to try using drawings instead of cut-outs. "I wanted to experiment but the boss didn't want to go for it. He said, 'It's all right. They're good enough for now.'"

Still, Vern Cauger, who owned the company, was willing to let Walt borrow a camera. At home in his family garage, Walt began experimenting with various ways of doing animation. He also visited the Kansas City Public Library in search of books on animation. Two books were particularly useful. "One was the book on animal and human locomotion by [Eadweard] Muybridge," Walt recalled. "That was invaluable to us. And the other was by Carl Lutz on the tricks of the animation trade. Now, it was not very profound; it was just something the guy had put together to make a buck. But, still, there were ideas there."

"I can remember him doing cartooning and experimenting with the movie camera," says Walt's niece Dorothy, who was five years old at the time. "He had me stroll down the walk in front of the house carrying a full milk bottle and wheeling my baby dolly carriage. I pretended to accidentally break the bottle, spilling the milk over everything. And then he reversed the film so that I backed up, and the milk came back up into the bottle."

TOP: *Walt designed this cover for a local theater.*

CENTER: *The staff of Kansas City Film Ad, c. 1921*

ABOVE: *Kansas City Film Ad artists at work: Walt in back row by window; Ub Iwerks in middle of center row*

Pretty soon, Walt felt he'd gotten far enough along with his experiments to go into business for himself. He thought that the Kansas City theaters, which featured cartoons made by the big East-Coast studios, might be willing to buy some with a local twist. Walt created a few and brought them to the Newman Theater. He called his new creation "Newman Laugh-O-grams," and made the sale. Unfortunately, he priced his new product badly—he charged the theater exactly what it cost him to create it. "I was stuck with it," he said. "But I didn't care. It was paying for my experiment."

Walt attracted some other young men to join his fledgling enterprise—at no pay, of course—and soon he decided to quit his day job and become a professional cartoon maker. Ever the salesman, he convinced local businessmen to invest some $15,000 in his enterprise. He rented space in a Kansas City office building. He bought his own movie camera.

"They made films which are referred to today as modernized fairy tales," says J. B. Kaufman, co-author of *Walt in Wonderland*, a book about Walt's silent cartoons. "Basically, they would take a fairy tale and add a contemporary spin to it. This is the kind of thing that a lot of other people are given credit for doing decades later. Disney was doing it in 1922.

His version of *Puss in Boots,* for example, doesn't have much to do with the original story. It's about a cat and his master going to the movies and seeing a parody of the latest Valentino picture. It doesn't have much to do with the original story at all."

While Walt and his staff—including Ub Iwerks—were turning out films like *Puss in Boots* and *Little Red Riding Hood,* he was also busily trying to sell the product. Soon enough, he succeeded.

He signed a contract to create a series of Laugh-O-grams for a company called Pictorial Clubs for $11,100. This was a wonderful deal, save for one problem. Kaufman: "What they actually got was $100. That was it. The contract was set up so that they were supposed to get the rest of the money a long way down the road, but Pictorial Clubs went out of business."

That was the beginning of the end for Laugh-O-grams. Walt tried to come up with ways to supplement the company's income, including taking movies of local children for their parents and signing up to provide newsreel footage for national syndicates. But it was a losing battle. His staff left for greener pastures. Walt couldn't pay his rent, and he wound up living in his Laugh-O-grams office. He ate on credit at a little coffee shop. "I was all alone," he said years later. "It was lonesome. When my credit ran out, I was tempted to go into a restaurant and eat, and then tell

ABOVE LEFT: Little Red Riding Hood *was one of the hot products of Laugh-O-gram Films.*

LEFT: *In* Puss in Boots, *a boy and his cat go to the movies.*

them I couldn't pay. But I didn't have the nerve. I was so damn hungry."

In December 1922, Walt caught a break. A local dentist, Dr. Thomas B. McCrum, agreed to pay Walt $500 for a short film about dental hygiene. Walt came up with a story about Jimmy Jones, a dental misfit, and his counterpart Tommy Tucker, a child with great faith in the power of the toothbrush. All of life's rewards came to hygienically correct Tommy, while Jimmy stumbled on the cavity-laden path to doom. Then Jimmy started brushing. And all ended well.

Kaufman: "Part of the money from *Tommy Tucker's Tooth* enabled Disney to get a few other ventures going, and one of them turned out to be the salvation of his career, if not of Laugh-O-grams itself. It was a film called *Alice's Wonderland*. This is another one of those wonderful things that Disney would do. He was in desperate financial straits; almost everything that he did was failing. A lot of people would be tempted to become very conservative and do something easy and safe. Disney blows it all on the most lavish film he can possibly make. There had been a number of films before that in which a cartoon character would jump off the drawing board and go into the real world. Disney turned that around and had a live-action character going into a cartoon world."

Inside the Laugh-O-grams office in the McConhay Building

Professional Pitfall

When a local dentist asked Walt to make a film for him, Walt was eager to take him up on the offer. But, as Walt told the story, there was one obstacle:

"One night he called me. He said, 'Come over here tonight and we can get it all wrapped up.' I said, 'I can't come tonight.' And he asked, 'Why not? What are you doing?' 'Nothing,' I replied. 'Well,' he said, 'why can't you come?' And I said, 'I haven't any shoes.' He said, 'You haven't any shoes? Where are they?' 'They were falling apart,' I said. 'I left them at the shoemaker. They're fixed, but he won't let me have them unless I pay him and I can't pay him. I have to wait until I can dig up a dollar fifty somewhere.'

"He had a car, and he asked, 'Is the shoemaker still open?' I said, 'Yes.' He said, 'I'll be right over.' Dr. McCrum came over, went in and paid the shoemaker, gave me my shoes, and then we sat down and struck the deal to make the little film."

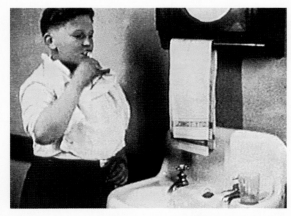

Tommy Tucker's Tooth brought Walt a much-needed $500.

The film starred a four-year-old charmer named Virginia Davis, who was already a professional model. "In fact," says Kaufman, "Walt saw her in an advertisement for Wernecker's Bread in Kansas City. She had been taking acting, dancing, and singing lessons. So at the age of four, she was a trouper."

Today, Virginia Davis McGee's eyes sparkle like those of the four-year-old featured in Walt's film. As a little girl, she was enchanted by her new boss. "I don't think I really realized, at four years of age, that it was going to be a motion picture," she reflects. "I really did not. I had posed for still pictures before, so I was just doing what I was being told to do. It was all 'Let's pretend. Let's have some fun.'"

Says Virginia, "He would tell me, 'Pretend that you're running.' And of course I could pretend. And he'd say, you know, 'Run, move your arms, move your arms, like you're running. Look scared, look scared. Look back, look back.' I'd look back and that was the way it was done. It was wonderful. I looked forward to going to work. It wasn't work, it was play."

RIGHT: *Little Alice (Virginia Davis) visits a cartoon studio, sparking her adventures in a two-dimensional world.*

BELOW: *Walt (standing) and the struggling Laugh-O-grams company earned some money taking "home movies" of local children.*

I got this company going—I was made president of it—and I was only 20 years old. I suppose it was illegal for me to have been president at age 20. If we ever wanted to get out of anything, I suppose we could have gone to court and claimed that I was a minor.

W A L T D I S N E Y

ALICE'S WONDERLAND

LAUGH-O-GRAM FILMS, INC.

P R E S E N T

Produced by a
Laugh-O-gram Process

LEFT: *Walt and Virginia Davis in* Alice's Wonderland

ABOVE: *Alice meets some friends.*

Walt wrote to New York distributors while he was working on the film. "We have discovered something new and clever in animated cartoons!" he declared. But unfortunately, with *Alice's Wonderland* half finished, he simply couldn't afford to forge on. He declared bankruptcy and made plans to move to Hollywood.

He sold his camera and "for $5 I got a nice pair of shoes. I didn't have a suit; I had a pair of trousers and I had a checkered coat. And the suitcase was kind of a frayed cardboard one. Everything had gotten threadbare.

"And I came to Hollywood. I was just free and happy. I was 21 years old. But I'd failed. I think it's important to have a good hard failure when you're young."

If Walt had gone on like that in life, he never would have gone anyplace.

ROY DISNEY,
on his brother's early business skills

*Walt's parents,
Flora and Elias
Disney, in 1913*

FLORA AND ELIAS

WHILE IT'S IMPOSSIBLE to pin down the roots of Walt's greatness, elements of his mother, Flora, and his father, Elias, emerge clearly. Says Walt's daughter Diane, "I think that what Dad got from his father was a strong work ethic, a sense of using time wisely, and not wasting it. From his mother I think he learned warmth and humor."

Elias held a series of jobs in his lifetime. He was a carpenter, farmer, newspaper-route owner, jelly-factory manager, and more. Although none of his jobs yielded great fortunes, Elias Disney took pride in all he did, worked as hard as possible, and never gave up, even when sickness and other misfortunes hit him and his family.

His sons often worked for him though they were never paid. For six years, Walt and Roy rose hours before dawn to deliver newspapers for their father. "He said I was part of the family," reported Walt. "He said, 'I clothe and feed you.' So, he wouldn't pay me." But pay or not, Elias required his sons to give total dedication to the task. He was a perfectionist in all he did, a trait that Walt seemed to inherit. "In the winter," said Walt, "my Dad would insist that every paper had to go behind the storm door, not just thrown on the porch."

In later life, Walt enjoyed telling stories about his father's temper and his inclination to strike his sons when provoked. It appears that Elias didn't hesitate to give his children—particularly his oldest sons—a good licking with a hickory switch, if he thought they deserved it.

But that was only part of the story. Elias was a socialist, deeply concerned with society's fairness to the common man. He was a fiddler, and often spent Sundays making music with neighbors. If he encountered a musician in need of a good meal Elias would invite him home for dinner. "He'd bring home some of the weirdest characters," remembered Walt. To this Walt's

*Elias in
later years*

younger sister, Ruth, added, "My father was a social person, very sociable. He was very gracious to people who came to our house. I always wanted to be like that myself." According to older brother Roy, "He was strict and hard, with a great sense of honesty and decency. He never drank. I rarely even saw him smoke."

Walt also told tales that made Elias seem tight-fisted, but when it came to things he thought were important, Elias was hardly penurious. "He bought a fine piano for me when I was nine years old," recalled Ruth. "My mother and father gave us every opportunity for education, and for extra education when we showed interest and talent." Continued Walt, "The only way I could go to the show at night was to tell my Dad it was an educational picture that I wanted to see.

And my Dad would shell out." In fact, although Elias didn't think a career in art was very practical, he hardly hesitated to pay for art lessons when Walt wanted them. "I had tremendous respect for him," said Walt. "I worshiped him. Nothing but his family counted."

"My father adored Flora," says Diane. "She cherished her family and her husband." She also loved a good laugh. Once Walt brought home a store-bought practical joke called a "plate lifter." When you squeezed a little rubber bulb connected to a mechanism under the plate you could make the plate jiggle up and down from across the table. Flora was eager to pull the joke on Elias. She squeezed the bulb, making her husband's plate dance merrily about on the table, but Elias didn't seem to notice. "My mother was just killing herself laughing," recalled Walt. "She kept pumping the bulb until finally my Dad said, 'Flora, what is wrong with you? I've never seen you so silly.'" Flora was laughing so hard that she finally had to leave the room. According to Roy, "We had a wonderful mother who could kid the life out of my Dad when he was peevish."

As a grandmother, Flora retained her sense of fun. Says her grandson, Roy E. Disney, "Flora was more fun than a barrel of monkeys. And she loved kids, like the way Walt did, I think. Kids responded to her. She'd get down on the floor and play games with your toys with you. She was great."

Not only was Flora a fun-loving mother and grandmother, she was instrumental in holding her family together. As Ruth wrote in 1988, "She was a great family manager and very capable of doing anything she undertook. My father liked to have her take care of most of the money matters. She had a very even temperament, never displaying anger or lack of self-control, yet she held her own in any situation requiring it. Before her marriage she had taught school. . . . Mother loved to read. She did sewing of every description, making most of our clothes, men's shirts, quilts, was a great cook, a lover of babies, excellent with children. She was loved by everyone who knew her."

TOP: *Walt and Ruth with their mother, Flora*

CENTER: *Flora brought warmth and humor to the Disney home.*

ABOVE: *Flora and Elias with their new grandchild, Diane*

27

"DURING THE 1920S, the American animation industry was centered in New York City," says Charles Solomon, animation historian and author of *Enchanted Drawings: The History of Animation* and *The Disney That Never Was*. "New York is where the first studios had been established and where the great majority still were. At that time, an enormous number of silent one-reel comedies were being released to movie theaters. If you were going to pick artists in the late '20s who was going to revolutionize the animation medium, you would probably have looked to Max and Dave Fleischer, who were doing the *Out of the Inkwell* series, or to the Sullivan Studio, where the first real cartoon superstar, Felix the Cat, originated.

"Felix set the pattern not only for the merchandising of animation but also for the basic design of a great many early animated characters. Oswald the Lucky Rabbit, Bosco, Bimbo, and the Fleischer shorts are all pretty much derived from Felix's basic design and from the fact that he was solid black. Otto Messmer discovered that a solid black mass moved better on the screen than a line drawing, particularly at the speed at which silent films were projected. Lines tended to strobe and to flicker on the screen, whereas the black masses would flow into each other when they were projected."

With Felix and others dominating the cartoon scene, Walt determined that he was not going to continue in animation when he first arrived in Hollywood.

"*Aesop's Fables* were very successful, *Felix the Cat* was going strong, so I just said it was too late," remembered Walt. "I should have been in the business six years before. I was through with the cartoon business. I honestly felt that I was too late."

Walt's new ambition: "To be a director."

He knew, of course, that he wasn't going to find any "director wanted" ads in the newspaper. "It was hard to get jobs then at studios. I wanted anything. . . . That was my feeling. Get in. Not choose, but get in. Be a part of it and then move up. I've always had that feeling about things. It upsets me so much when people want to get into something but they're too darn choosy about what they do. What the hell, sweep the floor. I don't care, you know what I mean?" But Walt couldn't even find a job sweeping floors. "I went from one studio to another and I went to the personnel departments and it was pretty cold."

He did get one chance—as an extra in a film. "They were hiring guys who could ride a horse," he said, "and I went and hung around and got signed. Well, it rained like hell. So I didn't get to go. And that was the end of my career as an actor. When they started all over again, they hired a whole new bunch." Finally, even Walt had to concede that he needed to look elsewhere. "I just couldn't get anywhere," he said. "Before I knew it, I was back with my cartoons."

Alice's Day at Sea, the first Alice cartoon on the West Coast, was animated entirely by Walt.

Walt.Disney
Cartoonist

4406 KINGSWELL
LOS ANGELES

Aug. 25, 1923

Miss M. J. Winkler,
220 West 42nd St.,
New York, N.Y.

Dear Miss Winkler:

This is to inform you that I am no longer connected
with the Laugh-O-Gram Films Inc. of Kansas City, Mo.
and that I am establishing a studio in Los Angeles
for the purpose of producing the new and novel series
of cartoons I have previously written you about.

The making of these new cartoons necessitates being
located in a production center that I may engage trained
talent for my casts, and be within reach of the right
facilities for producing.

I am taking with me a select number of my former staff
and will in a very short time be producing at regular

ABOVE: *Uncle Robert's garage, where Walt was "establishing a studio"*

RIGHT: *Ever the salesman, Walt puts an optimistic spin on his move to the West Coast following the bankruptcy of Laugh-O-gram Films.*

FAR RIGHT: *Margaret Winkler, Walt's first distributor*

The obvious place to start was with the half-finished *Alice's Wonderland*, which Walt had brought with him from Kansas City. While he was still in Missouri, one distributor, Margaret Winkler, had indicated she was interested, so he contacted her again, with a sample of the work he had done. He set up a makeshift studio in his uncle Robert's garage, which he described to Winkler as "establishing a studio in Los Angeles for the purpose of producing a new and novel series of cartoons." Winkler, who presumably never saw his headquarters, agreed to pay him $1,500 each for six cartoons. She was particularly taken with little Virginia Davis and required that Walt sign her up for the series. "Walt agreed with that," says Disney archivist Dave Smith, "and so he wrote back to Kansas City to Virginia's parents and said, 'Why don't your bring her out here to California? We'll make her into a movie star.'"

Recalls Virginia Davis McGhee, "My mother was very excited about the letter that came from California. Walt wrote that he had a distributor and proceeded to do a great selling job to my mother, that this would be a great opportunity for Virginia, and so forth. Also, I'd had double pneumonia and the doctor always said I'd be better in a drier climate than Kansas City. I think it was the combination of several factors that made it worthwhile to move to California. The first picture was *Alice's Day at Sea*. I'd never seen the sea. That was a big experience for a youngster, all these waves. It was wonderful, and there again was Walt with his stories and his direction."

At this time, big brother Roy was in a sanatorium near Los Angeles, recuperating from a case of tuberculosis. Explains Bob Thomas, an eminent Hollywood historian who wrote biographies of both Walt and Roy, "Walt came out to the sanatorium, woke Roy in the middle of the night, and said, 'Roy, I've got a deal with a New York distributor and I want you to come in with me. I need your help.' And Roy said, 'Okay.' The next day, against doctors' advice, Roy left the hospital. He never went back, never had a recurrence of TB, and that's how the Disney Brothers Studio was formed."

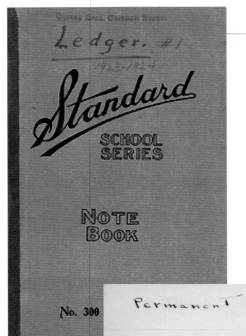

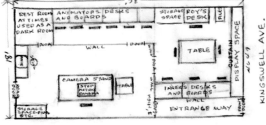

Walt later explained, "The government did play a part in subsidizing the first studio because my brother was discharged from the service with a partial disability allowance. I think it was about $65 a month. My brother and I lived on that while we started our studio."

With the commitment from Winkler, Walt was able to move from his uncle Robert's garage to a small studio of his own. He began to hire staff, soon bringing Ub Iwerks in from Kansas City. For some time, Iwerks would be Walt and Roy's single most important staffer. Says Don Iwerks, Ub's son, "My Dad concentrated on his work as the most important part of his life. His father left the family when he was about 12 years old. He had to go to work to support his mother. He knew responsibility at a very early age."

"The Disney studio was located on Kingswell Avenue in a tiny office," relates author and historian J. B. Kaufman. "They also rented a vacant lot, which they intended to use for the live-action scenes. They brought in a big white backdrop, which they let down on the side facing the street so they wouldn't pick up traffic going by, and they would film Virginia going through her paces in front of this white sheet." Virginia Davis McGee remembers the shoots: "They didn't have enough film for more than one take. It had to be right the first time. Walt was always very pleased that I could do what he told me to do in that first take."

"Virginia Davis played Alice throughout the first year," continues Kaufman. "After that, her mother and Walt had some disagreements over financial terms. As a result, the Davis family went its own way and Disney needed to find somebody else to play Alice." A child named Dawn O'Day appeared in one film, and she was then replaced by young actresses Margie Gay and Lois Hardwick, who played Alice for the remainder of the series.

Although the Alice Comedy series didn't generally appear in first-run theaters, the films were reasonably successful. Alice appeared in some 56 silent cartoons made between 1924 and 1927. The cartoon situations are reflected in their titles: *Alice Foils the Pirates, Alice in the Klondike, Alice in the Jungle, Alice on the Farm, Alice the Piper, Alice the Toreador, Alice the Whaler, Alice the Lumber Jack,* and on and on.

It was inevitable that the series would eventually run out of steam. Says Charles Solomon, "They had basically exploited all the situations and gags that the live-action little girl could play with the animated characters, and it was becoming formulaic. If you look at some of the later ones, such as *Alice Rattled by Rats,* you'll see that Alice tends to come in at the beginning, set up the premise of the film, then leaves. You have the animated portion, and

TOP TO BOTTOM:

Roy kept the books in this modest ledger.

'Initial purchases of the Disney Brothers Studio,' as recorded by Roy in early 1924

Walt (right) with his first animators, Ub Iwerks (left) and Rollin Hamilton (center)

Floor plan of the Kingswell studio—the rest room doubled as a darkroom

I made the first six Alice cartoons practically alone. At that time, I was able to get some of the boys who had been with me in Kansas City to come out to California. From the seventh cartoon on, I had some help. . . . I had to drop the drawing end of it myself. But I've never regretted it because drawing was always a means to an end with me. . . . And if I hadn't dropped the drawing end of it myself, I don't think I'd have built this organization.

WALT DISNEY

Alice comedies were churned out at a remarkable clip.

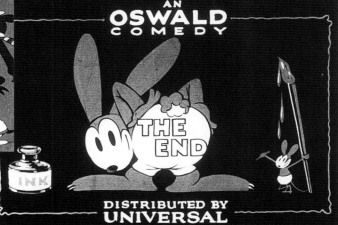

then Alice returns at the very end to close the bookends."

By this time, Margaret Winkler had married Charles Mintz, who essentially took over her distribution business. "Mintz wanted a series that would be purely animated," says Solomon. "I don't know who actually suggested a rabbit or who thought up the name Oswald, but Oswald the Lucky Rabbit was the character they came up with, and he was, not surprisingly, a solid black rabbit. He's actually kind of dumpy in the first couple of films, but I suspect Ub Iwerks redesigned him to be a little more appealing and easier to animate. With Oswald, they launched their first series of purely animated shorts, which received good reviews and did fairly well financially." J. B. Kaufman adds that "the films were distributed by Universal, which represents the first time a major company distributed Disney's cartoons. They were being shown in major theaters with first-run films.

A trimmer, redesigned Oswald

"What distinguishes Oswald the Rabbit," Kaufman continues, "is that he is the fullest expression of Walt's personality to date. A lot has been said about Mickey Mouse being the personification of Walt Disney. To an extent that's true, but I think you see Walt in a number of his characters, even in his earliest films. Basically, it's not too much of a stretch to say that Mickey Mouse is Oswald the Rabbit with round ears. The two personalities are very similar. In fact, a number of the Oswald films were later remade as Mickey films. One of the most brilliant gags in *Steamboat Willie* is the goat eating the sheet music while his tail is being cranked as if he were a hand organ and the music is coming out of his mouth. The same gag had been used earlier that year in one of Disney's Oswald films called *Rival Romeos*. It's really interesting to see that spunky optimism, that resourcefulness you always associate with Mickey Mouse, also showing up in Oswald the Rabbit."

In spite of (or perhaps because of) Oswald's success, Charlie Mintz wanted to change the status quo. Explains Kaufman, "Mintz wasn't the first to underestimate Walt Disney and he wouldn't be the last. He figured he could

32

The entire staff of the Winkler Pictures Corporation, makers of Oswald the Lucky Rabbit Cartoons, released by Universal. Charles Mintz, president of the company, is the man with the cane in the center of the picture.

WHO PUTS ANIMATION IN OSWALD CARTOONS?

Comedy Cartoon Tricks Little Known in the Trade That Make the Lucky Rabbit Do His Stuff

Charles Mintz (center, with cane) took Oswald and animators away from Disney.

A Turn of Fortune

Although Charles Mintz became the producer of the Oswald films, he didn't retain them for very long, because Universal very quickly took the series away from him. Mintz wound up producing *Krazy Kats* all through the '30s and worked for Columbia. It's rather sad to see what happened to his career. One day Walt ran into Mintz in a distribution office where he was trying to sell *Steamboat Willie*. Both Walt and Mintz were coming to the office with their hats in their hands, except that Walt had something good to sell and Mintz didn't. Walt could have been pardoned for being a little vindictive by taking some pleasure in Mintz's turn of fortune. But Walt wasn't like that. He wrote a letter to Roy saying, "Poor old Charlie. It was sad to see him this way." That says a lot for Walt.

J. B. KAUFMAN

produce the Oswald cartoons just as well as Disney, so he went behind Disney's back to all of his top artists and managed to sign up most of them to come to work for him. Disney didn't find this out until he went to New York to renegotiate his contract." Mintz made something else clear to Walt. As distributor, he controlled the rights to the Oswald character. Walt controlled nothing. Mintz gave Walt two choices: either Walt could work directly for Mintz or he would lose both his staff and the Oswald character. Walt chose the latter.

What happened next has become one of the most famous stories in the history of animation. As Walt's daughter Diane tells it, "That train trip to New York was very critical. Dad learned he didn't own Oswald, which caused a real crisis. But, typically, Dad was unstoppable. He wired Roy: 'Everything okay, I'll explain when I get home,' or something to that effect. On the train returning to California Dad brainstormed with my mother, which was fortunate because she usually didn't accompany him on these trips. And he said, 'I need a new character. I think it will be a mouse. And I think I'll call him Mortimer.' And Mother said—and she was so proud of this moment—'Mortimer? I don't like Mortimer. What about Mickey?'"

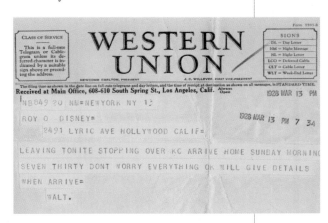

March 1928 telegram from Walt to Roy

LILLY

TOP: *Jeannette Bounds
(center) with daughter Lilly,
son-in-law Walt, and dog
Sunnee in the backyard
of their first home*

ABOVE: *Lilly, c. 1917*

SOON AFTER WALT OPENED his first real studio on Kingswell Avenue in Los Angeles, he began to hire staff. He was in the market for someone to help ink and paint the cartoon cels. And then, as the cliché goes, fate stepped in, in the form of a pretty young woman named Lillian Bounds, who had been brought up in a small town in rural Idaho. "Lilly was warm. She was gentle," said her niece Marjorie, "a real lady, and a very caring person. My mother and her three sisters all had beautiful voices. My mother played the guitar. The family never had much training but it was very musical."

Explains Diane, "My mother went down to Los Angeles and moved in with her sister Hazel and Hazel's daughter, Marjorie, who at that time was about seven years old. A friend of Hazel's said to my mother, 'I can get you a job. There's a young guy down the street who's making cartoons.'" Lillian recalled that her friend added, "You can come if you won't vamp the boss."

The next morning, Marjorie walked with her aunt for a couple of blocks to the little storefront that was Walt's studio. The admonition against vamping seemed not to be an issue for Lilly. "I had no idea of vamping him," she said. "I never had such a thought in my mind. The guy didn't even have a sweater to take you out any place. . . . When I first went to work for him, I made $15 a week. And sometimes he and Roy would say, 'Lilly, have you cashed any checks?' And I'd say, 'No.' And they'd say, 'Well, hold them off for a while, will you?' So I'd keep 'em. I didn't need 'em. I'd put away the checks and they would use that little bit of money to pay their expenses."

Walt seemed taken with Lilly immediately. "He had a little car," says Diane, "and he would drive Mother and another young woman who worked for him then home every evening. Mother took great delight in the fact that even though Mother lived nearby, he would take the other girl home first and then drop Mother off on the way back."

Lilly described these early days of courtship: "One day Walt said to me, 'I'm going to get a new suit. When I do, is it all right if I come and call on you?' I said it was all right. Walt and Roy both went to Foreman and Clark to buy suits. This shows you the difference between the two men, even at that time: Walt got a suit with two pairs of pants. Roy bought only one.

Lillian Bounds, a Disney Brothers employee, stands next to her boss, Walt, in the doorway of the Kingswell Avenue office.

"The next night Walt came in the house and said 'How do you like my new suit?' And he modeled it for us. It was sort of a gray-green suit and he looked very handsome. . . . The family liked him immediately. There was never any embarrassment about Walt. He met people easily. . . . He just had no inhibitions. He was completely natural."

About that time, Walt bought a second-hand Moon automobile, dark gray with a dramatic hood ornament. "We used to take rides in it out to Pomona and Riverside, driving through the orange groves. And Walt would take me out to dinner at tearooms on Hollywood Boulevard. He also would like to take me to shows. Our first big date was *No, No, Nanette,* which was appearing in L.A."

Recalled Marjorie, "All of a sudden, Walt was at our house an awful lot. My mother was an excellent cook. They never could really decide whether he was there because of Aunt Lilly or because of my mother's cooking. But I guess it was Aunt Lilly. I slept on the sofa in the living room, but I was moved into Aunt Lilly's bedroom while she and Walt would stay up talking. When he was ready to go he would make up my bed on the sofa. He was the only one who could make up the bed so that I wouldn't fall out. He fixed it so and tucked it so that I never fell out of bed. Otherwise, I would always wake up in the morning on the floor."

In many ways, Lilly's family was different from Walt's. Says Diane, "My mother's family was large, double the size of his, and they really enjoyed laughing. Elias Disney was a very duty-oriented man, but my mother's father was, as she described him, a good-time Charlie. They never had much money, and when her father made a little he bought them all presents. It was a family full of laughter, full of music. They really knew how to have a good time. Dad really enjoyed Lilly's family, especially her mother. He never knew her father, but her mother was very warm and told wonderful stories about coming to the West in a covered wagon, and the Indians, and all kinds of bits of Western history that Dad loved to hear."

At the time, Walt was living with Roy in a tiny rental on the second floor of a house near the studio. Working and living together was a bit too much closeness for the brothers.

Roy got to thinking that, on the whole, he would far rather be spending time with his longtime girlfriend, Edna, who was still in Kansas City, than with his younger brother. "One night they had a little blowup," says Diane. "Dad complained about the meal Roy had prepared and Roy said, 'Okay, this is it.' And he wrote to Edna, saying, 'I think we ought to get married.' I don't know exactly what he said in the letter but that was the gist of it.

"The wedding was at my uncle Robert's house just down the street. In looking at the home movies from that day . . . Dad is obviously so delighted with my mother that he makes any excuse to hug her. She looks very pleased to be the object of his affection, and not long afterwards they decided to get married, too."

Walt and Lilly were married on July 13, 1925, at her brother's home in Lewiston, Idaho. Marjorie reported that her aunt giggled throughout the entire ceremony. After the wedding—on the way to a honeymoon at Mount Rainier—Walt and Lilly stopped off in Portland, Oregon, where Walt's parents had moved, and Lilly met Flora and Elias for the first time.

"They were very warm and friendly and loved Walt very much," said Lilly. "They wanted him to be happy, which is why they were so happy with me."

When Walt and Lilly returned from their honeymoon, the newlyweds moved into a small apartment near the studio that overlooked an alley. Soon, they rented a slightly larger place. "After we had dinner, Walt used to drive around to catch the cartoons at the theaters," said Lilly. "He knew what time they were going on, and he would drive to each theater and leave me in the car while he watched the cartoons. He studied them all—*Felix the Cat, Out of the Inkwell*—and tried to learn from them.

"Often, he'd go to the studio at night. He had a little office there and I would sleep on the davenport while he worked. Sometimes I would wake up and ask, 'How late is it?' 'Oh, It's not late,' he'd say, even though it was three o'clock in the morning.".

By 1927, the studio had expanded to much larger quarters on Hyperion Avenue. Walt and Roy were successfully selling their *Oswald the Lucky Rabbit* series and began to feel a sense of economic security. According to Diane, "They bought adjoining lots on a little hillside street not far from the Hyperion Studio. They ordered identical homes from Pacific Ready-Cut Homes and the houses went up. My cousin Marjorie remembers that was the most exciting home she'd ever seen. It was probably the finest home that anybody in their family had ever had up to that point."

Soon afterward, Lilly's mother moved in with them. Marjorie: "Walt was so good to my grandmother. He treated her like she was a queen. That's how he treated Aunt Lilly, too. We used to go for rides on Sunday, because Grandmother loved that. And we would always stop in an ice cream parlor on the way home. Walt and I

TOP: *Roy and Edna at their wedding, April 11, 1925*

CENTER: *Lilly and Walt at Roy's wedding*

ABOVE: *Lilly and Walt on their honeymoon at Mount Rainier*

would go into the ice cream parlor and bring out ice cream cones, including one for the dog. And Walt would stand by the curb and feed the dog her ice cream cone."

The health of Lilly's mother's declined, however, and she moved in with another relative. But Walt and Lilly weren't alone in their house for long. By the late 20s Hazel was divorced, and she and Marjorie moved in with them. "Walt was very fond of my mother and he was very good to me," recalled Marjorie. "He used to wait up for me to come home. He'd be at the top of the stairs when I came in at night, especially if I was very late. I was going to boarding school at the time. I'd come in from school on weekends, and he would get annoyed if I had plans for the weekend. 'Why'd you bother to come home? Why'd you bother, if you're not going to be here?' I tell you, I broke the ice for his girls.

"I'll never forget one time when I came home from boarding school. I don't know why, but I was feeling pretty full of myself at the time. We were sitting at breakfast—just Walt and me. I don't know what came up, but he said, 'Well, you disappoint me.' I stood up and my chair fell over backwards. That was a little deflating, I must admit, but I declared, 'Well, you're a self-made man, and you worship your maker!' I don't know where I'd heard this. I'm certain I didn't think of it myself. I turned and stomped out of the room. The worst thing was that by the time I got to the bottom of the stairs, I heard him laughing. And that just undid the whole scene."

ABOVE: *Lilly's niece Marjorie*

LEFT: *Marjorie and Hazel (far left) with Walt and Lilly at their new home in Los Feliz.*

MICKEY AND MORE

IN 1928, WALT HAD LOST most of his staff as well as the rights to his character, Oswald the Lucky Rabbit, to distributor Charlie Mintz, but he was still obligated to complete the last several Oswald cartoons. Fortunately, master animator Ub Iwerks had stayed loyal to Walt, so while his former staff was finishing up on the Oswalds, Iwerks hastily animated the first Mickeys. At night Walt brought home his drawings and handed them over to Lilly, her sister Hazel, and Roy's wife, Edna. They were his inkers and painters. "Walt didn't want anybody to know that he was doing something else," recalled Hazel's daughter, Marjorie. "He just didn't trust anybody at that time. He'd been so badly cheated."

Meanwhile, Walt was trying to sell the Mickey Mouse character. This wasn't easy. Walt reported that he was told, "The public doesn't know you and they don't know your mouse." Clearly, Walt needed something extra to generate interest in his new character. The answer? Sound. He had three Mickey cartoons in hand, *Plane Crazy*, *The Gallopin' Gaucho*, and *Steamboat Willie*. He decided that *Steamboat Willie* would be the test.

As animation historian Charles Solomon explains, "During the '20s there had been several experiments with sound and animation, attempts to coordinate sound cartoons with phonograph systems, but the synch was always a problem. Disney went ahead anyway, making sure he could do it better and more effectively than anyone else had up until then. Working with his friend Carl Stalling, who had been a theater organist in Kansas City, Walt created a soundtrack that was basically 'Steamboat Bill' and 'Turkey in the Straw,' songs that were popular and in the public domain."

ABOVE: *Ub Iwerks at his drawing table*

RIGHT: *Pat Powers*

Walt headed off to New York City to find people who had the technology necessary to make a sound cartoon. "I went to Fox," he said, "and got the brush-off. I went to RCA and they listened to me. I saw the head guy and they were agreeable." Unfortunately, RCA insisted on utilizing a simplistic technique for putting sound on cartoons that simply wasn't good enough for Walt. "I said, 'No, I don't want to do it that way.' And they said, 'Well, we're just too busy to monkey around with anything new and experimental around here.'"

Walt kept hunting and finally ran into a fellow named Pat Powers, "who had what they called at that time a sort of outlaw sound equipment—that is to say, not properly licensed," remembered Walt. "Powers had formerly been a policeman in his early days in New York. He was a big lovable friendly Irishman. You couldn't help but like him. He just took me in with open arms."

The first recording session, featuring 30 musicians, was an unmitigated disaster. "Let's face it," said Walt, "30 musicians is a lot of dough. I was the first one to the recording studio, and the sound men were just then

Mickey Mouse in Steamboat Willie

warming up. I was waiting because, gee, we were putting out a lot of money. The first musician to come in was the bull fiddle player. He was a little short guy and he had this great big bull fiddle. He had just gotten off the train from Camden, New Jersey, after recording all night! And when he arrived he opened his bull fiddle case, where he had a bottle of whiskey, and he had a drink!"

There was no margin for error. "In those days," said Walt, "you had to do it all on one piece of film. There was no dubbing. Today we can put it on 20 films and blend them all together, but not then." Unfortunately, there were plenty of errors. The conductor didn't want to follow Walt's carefully marked-up score. The bull fiddle player drowned out the rest of the orchestra (and was eventually sent to play out in the hall), and the musicians lost the precise beat necessary to follow the animation. When the first recording session was over, Walt didn't have a sound cartoon. He was also out of money.

Powers had confidently guaranteed Walt that he'd pay for a second session if one was needed. One was needed, and Powers reneged. "I had to wire Roy," Walt said, 'No good. We got to do it over again. Need another twelve hundred bucks.' " Back home, Roy sold Walt's car. In New York Walt cut down on the number of musicians and sound-effects men. And he convinced the conductor to follow his notations.

> ✳ **I think Walt had a sense of destiny. He always knew where he wanted to go and he wanted to get on with it.**
>
> Artist and Imagineer JOHN HENCH

Mickey is buried in fan mail in a promotional shot from the 1930s.

This time, Walt emerged with a usable print. "Mickey seemed to be tap dancing and whistling and singing to the music in a way that no character had ever done before," says Solomon. "And that made the film enormously appealing and very novel. When you look at *Steamboat Willie* today, it's hard to imagine how fresh and how different it must have been from the other animated films of that era."

Harry Reichenbach, a publicist and manager of New York's Colony Theater, agreed to show the film for two weeks. Walt hoped that distributors would come and decide to place *Steamboat Willie* in other theaters. Solomon: "If you were in the audience in New York's Colony Theater on November 18, 1928, you were seeing something new for the first time. Audiences were delighted. They immediately took to the character, who was very likable, very jaunty, rather mischievous at that point in his career. And the rest is cartoon history."

Mickey Mouse was, in Walt's words, "an instantaneous hit. It hit them with a bang. . . . Bookings! Theaters wanted them!" Pat Powers agreed to furnish the sound equipment and distribute the films, as well. Walt's studio expanded. He started a comic strip based on the Mickey character. The first 18 were penciled by Iwerks and written by Walt. For a brief while another staffer took over the art work, while Walt continued to write the strip. Finally, Walt turned the whole thing over to artist Floyd Gottfredson, who told the *Comics Journal*, "Walt had said, 'Just take it over for two weeks until I find someone.' By the end of a month I began to wonder if he was looking for anyone. And at the end of two months I began to worry that he was going to find someone, because now I had adjusted to the strip and was beginning to like it. So I continued for 45 and a half years."

Mickey was wordless in the first cartoon, but Walt provided the voice of Mickey in the second cartoon and he continued to do so. Solomon: "He couldn't find an actor who did it the way he liked. He would say, 'It's high, but it's not falsetto. It's like this.' And everyone finally agreed that Walt should keep doing it. And many of the artists maintained that Mickey was really kind of an alter ego for Walt."

John Hench, who started working for Walt in 1939, painted the official portraits of Mickey for his 25th, 50th, 60th, and 70th birthdays. "Walt's relationship with Mickey was hard to miss," he says. "In a way, he was the personification of Walt. He had Walt's optimism. We couldn't have known Mickey any better if he was really a small boy running around the studio with us every day. We knew how he'd react to every situation. He was constantly evolving, from the very first Mickeys to later ones, and we were watching him grow. I don't think Walt felt quite the same about any of the other characters as he did about Mickey."

Meanwhile, Walt decided that it was time to broaden the horizons of his team. Why was it necessary to have a company of well-known characters for animation to work as entertainment? Wouldn't audiences enjoy beautifully drawn animation with a lush musical background? Solomon: "The idea for *Silly Symphonies* was suggested by Carl Stalling, the theater organist

from Kansas City, Walt's good friend who had worked with him on *Steamboat Willie*. *The Skeleton Dance* was the first film in that collaboration. It really doesn't have much of a plot. Basically some skeletons emerge from their tomb at night and dance some rather jaunty routines, smashing each other, bouncing up and down, and having a good time."

In what was becoming a pattern, few others saw the potential in *Silly Symphonies*. "I sent it back to New York," Walt said. "Powers showed it around, and he got turned down everywhere on Broadway. He sent it back, saying 'They don't want this kind of stuff. More mice.'"

Walt eventually convinced a Hollywood theater to give the film a try. It was a huge success. Once again, Walt had demonstrated that he had a better understanding of audiences than did the theater owners or film distributors. Author Ray Bradbury, who became a close friend of Walt's in later life, recalls seeing *The Skeleton Dance* as a child when it first came out in the summer of 1929. "I went to the movies to see *Skeleton Dance*. It was a matinee. I stayed through the feature film—a dreadful film, really, probably something with lots of mush, you know. But I stayed through it to see *The Skeleton Dance* so many times that my father had to come and drag me out of the theater."

Just when Walt's professional life should have been moving ahead without difficulty, "trouble began to loom up for us," he said. Roy suspected there was something amiss with Powers. "I came back from New York one time," Roy said in a 1968 interview, "and I said, 'Walt, that Powers is a crook. He's a definite crook. He won't give me satisfaction. I can't find out what we've got coming to us.' Walt was upset with me and he said I was a troublemaker, that I was suspicious, that I didn't believe in people, and so on."

Soon enough, however, Walt was convinced that Roy was right. "We got word that Powers was conniving in some way with one of my boys," he said. "He refused to give us reports

ABOVE: *A reference sheet for animators from the late 1930s.*

RIGHT: *Walt and his new star*

BELOW: *Mickey Mouse drawn by Walt himself for his old boss, Vern Cauger, from the Kansas City Film Ad Company*

on what we were earning. He would just send us these little checks of $3,000 or $4,000 to keep us going. But he wouldn't give us any reports. We began to suspect there was something wrong there."

It turned out that Powers—something like Charlie Mintz before him—wanted to take over Walt's operation, guaranteeing Walt a hearty salary to come work for him. As leverage, Powers had hired Ub Iwerks away, offering to set him up in business animating his own character. Walt and Roy had given Ub a 20 percent interest in their studio, and were paying him better than they paid themselves. Nonetheless, this was simply an offer Iwerks felt he couldn't refuse. As Roy recalled, "When Ubbie got the offer of his contract with Powers, he felt he had to take it. We hated to lose him, but we weren't mad at him for it. He drew Flip the Frog for Pat Powers. As I remember, I paid him $2,940 for his share of the company when he left."

Walt, of course, refused to go with Powers. And while Flip the Frog never made it into the pantheon of cartoon greats, Mickey Mouse and the *Silly Symphonies* continued to thrive. The ensemble of characters who worked with the mouse grew as time went on. Minnie was featured in *Steamboat Willie* in 1928. She was originally voiced by Marcellite Garner, an inker and painter who worked for Walt. Over the course of years, she appeared with Mickey and Pluto in scores of cartoons .

Donald Duck first appeared in 1934 in a *Silly Symphony* called *The Wise Little Hen*. He would go on to become as popular as Mickey, starring in about 128 cartoons and for some 50 years voiced by Clarence "Ducky" Nash. Goofy, meanwhile, debuted in *Mickey's Revue* and soon became part of the regular gang. Pluto—like Goofy a dog, but without benefit of voice—appeared with Mickey and Donald in many of their shorts but also starred in about 48 cartoons of his own, beginning in 1937.

The *Silly Symphonies* gave Walt the opportunity to experiment with different kinds of animation and to educate his artists. The introduction of color into his cartoons represented one of the biggest innovations. As Charles Solomon describes it: "Disney somehow learned about the Technicolor process, signed a deal for its exclusive use in animation for two years, and then announced to his brother Roy that they were going to reshoot in color a film that was half done. This probably trebled the costs and sent Roy's blood pressure up a number of degrees."

ABOVE: *Walt and Ub*

RIGHT: Silly Symphony *artists at work*

*T*he whole idea of the Symphonies *was to give me another street to work on, you know? Getting away from a set pattern of a character. For each Symphony, the idea would be a different story based on music, with comedy and things.*

WALT DISNEY

Donald Duck in his screen debut

As Walt said, "My brother was very much against it. The reason was, he always lived with figures and calculations. . . . I said, 'I want color.' And his reasoning was that we'd already sold the series of cartoons, and, once you made a deal with the theater man, you had to deliver all 12 at that price. Changing in the middle of the series would get us no more money from the theater man to pay for the extra costs."

The first color film Walt made was called *Flowers and Trees*. "And fortunately for me, it did hit," he said. "It did create excitement. It brought on an avalanche of orders and bookings and started a whole new thing." It also won Walt the first Academy Award for an animated film."

Perhaps the most important advance Walt made in animation during these years was neither artistic nor technological. Instead it was in the development of genuine characters

BELOW: *Goofy in* Father's Day Off *(1953)*

RIGHT: *Mickey and Pluto in* The Pointer *(1939)*

Flowers and Trees *(1932) was the first color* Silly Symphony.

with real personalities. *Three Little Pigs*, an eight-minute *Silly Symphony*, was notable in this way. According to Walt, he had achieved "a certain recognition from the industry and the public that these things could be more than just a mouse hopping around."

Three Little Pigs also featured the song "Who's Afraid of the Big Bad Wolf?" which captured a spirit of hope and determination that struck a responsive chord during the height of the Depression. All in all, it was an enormous success. In fact, recalled Roy, "There was a theater in New York where it ran so long that they took the picture of the pigs in front and gradually put whiskers on them. And the longer they stayed there, the longer the whiskers got."

Three Little Pigs *(1933) was a major success.*

POLO

IN THE EARLY 1930S, largely as a result of work pressures and the emotional pain of Lilly's suffering two miscarriages, Walt's doctor suggested that he get exercise to help relieve stress. "I took up wrestling," he said, "but I didn't like having to stay for ten minutes in somebody's crotch with the same smelly sweatshirts and sweat trousers. So I took up boxing, because at least you had a chance to get a little air, you know? Then, I took up horseback riding, and that led to polo."

In those years polo was *the* game in Hollywood. Actor Robert Stack was a teenager, but, being a member of a show business family, he played polo with many of the celebrities of the day, including Walt. He explains, "Remember, this is the macho time for film. This is when the men tried to simulate the characters they played on film."

That description may not have been true of Walt, but he jumped into the game with both feet. He recruited a team from the studio that included Norm Ferguson, Les Clark, Dick Lundy, Gunther Lessing, Bill Cottrell, and even Roy. Then he hired a polo expert, Gil Proctor, to work with his team. The practices started at dawn and ran until it was time to start work. He began to acquire polo ponies—a rather expensive collection. As he wrote his mother, "Don't fall over dead when I tell you I have six polo ponies now. After all, it's my only sin. I don't gamble or go out and spend my money on other men's wives or anything like that, so I guess it's okay. Anyway, the wife approves of it." Eventually Walt wound up with 19 ponies.

When his team was deemed ready by Proctor, they started to compete. First, they played at Victor McLaglen's stadium, and later Walt and Roy joined Riviera Club luminaries like Will Rogers, Spencer Tracy, and Darryl Zanuck.

"Everybody in Hollywood was playing polo," says Roy E. Disney. "Many times I was in the stands not understanding what I was looking at. Once somebody was introduced to my mother and me, and he asked, 'Oh, is your father out there playing?' And I said, 'Yes. He's the one who just fell off his horse.'"

Recalls Stack, "Walt was a good player and he loved the game. I have a couple of trophies at home with Walt's name on them. We didn't win the world's championships but we had an awful lot of fun."

The end to Walt's polo years came rather suddenly. Mel Shaw was a studio artist and polo player. Shaw says, "Walt arrived at a point where he wanted to play with the better players. The South American team, the Argentines, were scrimmaging on the practice field at the Riviera. Walt wanted to scrimmage with them, and the man who was the head of polo at Riviera told him that he could. While he was riding with the Argentine team, one of the players backed a ball and Walt turned around just about the time that the ball hit him. These balls are hard wood objects and Walt was badly hurt. And at that point the insurance company told Walt that he had to quit playing polo."

TOP: *Walt (foreground) in action on the polo field*
ABOVE: *Walt and fellow polo player Spencer Tracy*

PART TWO

WORLDS TO CONQUER

From 1933 to 1946 Walt's life was a dizzying roller-coaster ride. These 13 years included some of the greatest personal and professional thrills of his life, as well as its two greatest tragedies.

The first of the personal highs was the birth of Walt and Lilly's daughter, Diane, in 1933, and the adoption of their second daughter, Sharon, in 1937. Walt loved being a father and reveled in playing with his two little girls.

The year of Sharon's birth, Walt's feature-length animated film Snow White and the Seven Dwarfs was released and was a smash hit, despite the negative predictions of skeptics. Walt followed up with three major animated features—Pinocchio, Fantasia, and Bambi. Although these were creative wonders, the onset of World War II and the loss of European markets meant they were financially unsuccessful. Disney suspended animated feature productions after the United States entered the war, when Walt's studio largely turned over its operations to defense-related work.

The loss of the European markets and the attendant money crunch led to an ugly strike in 1941, an event that shattered Walt's idealistic notion of him and his employees as a big happy family.

Further tragedy occurred with the death of Walt's beloved mother, Flora, who was asphyxiated by a malfunctioning gas furnace in the small home Walt and Roy had given their parents.

SNOW WHITE

AFTER MICKEY MOUSE AND THE *Silly Symphonies* hit the jackpot, it would have been a simple matter for Walt to live the life of an animation giant, watching the money roll in. If he had done so, he would still be an important part of animation history, similar to Walter Lantz, creator of Woody Woodpecker, or Max Fleischer, who brought Popeye, Betty Boop, and others to the screen. But one of Walt's career characteristics was his restlessness, almost an impatience with success. Like a gambler who can't resist pouring a jackpot back into the slot machine, Walt was perennially looking to parlay his prior achievements into something bigger and better.

And so, in the early 1930s, Walt began to think about bringing the art of animation a giant step forward. Today, nearly 70 years later, people may consider the idea of feature-length cartoons as fairly commonplace. After all, they've been with most people for a lifetime. But when Walt first started to move down the path that led to *Snow White and the Seven Dwarfs*, a feature-length animated film was revolutionary.

Animation historian Charles Solomon puts *Snow White* into historical context by explaining, "It wasn't the first animated feature. There had been a couple made in Argentina in the teens, which had been forgotten by the 30s. In Europe there had been Lotte Reiniger's *Adventures of Prince Achmed*, which was known little in this country. But the idea that a full-length, spectacular, Technicolor, fully animated film could be made was an extraordinarily bold yet very logical move for

As a teenager, Walt saw the silent film Snow White *starring Marguerite Clark.*

"There are no left-handed animators"

✳ It was fantastic how long Walt would remember things. Larry Clemmons was a fellow who went from animation into story work. Because Clemmons was left-handed, Walt insisted he'd never be an animator. "There are no left-handed animators," Walt said. Clemmons left the studio to work in radio and was gone for nearly 30 years, after which he returned to the studio as a writer. One day he was scribbling on a notebook and Walt commented, "I told you that you'd never make it as an animator! There are no left-handed animators." Thirty years later!

FRANK THOMAS

Walt. The silent comics whom Walt admired and knew—Charlie Chaplin, Buster Keaton, Laurel and Hardy—had all moved from shorts to features. Features commanded more respect, a higher price, and allowed for a much greater development of the material. I think those reasons moved Walt to the idea of a feature."

As Walt explained, "I saw the handwriting on the wall. My costs kept going up and up, but the short subject was just a filler on any program. And so I felt I had to diversify my business. You could only get so much out of a short subject. . . . I don't know why I picked *Snow White*. The story is something I remembered as a kid. I once saw Marguerite Clark performing in it in Kansas City when I was a newsboy back in 1917. It was one of the first big feature pictures I'd ever seen. That was back in 1917. . . . I thought it was the perfect story. It had the sympathetic dwarfs, you see? It had the heavy. It had the prince and the girl. The romance. I just thought it was a perfect story."

Outside of Walt's imagination, the story of *Snow White* began in a dimly lit soundstage in 1934, when he first introduced his plans to his animators. Ollie Johnston and Frank Thomas were both there. The relationship between these two men is legendary. They first met as students at Stanford University, worked together at the studio for over four decades and then went on to co-author four books, including *The Illusion of Life: Disney Animation*. "We were pretty confused about what Walt was doing," admits Thomas. "Why was he doing a feature in the first place? What made him think he could sustain the audience interest for a whole feature length? We were all pretty nervous about it. Then he started telling the story. Of course, typical of Walt, he was a terrific actor, but he couldn't perform by memorizing lines or by doing anything he'd rehearsed. He just acted out every part spontaneously. 'The queen gets up here and does this, and Snow White's down here, and here comes the prince on his horse.'" Johnston agrees: "I was just spellbound by it. Walt was a great actor. A wonderful, spontaneous actor. He'd be telling something and say, 'Like this!' and he'd get up and act it out and have you laughing at what he was talking about, and, sure enough, you could visualize what he was presenting to you. It was amazing."

By the time the evening was over, Walt's staff was convinced that *Snow White* would make a perfect feature-length animated film. Others in Hollywood were skeptical about the project for years to

An original theatrical poster for Snow White*'s 1937 release*

From Snow White to Toy Story

✴ **The film we created at Pixar, *Toy Story*, was the first feature film made with computer animation. At the time a lot of people said it couldn't be done—no one would watch it. It's cold. No one would sit through it. But we were convinced that the film is about the story and characters, not about the technology. We persevered. And *Toy Story* became the number one movie of 1995.**

I was reading a book about Walt and realized people were saying the same thing about *Snow White*. They predicted that no one would sit through an hour and a half animated cartoon. Walt persevered, making the film without listening to his detractors. He didn't listen to anybody. And of course it became the number one movie in 1938.

JOHN LASSETER

come, calling the film "Disney's Folly." The very idea of making a cartoon that ran longer than a few minutes seemed like the height of hubris.

Walt forged ahead, paying little attention to his detractors. He continued telling and retelling the story of *Snow White*, and the plot evolved with each rendition. Says Joe Grant, artist and storyman, "I think I probably heard the entire story of *Snow White* three or four dozen times. Walt would go from room to room, describing sequences. Whatever we added would be incorporated into his next narration. He repeated the story to as many people as possible and gathered up as many ideas as he could. It was a verbal process, the old storyteller, and that technique seemed to work very well."

Creating *Snow White* necessitated the development of a variety of new animation techniques, and Walt knew his staff needed training for the effort. So, in the years prior to its creation, he used his *Silly Symphonies* to hone animation techniques and style. Explains Charles Solomon, "Before they started *Snow White*, the Disney team created several films with heroines, as a way of learning how to draw a convincing female character for the screen. The first in that series is *The Goddess of Spring*, a rather rubbery-limbed version of Persephone. Her arms tend to ripple when she moves, but she was an admirable first attempt. Compare that to another film a year or two later, *The Cookie Carnival*, and you see that the sugar

ABOVE LEFT: *The "rubbery" Goddess of Spring*

LEFT: The Cookie Carnival *helped to advance the animation of human figures.*

INSIDE THE DREAM

cookie girl, the heroine, is much more feminine, more solid, more believably female. The sugar cookie girl was animated by Grim Natwick, who would be the lead animator of the heroine in *Snow White.*"

One of the keys to *Snow White*—and, in fact, to all of Walt's work—was his ability to use animation to create convincing individual personalities. "The effort to give cartoon characters personality goes back to Winsor McCay's *Gertie the Dinosaur* in 1914," says John Canemaker. Known throughout the world as one of the leading authorities on animation, Canemaker has written eight books on the subject, created award-winning animated films himself, and is head of the animation program at New York University. "But the Disney studio, under Walt's direction, really developed this talent to its highest point in the 1930s with *Snow White and the Seven Dwarfs.* It's quite amazing. Although the Dwarfs look very similar, they have distinct personalities. Grumpy doesn't brush his teeth like Dopey. Bashful puts on his pants in a way that is different from Happy or any of the other dwarfs." All of this, according to Canemaker, was to advance one goal: "Walt was convinced that story was king."

In service to that monarch, Walt was willing to make any changes necessary to his film. Recalls animator Ward Kimball, "I created a soup sequence for *Snow White.* It was very funny and everybody laughed, including Walt. Right after the dwarfs wash up, Snow White calls them in, hitting a pot with a spoon—dang, dang, dang. And then we animated all the funny ways they slurp the soup, especially Dopey. Walt called me up to his office and declared that he'd been looking at the film and decided that the soup sequence would have to come out. I'd spent eight months on it! He explained his reasoning: 'We've got to get back to the witch.' I was disappointed and kind of hurt, but he turned out to be right."

TOP: *Dopey prepares to "slurp the soup" in Ward Kimball's soup sequence.*
CENTER: *"I'm going to have to take out the soup sequence," said Walt.*
BOTTOM: *"We've got to get back to the witch," insisted Walt.*

hen they wanted more Snow White*s, the same as they wanted more* Three Little Pigs. *I remember the ones that followed were disappointing in a way. And for years afterwards I hated* Snow White, *because every feature I made after they'd always compare it to* Snow White.

WALT DISNEY

TOP: *An innocent Snow White, about to be threatened by the huntsman*

ABOVE LEFT: *Snow White*

ABOVE RIGHT: *"The "unique and distinct" Seven Dwarfs*

BELOW: *Shirley Temple presents Walt with the special Oscar.*

Walt was relentlessly critical. "He'd pick on everything," recalls Ollie Johnston. "For instance, we were running through one scene created by the great Fred Moore, when Walt commented that Grumpy's finger was too big. Walt called out, 'Hey, Fred, that finger's too big. Run it again.' And they ran it again. 'Yep, Fred,' Walt said, 'that's it.' And Fred said, 'Right here? That finger's too big?' 'That's it,' Walt replied. 'You gotta make that finger smaller.' So when we were getting ready to run the next scene here's the finger again and Walt says, 'Hey, Fred. See, that's it. That finger's too big!' 'I know Walt. I know! I'll fix it!'"

Over the course of months, such perfectionism naturally became pretty expensive. "Walt was literally mortgaged to the hilt," explains Charles Solomon. "He put into the film every nickel he could raise, borrow, or beg." As time went on, even that wasn't enough. Costs had soared from an estimated half-million dollars to three times that much. Says Card Walker, one of Walt's top executives, "Joe Rosenberg was with Bank of America in charge of motion picture loans. He came out to see the picture in order to evaluate how much money they could give Walt. The last part of the picture was not yet finished, so Walt ad-libbed the scenes and showed him stills. After the meeting was over, they walked out to Joe's car, and Joe said to Walt, 'Don't worry about the money a minute. This picture is going to make a potful of money.' Here was a banker Walt really liked."

Of course, Rosenberg was right. A glittery Hollywood premiere attracted the biggest stars. "All the Hollywood brass turned out for my cartoon," Walt later boasted. "That premiere was really exciting. And, gosh, that darn thing went on to gross eight million dollars around the world."

According to Solomon, that money "enabled Walt to continue experimenting, training, educating, exploring, and pushing the boundaries of the medium." What's more, *Snow White* set the pattern for animated features in the United States and much of the world. "We're still seeing animated features as musicals because *Snow White* was a musical. The idea that these should be based on fairy tales comes directly from *Snow White.* The kind of storytelling you see in *Snow White* is still the goal aspired to by animators. *Snow White* is one of the watersheds in the history of animation."

TOP: *The industry hails* Snow White.

ABOVE: *Walt on the cover of* Time, *December 1937*

"HE WAS DADDY"

IN 1930, ROY AND EDNA HAD A SON, whom they named Roy E. Disney. In the early years of her married life, Lilly wasn't ready to start a family. According to Diane, "Mother didn't want children at first. I learned many years later that my dad had wanted ten children, but Mother, as the youngest of ten, had seen her mother and sisters work too hard. She wanted to enjoy life, especially as my Dad was more and more successful. Life had become pretty exciting for them."

As it happened, when Lilly was ready to start a family, things didn't go easily for her. She suffered two miscarriages. "We were all very concerned about the miscarriages," says Walt's niece Dorothy. "You worried they might not be able to have their own child." Lilly's niece Marjorie recalled, "I took care of Aunt Lilly after both miscarriages. It was very sad."

These losses hit Walt hard. Although Mickey Mouse had made the studio wildly successful by the early 1930s, Walt was unremittingly tough on himself. He continued to work ceaselessly, never content with his products, no matter how successful they were, and he drove himself beyond the limits of most men. "As we got going, I kept expecting more from the artists and when they let me down I got worried," said Walt. "Just pound, pound, pound. . . . I was very irritable. I got to a point where I couldn't talk on the telephone without crying."

TOP: *Diane and Walt*

ABOVE: *Walt and Lilly relax on deck chairs during their 1931 cruise.*

The advice from Walt's doctor was clear: "I can't do anything for you if you don't just drop everything now and get away."

In the fall of 1931, Walt and Lilly left for a "gypsy jaunt" that included stops in Washington, D.C., Florida, and Cuba and concluded with a 5,000-mile cruise from Havana back to Los Angeles. "We had the time of our life," Walt said. "It was actually the first time we'd ever been on a true vacation since we were married."

When they returned home, Walt was his old energetic self again. In 1933, he and Lilly moved into a beautiful new home in Los Feliz Hills. "The house was in the English Tudor style and was on a hill," recalls Diane. "It had a big lawn that kind of rolled down to a huge swimming pool. And on many wonderful Sundays, animators and others who worked with him would come with their families and have lots of fun and games with the swimming pool. Barbecues, too."

The new house cried out for a larger family to fill it. And, in mid-1933, Lilly told Walt she was expecting again. Walt was understandably nervous. "Lilly is partial to a girl baby," he wrote his mother. "She seems to feel that she could get more pleasure out of dressing up a little girl than a boy. Personally, I don't care—just as long as we're not disappointed again."

They weren't. On December 18, 1933, Lilly gave birth to Diane Marie Disney. Marjorie, who was still in boarding school at the time, recalled, "Wow! She was the cutest baby. And so loved and welcome. I just kept calling home every day until she was born. Everybody in my school was saying 'Yay, it's a girl!'"

After the birth of Diane, Lilly suffered another miscarriage, and her doctor told her that it would be unwise to try to have another child. Knowing this, Walt and Lilly decided to adopt. In January 1937, two-week-old Sharon Mae Disney was brought home, but not without some anxiety. Marjorie: "She arrived and got pneumonia. We were all scared to death." Sharon recovered, and Walt's family was now complete.

It must have been tempting for Walt to use his daughters to help garner publicity. After all, what would have been easier than to have newspaper photographers taking pictures of two beautiful little girls attending a film or holding a Mickey Mouse doll? But Walt decided against this, in part because of fear of kidnapping. "The Lindbergh kidnapping occurred just before I was born," says Diane, "and because of it Dad would never permit any publicity. Even later he felt that we should be allowed to live our lives away from the

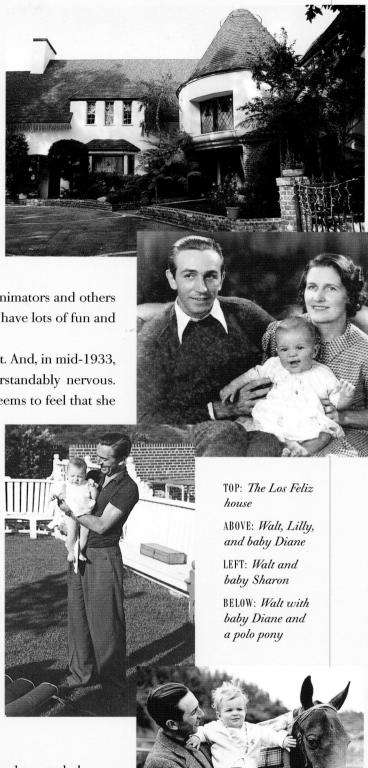

TOP: *The Los Feliz house*

ABOVE: *Walt, Lilly, and baby Diane*

LEFT: *Walt and baby Sharon*

BELOW: *Walt with baby Diane and a polo pony*

TOP: *At home, Walt was an avid photographer and home-movie maker.*

ABOVE: *Sharon (left) and Diane in their playhouse*

BELOW: *Sharon and Diane on Christmas morning in the early 1940s*

limelight without having people regard us as personalities." As Walt said, "I've never brought my family much in on the studio. In fact, there's hardly any evidence of the Mouse or anything around the place. I've lived with it too much and I just did not want to live with it at home. I tried to set up my home as something apart. I've kept the press away. . . . And they grew up in a way not knowing what part I played in the darn thing."

In fact, soon after Diane started school, she came running up to Walt one evening and called his name. "She was looking at me in a very serious way," recalled Walt. "And she says, 'Are you Walt Disney?' I said, 'Yes, honey.' She said, 'Give me your autograph.' And I said, 'Honey, what do you want my autograph for?' She said, 'A little girl from school asked me whether my daddy was Walt Disney, and she said she wanted me to get his autograph.' I guess she didn't quite understand what an autograph was then. . . . But she'd heard the kids talking. I got quite a thrill out of that."

✳ **He would collect all my drawings and encourage me and make me think I was wonderful.**

DIANE

Hazel and Marjorie had moved out shortly after Diane was born. As was customary at that time, a nurse was hired to care for the Disney girls. In the early 1940s, Lilly's oldest sister, Grace, moved in and helped with child care and babysitting.

Both daughters remembered Walt's role in those early years as someone who could be counted on to provide fun. "From the word go, Daddy was our playmate," Diane once told an interviewer. "He was the person you wanted. When Daddy came home at night that was the fun time. He could do anything. We thought he was the man with the most endurance. He could throw us around by our heels, you know, just spinning and spinning and spinning."

In spite of Walt's busy schedule at work, he gave the impression that time was endless whenever he was playing with his daughters. He drove them to school every day and rarely missed a school event. The family had dinner together every night, prepared by a cook, as Lilly rarely set foot in a kitchen. On the cook's day off, the Disney family would drive to the Tam O'Shanter, in Glendale, or to the Brown Derby, on Los Feliz Boulevard.

On many weekends Walt took his girls to local attractions like the carousel at Griffith Park—trips that inspired his first ideas about Disneyland. On occasion he'd come up with something special. "One time," said

> ✳ **It always made him mad that we had homework. I remember when he went to the principal of my school saying, "You've got my daughter in this school from 8:15 in the morning to four in the afternoon. I don't think it's fair that she should have to come home and do homework rather than be with her family."**
>
> SHARON

BELOW: *Diane and Walt*

BOTTOM: *Diane (left), Sharon, and their father by the playhouse that Santa brought one Christmas*

Diane and Walt at the Pasadena Rose Parade, New Year's Day 1939

Lilly, "when Diane, Walt, and I were going someplace in the car, we saw a blimp in the air. Walt wanted to go look at it when it landed. So we went over and the guy asked if we'd like to take a ride in it. Walt said, 'Sure.' Diane said, 'I will, too.' I thought, 'Well, my God, if they're going, I'm going, too. . . . If it goes down, I might as well be with them.' But I hated it. I remember the seat—there was no place to hang on. Another time Walt took us to a carnival where there was an elephant. As he was taking pictures, the keepers had the elephant raise its foot, and Diane was under it while Walt took a picture. I nearly died."

The Los Feliz house was up on a hill and somewhat isolated. With the fear of kidnapping, Walt would not allow the children to stray far from home. But early in their lives, Walt fell in love with the desert and began vacationing at a dude ranch in Palm Springs.

Diane: "There is something about the desert that Dad loved. It's peaceful. It smells good. The air is fresh. Smoke Tree Ranch was well located, with a back-drop of purple mountains whose foothills provided beautiful, verdant canyons that were only about an hour's horseback ride away. We enjoyed all of this, especially the freedom provided by the feeling that we were safe there. Sharon and I could go anywhere on our bikes. We could go down to the stables with our friends whenever we wanted and go for a ride in the desert. This was as wonderful for our parents as it was for us, I'm sure."

Walt spent hours in the water with the girls. He taught them to dog paddle and be "water safe," though proper swim strokes were not his strong point. He also taught them to ride horses and, when they were 12 or 13, to drive cars. "He was very patient and understanding," said Sharon. "Even when I got the car stuck in the sand, he didn't get mad."

Naturally, even on weekends at home Walt had a hard time staying away from the studio and was inclined to spend hours prowling around. As artist and writer Joe Grant recalls, "He made these sorties into the studio on Saturdays and he'd go from room to room, poking through the artists' desks and wastebaskets. Walt was hungry to see the ideas that might have developed outside the daily routine." The girls would often accompany him and ride their bikes around the studio lot. "We weren't raised with the idea that this is a great man who was doing things that no one else has ever done," said Sharon. "He was Daddy. He was a man who went to work every morning and came home at night."

> ✳ **He always told stories. At the dinner table he would tell the story of whatever he was working on. That was his forum.**
>
> DIANE

From "The Sorcerer's Apprentice" sequence in Fantasia

A NEW ART FORM

AFTER *SNOW WHITE'S* HUGE SUCCESS, many Hollywood experts thought they knew exactly what Walt should do next: a sequel. They wanted "more dwarfs." Walt did, in fact, make some sequels over the course of his career, but they never excited him. He wanted to move his fast-growing studio into entirely new directions in animation. So, with the money from *Snow White* in hand, Walt began production on three new animated films at the same time: *Pinocchio, Fantasia,* and *Bambi.*

All three required his artists to push themselves beyond past successes. Walt wanted to improve the quality of artwork in all of his pictures and he wanted his animators to truly understand animation as an art form. Fortunately, even before *Snow White* was completed, he had begun putting the apparatus in place to give his staffers all the skills they'd need.

"He knew his artists weren't trained enough for what he wanted to do," said Marc Davis, one of Walt's finest animators and Imagineers. Walt was initially impressed with Davis's ability to animate animals, and Davis would go on to create some of Walt's most memorable women, including Tinker Bell, Maleficent in *Sleeping Beauty,* and Cruella De Vil in *101 Dalmatians.* "So he visited the different art schools in Los Angeles to ask if they would train his artists. But he also asked if they would carry him for a while, because he didn't have the money to pay. The first few schools he approached just laughed at him. Eventually, he turned to Mrs. Chouinard of the Chouinard Art Institute. She looked at him and said, 'Mr. Disney, I admire what you're doing. You send down your people and we'll take care of the bill later.' And so she carried him for two years before he was able to pay her. He never forgot this."

Meeting Walt

Soon after I started, I was told, "If you bump into Walt, you should say, 'Hi, Walt.'" I'm coming down this hall, and here comes Walt Disney. But I'd been briefed. So he gets closer and walks by me and I say, "Hi, Walt."

And he went by me like there was nobody in the hall. And I thought, "Oh, those dirty bums. They set me up and I walked right into it." Well, some minutes later, I'm coming down this same hall and here comes Walt again. So, this time I walked right by him. And just as I went by, he grabbed me by the arm and says, "What's the matter? Aren't we speaking?"

BOB BROUGHTON

Walt was impressed with the results and resolved to step up his training program. He brought in an art instructor named Don Graham to teach at the studio after work. Mel Shaw was a young artist with the Disney Studio at the time: "Walt's idea was to get all of his artists to draw in the way of the Old Masters and then put those skills to work in animation. He wanted to capture the storybook quality that the famous illustrators had established through the years. Don would bring in paintings by El Greco and other Renaissance painters and he would analyze the paintings, explain their composition and use of color, and discuss the way their scenes were staged."

Don Graham's enthusiasm impressed his students. "They started bringing in real animals for us to draw and kept them in cages on the sound stages," Shaw recalls. "It became a zoo. Even so, Don kept encouraging people like Marc Davis and myself to also visit the real zoo, which was just down the road. We'd go over there at lunch hour."

Walt's efforts to cultivate his staff went beyond technical art training. Shaw: "Walt brought in top story people. He brought in H. G. Wells, who lectured on story development, and Alexander Woollcott, who was a great short story writer. He even had Frank Lloyd Wright to the studio to talk about inspiration and art. Walt was really imbuing all of us with something that made us feel we were part of a movement that could be considered a Renaissance in the animated cartoon business."

Joe Grant holding a model for Fantasia

Walt constantly strove to improve not just the skills of his artists and animators but also the way they worked. And when he was convinced of the need for change, he acted quickly. During the planning for *Pinocchio*, he determined that his artists needed better preparation for their animation and that models were superior to sketches. Thus the birth of the model shop. Recalls Joe Grant, who founded that operation: "It happened during one of those conferences you'd have with Walt in the hallway. We had finished *Snow White* and he asked, 'What are we going to do for an encore? Let's do some experimenting. Let's do some

research and see what we come up with.' We said, 'Let's create a model department.' And so we did. There was never anything ceremonious about him."

The studio became almost zoolike as animators studied deer and other animals for Bambi.

Aided by a series of remarkable models, the studio forged ahead on *Pinocchio*. The film is remembered today as one of the great triumphs of Disney animation. Comments Charles Solomon, "I think you could find among animators and animation historians that *Pinocchio* is as perfect as an animated feature has ever gotten. It's one of the very few films in which all of the characters are interesting, even the good guys. In terms of its art direction, its animation, its layout, its special effects, it's a gorgeous film and done with a fraction of the technology that's available to artists today. Yet it's still so far superior to virtually everything else, it's amazing."

When Walt was in the midst of *Pinocchio*, though, he realized that the film seemed to lack the kind of heart it needed. The marionette just couldn't carry the film on his own. Walt halted production while he worked out a solution: Jiminy Cricket. "The cricket is smashed on the third page of the original story," recalls Grant, "but Walt came to the idea that the cricket could be Pinocchio's conscience. That was the origin of Jiminy Cricket—purely in Walt's imagination."

Marc Davis

✳ **Thank God we did not wait longer to begin filming our interviews. Marc Davis's presence is a precious part of our film. We interviewed Marc and his talented wife, Alice, on the first day, December 4, 1999, along with Frank Thomas, Ollie Johnston, Joe Grant, and John Hench. It was a wonderful day for me and a wonderful beginning. Marc died a little over five weeks later.**

DIANE DISNEY MILLER

Initially, the cricket looked entirely too buglike to draw much audience sympathy, so animator Ward Kimball was given the assignment of personifying the creature: "At first, Walt said he looked too much like an insect, and I didn't catch on right away that Walt was kind of telling me that we can't have an insect running through the whole picture. So he ended up not being an insect. We finally ended up with a little man. He was cute. His head is an egg. He has no ears—that's the only thing you could construe as being cricket-like; he didn't have the big bug eyes and the funny little teeth. Walt wouldn't necessarily create the character, but he would tell you when he liked it. He did that always. He wasn't drawing. But he was giving us input."

Walt constantly tinkered with the stories he was trying to tell in his films. "Walt usually took home a briefcase full of material—books and whatnot," reports Grant, "and it was always a pleasure on Monday morning to see what he'd come up with over the weekend. In the case of *Pinocchio*, which is an oversized volume, I always had the feeling he never read the entire story. But I think he came back with a much better story, one full of his own improvisation. For instance, there's a scene where Pinocchio and Geppetto are locked inside of the whale. They do something in there to tickle him and the whale sneezes both of them out into the water. Walt looked at it and said, 'Well, that's interesting, it's not bad. But how about them saying *Gesundheit*?' It was one of the biggest laughs that picture ever got."

Just as with *Snow White*, Walt enjoyed telling the story of *Pinocchio* over and over again, seemingly developing it as he retold it. His nephew Roy E. Disney was about nine years old when *Pinocchio* was in production: "I had the chicken pox. I was up in my mother's bed being pampered by her when Walt and Lilly came over to have dinner with Mother and Dad. Walt came up to say hi and he said, 'Say, we're working on a new show right now, let me tell you a little bit about it and see what you think.'

"I've realized in the years since that he did this to every kid he could get his hands on. He'd test out some part of a story on them. So he started with the story of *Pinocchio*. He wound up sitting on the edge of the bed telling me the entire story, beginning to end. And it was great. I couldn't wait to see the movie. When I did, it was nowhere near as good as Walt telling it to me. And the story he told me was different from the story I saw on screen. I put two and two together years later and realized he was trying out some version of it on me to see whether I reacted or not."

While the staff was hard at work on the new productions, Walt decided that they needed a new studio. He and Roy settled on Burbank, California, as the location, and they started pouring millions of dollars into a state-of-the-art facility, making plans for badminton courts, a gym on the roof of one building, a full-service commissary, carefully manicured grounds with benches, and offices with good views and plenty of natural light. What's more, the buildings would all be air-conditioned. "It was a wonderful place," says Betty Kimball,

An early, buglike Jiminy Cricket (right), and the less "buggy" Jiminy Cricket (below)

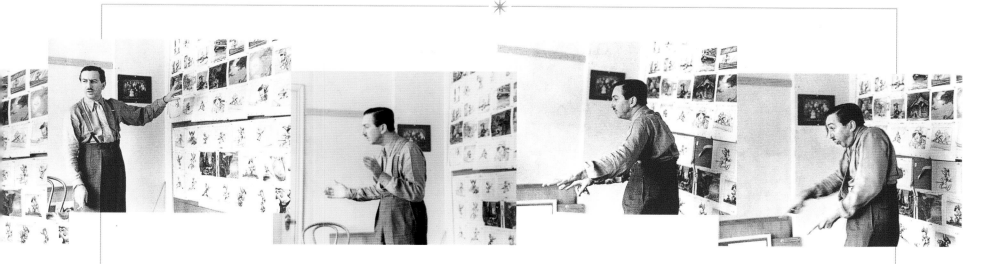

Ward's wife and former Ink and Painter. "Walt had new ideas and had all the furniture designed by someone special."

Even though much of the work on *Pinocchio* was being done in the old studio, a decision was reached to put a new animation camera into the new building. As a result, camera artist Bob Broughton and one other man, Berk Morrison, were the first two employees on the lot in the middle of 1939; the big move would come in 1940. Not only did Morrison work for Walt, but his father owned the stable where Walt had kept his polo ponies.

Recalls Broughton, "Well, there was no air conditioning yet, and there were a lot of flies in our room. On an animation camera you have a glass platen that comes down on the cels and the background. Well, when you'd bring that platen down and catch a fly, you'd squish it. That made a mess and it was a lot of work to clean up. So, Berk and I would turn off all the lights except one and we'd shoot the flies with rubber bands.

"One day we were doing this and, suddenly, there stands Walt with three bankers. He'd come to show them his new studio. Berk and I quickly turned all the lights on, showed them what we were shooting, how we were doing it, and so forth. Walt described the whole process to the bankers. And then they left.

"Well, about 30 seconds later, the door opened and Walt was standing there with a furious look on his face. He said, 'Berk! If I ever catch you in another stunt like this, you're gonna be back shoveling you-know-what in your father's stable!'"

During this period, Walt's team was also working on *Fantasia*. The project had begun as a short subject, starring Mickey Mouse as the Sorcerer's Apprentice. But after Walt got together with famed conductor Leopold Stokowski, the idea grew into something far more ambitious. It would eventually become a full symphonic concert performed by the Philadelphia Orchestra. Eight individual musical sequences—including pieces by Bach,

ABOVE: *Walt acts out instructions for his staff in front of a* Pinocchio *storyboard.*

BELOW: *The detail in* Pinocchio *was extraordinary.*

BOTTOM: Pinocchio's *nose grows and grows.*

Tchaikovsky, Stravinsky, Beethoven, and Schubert, were interpreted and brought to animated life by Walt's storymen and artists. In yet another step forward, studio engineers developed Fantasound, an early attempt to introduce stereophonic music into movie theaters.

"*Fantasia* may have been the most original and the most unusual project Disney ever undertook," says Charles Solomon. "It was basically a feature-length experimental film. Until that time, the only idea of putting together animation and classical music had been in Europe, where they were trying to bring movement to abstract painting. It was very much a high-art, high-culture, European phenomenon. In the United States, classical music was part of the fine arts. It was something elevated; it was something cultural. Animation was something to amuse people in the theaters, in movie houses—very different from an opera house or a concert hall. The idea that Disney could claim a place for this new art of animation as ranking with the traditional fine arts was almost sacrilegious."

Though Walt had no formal training in music, he worked one-on-one with his musicians and Stokowski to express musical images through animation. Recalled Walt, "We'd come to a big burst of a crescendo and I said, 'To me, that's like coming out of a dark tunnel and a big splash of light coming in on you.' We argued about it. Then I said, 'I see kind of an orange.' It's funny. Stokowski said, 'Oh, no. I see that as purple.'"

The results of this unusual collaboration redrew the boundaries used to define animation. Says animation scholar John Canemaker, "It's still astonishing to see that film. In fact, when he was doing storyboards for the 'Ave Maria' section of *Fantasia*, one of the story people said, 'You know, I don't think we're using the cartoon medium as we should be with this kind of thing.' Walt immediately turned on the guy and said, 'This is not the cartoon medium. We shouldn't be thinking of this as just a cartoon. We have worlds to conquer here.' That's how big his thrust was, his imagination for what animation could be."

TOP: *Walt surveys the progress of construction from inside the new Burbank studio.*

CENTER: *Walt's plans for the new studio included many amenities for the employees.*

ABOVE: *Lilly and Walt at the* Pinocchio *premiere*

Pinocchio and *Fantasia* were both released in 1940. Unfortunately, neither duplicated the success of *Snow White* at the box office. Like many American businesses that year, the Disney studio suffered with the outbreak in Europe of World War II. Though the United States wouldn't become directly involved in the war until 1941, the studio's revenues declined about 40 percent with the loss of its overseas markets.

Walt was particularly hurt when financial stress limited his ability to do everything that he had wanted with *Fantasia*. He was unable to use his Fantasound system in more than a handful of theaters. Worse yet, the distributor, RKO, insisted that the film be cut from two hours to 82 minutes, so it could be part of a double feature. Walt: "They prevailed upon my brother to do an edited version of it. He came to me and wanted me to edit it for general distribution. I refused. I said, 'Yes, you can edit it. But I'm not gonna do it.'"

"Had *Fantasia* been as successful as *Snow White*, the entire history of animation would be very different," says Solomon. "Disney's plan for *Fantasia* was to add to it continuously. He wanted to be changing sequences all the time: dropping pieces, adding pieces, rearranging pieces, so that you would never see the same film twice. Had he been able to do this, he would have been able to continue to expand the boundaries of the medium in terms of aesthetics, animation, design, color, music, and technology in a way that he wasn't able to after that."

Adds Canemaker: "If financial troubles hadn't come along, and if he could have kept doing films that were as experimental as *Fantasia*, there's no telling what we would be seeing now in animated feature films."

Meanwhile, even though the outbreak of war in Europe had put the studio on perilous economic turf—made all the more so because of

FAR LEFT: *From "The Nutcracker Suite" sequence in* Fantasia

LEFT: *From the "Ave Maria" sequence in* Fantasia

ABOVE: *The Hippo Ballet from the "Dance of the Hours" sequence in* Fantasia

My daughter Diane had read Bambi. *And when I finished the picture I brought it home and ran it. And she cried—she cried when Bambi's mother was killed. And afterwards, she said to me, 'Daddy, why did you have to kill Bambi's mother?' And I said, 'Well, it was in the book, dear.' She said, 'There are plenty of things in the book that you changed. Why couldn't you have changed that?' She had me there.*

WALT DISNEY

the costs of the new studio—Walt's crew continued work on *Bambi.* Ollie Johnston not only helped animate the film, but later co-authored (with Frank Thomas) the book *Walt Disney's Bambi: The Story and the Film.* He recalls Walt's insistence that the animals look real, not just like cartoon characters. "It was a difficult picture. We'd never done any animal with anatomy before, and Walt wanted the deer to have personality and be believable."

In signature fashion, while Walt drove his animators to push their artwork farther than they had in the past, he obsessed over the story. Johnston: "The great thing in that picture was how he presented the death of the mother. The story guys had been saying, 'Walt, we gotta show the mother lying there after she's shot and Bambi comes back and sees this bloody mess there.'

"And Walt says, 'Gee, I don't know guys, that doesn't sound quite right.' About two months later they'd bring it up again. And he'd say, 'Well, maybe.' He kept putting them off, saying, 'Gee, I don't know guys—that might be too strong.' So finally he worked it out that Bambi comes back and searches and calls for his mother and cries out but he never sees her. And Walt says, 'This is the way to do it, because if you

TOP: *"Your mother can't be with you anymore."*

ABOVE LEFT: *Bambi and his mother*

LEFT: *Bambi and Thumper try out the ice.*

66

show her lying there, it would be too much. What we want to do is just show Bambi's feelings and how much he cared.'"

"Chaplin said that he believed that Walt knew more about story than anybody in Hollywood, at any time," says animation director Chuck Jones. Jones was the creator of a number of Warner Brothers' greatest cartoons, including many featuring Bugs Bunny, Daffy Duck, and the Road Runner; he worked for Walt for a brief period. "And I think that's probably true. He knew falseness when he saw it. And even though he was accused of being a little too cute some of the time, maybe he was, but what are we going to do? Throw him out the window because he was a little too cute?"

Bambi was released in 1942 and, like *Fantasia* and *Pinocchio*, was not an immediate moneymaker for the studio. It wasn't the commercial instinct of "more dwarfs" that inspired *Bambi*, *Fantasia*, and *Pinocchio*, but rather Walt's constant struggle to refine and advance the medium he loved. Although the films were produced by teams of highly skilled artists and

In the "sweat-box" with Walt

technicians, no one involved in their creation would dispute that they are a testament to the singular vision, work methods, and management style of one man. All three films would, however, validate Walt's commercial vision in the years that followed; through later re-releases, they recouped their investment costs many times over.

Walt Disney was not a typical boss. During the war, one of the Disney Studio's training films was called *The Importance of Good Management*. It featured a section called the "Ten Commandments of Good Management." Walt's staffers found this terribly funny because he consistently broke all the commandments.

Ollie Johnston: "Walt didn't do too much complimenting. He didn't come to you and say, 'You're doing great and I'm going to give you a raise!' He would say, 'I hear that you've done something pretty good!' He wouldn't say, 'I like it.' He'd say, 'I hear from the director that something you did was pretty good.'"

Says John Canemaker, "Some people found it quite unnerving to come before Walt Disney and present a storyboard. Joe Grant, of all people, said it was like a trial. He'd hunch forward on his seat, his very animated eyebrow would go up, and he'd scowl because he was concentrating so hard."

Don Peri is a Disney historian who interviewed many of Walt's earliest employees. Says Peri, "He was very good at chewing people out. He could be very rough with people if he was upset with something that they did. He was mercurial. His moods changed very quickly, and many of the people I talked to needed to learn how to work with him. If someone had a big ego they couldn't be there. . . . You had to be willing to be criticized and to criticize and to question everything that went on."

Canemaker: "Animator Bill Peet said that he was brutal in his criticisms. And it wasn't anything personal. He

When Bambi *was released there were some hunting groups that were really down on me, because they didn't dare come home and brag to their family that they'd shot a deer, you know. They were ostracized.*

WALT DISNEY

X Atencio

"Hi, X"

✳ **Walt was upstairs on the second or third floor, where the story people were, the directors and everything. So, I didn't have any personal contact with Walt during that period. The first time I really talked to Walt, I was waiting for the elevator to go upstairs. He walked up and began to wait, too. And I said, "Hi, Walt."**

And he said, "Hi, X."

I didn't even know he knew my name. I almost dropped on my knees and kissed his foot. I was so impressed. Hey! He knows my name. . . . The great man upstairs!

— Imagineer X ATENCIO

wasn't brutal to the people who did it, but to the work itself. There was a woman, Bianca Majolie, who was the first woman to work in the story department back in 1935. She was a very nervous person, with good reason, because she worked with a bunch of these big bumptious storymen. But she was so nervous that, after each story session in which she had to pitch a board to Walt, she would vomit."

Peri: "One of his nontraditional techniques was to put two antagonists together. He liked the friction that came with that. He felt something creative would come out of it. Also, if he had a team working together who liked each other too much, he would break them up."

Canemaker: "Joe Grant and storyman Bill Cottrell, for example, worked very well together on the shorts and then into *Snow White*. But then Walt decided he wanted to use Joe Grant to create the character model department, and so that team was split up. And they had been very successful. Joe Grant said that there was something in Walt that if you became too close, too chummy, and perhaps too successful, he had to break it up."

All in all, it was a difficult landscape. Some employees simply couldn't take it, and they left. Others stayed on for their entire careers. "Walt didn't like 'yes men,'" says Peri. "And he didn't like people to throw cold water on his ideas. So it was difficult to find the happy medium between those two."

The men and women who worked with Walt liked to know when he was around or might be approaching. As Ollie Johnston recalls, a sort of code developed: "You know that scene in *Bambi* where the animals say that 'Man is in the forest,' and the deer have to run and hide? Well that became a regular thing in the studio. Walt would be coming down the hall, and someone would say, 'Hey, everybody! Man's in the forest!' That meant that Walt was coming."

FLORA'S DEATH

"WHEN WALT AND ROY became more prosperous with the success of *Snow White and the Seven Dwarfs*, they wanted to get a nice place for their parents to retire," says Bob Thomas, Walt's biographer. "Flora and Elias had been living in Portland, Oregon, near their daughter, Ruth. Roy and Walt said, 'We want the folks to come down here, where the weather is better, and where we can keep an eye on them and they can watch their grandchildren grow up.' So Walt and Roy brought them down to Los Angeles and bought them a very nice little house in the valley, close to where Roy lived." Said Ruth, "Those boys would have done everything in the world for their parents."

Soon after Flora and Elias moved to California, Walt had an offer from the DeSoto car company. Recalled Ruth, "They said if he'd pose in front of a DeSoto, they would give him a car. Walt said he didn't drive a DeSoto and he wasn't going to claim he did. But Mother asked, 'Why not? You can give it to us!' So Walt did it and they loved that little car."

TOP: *The family gathers to celebrate Flora and Elias's fiftieth anniversary. Back row (from left to right): Ray, Roy, Edna, Louise, Charlotte Disney, Robert Disney, Jr., Robert Disney, Dorothy Disney Puder, and Glenn Puder; front row: Herbert, Flora, Elias, Walt, Roy E., Diane, and Lilly Disney*

ABOVE RIGHT: *Walt and his mother, Flora Disney*

RIGHT: *Flora and Elias with their sons; (from left) Herbert, Ray, Roy, and Walt Disney*

*"Those boys would have done everything
in the world for their parents," said sister Ruth.*

For some time the Disney brothers—Herb, Ray, Roy, and Walt—enjoyed spending weekend afternoons together. As Walt's nephew, Roy E. Disney says, "They were very close. Walt and Roy and Herb and his wife and Ray would all show up on Sunday, particularly during the summer, and they would have these vicious croquet games. . . . The day would usually wind up with barbecue of hamburgers and corn. It was very Midwestern." Now living nearby, Flora and Elias were happy to join in with the fun, playing with their younger grandchildren, Roy E., Diane, and Sharon.

Flora and Elias's new home was very comfortable for them, but there was something wrong with the furnace. Walt and Roy sent studio repairmen to take care of the problem, but they didn't do a good job. Flora even wrote to Ruth, who was still living in Portland, that she was concerned about the furnace. "One night," says Bob Thomas, "Flora was asphyxiated from the gas leak, and, if he hadn't been rescued by the housekeeper the next morning, Elias would have died, too."

"Flora's frightful death was heartbreaking to Walt and Roy," remembers Lilly's niece Marjorie. "His mother's funeral service was held in the Wee Kirk of the Heather, in Forest Lawn, the same location where I had been married. I remember Uncle Roy saying to me, 'This sure isn't the same, kid.'"

Elias never really recovered; the loss of his wife, combined with whatever damage was done to him by the fumes, left him a shell of himself. "He was just lost without her," said Walt. "I never felt so sorry for anybody in my life as I did for Dad. He was really a lost person."

Occasionally Elias would forget Flora had died. Recalls Glenn Puder, a minister who is married to Walt's niece Dorothy, "Elias was like a man lost in time. His other half was gone and he was older, so the family rallied and everybody took care of Pa to see that he wasn't alone and lonely." Walt remembered, "I used to take my kids over to see him every Sunday. And there was nothing. He was just lost. It was a very sad thing. But before my mother died they were happy and she was very proud of Roy and me and what we'd done. She'd go places and say her name was Mrs. Disney and they'd ask if she was any relation of the Disney boys, and she'd say, 'Oh yes. My sons.'"

"The loss was devastating for Walt and Roy," says Bob Thomas. "In later years they would rarely talk about it." Recalled Sharon, "One morning I drove Daddy to work. I remember driving down Sunset Boulevard and asking Daddy where his mother was buried. All he said was, 'She's in Forest Lawn. And I don't want to talk about it.' Tears came into his eyes. Nothing more was said."

WALT DISNEY PRODUCTIONS

WALT DISNEY

INTER-OFFICE COMMUNICATION
P-139

TO Bob Cook   DATE February 26, 1941.

FROM Walt   SUBJECT

Under present conditions, the laying out of cash for equipment is out of line. Our situation is plenty tough and after returning from a session with the Bankers we have to stretch things out as far as we can and we still have to cut further. So we will have to work as efficiently as we can with whatever equipment we have. Steve says the splicer situation can be worked out to his and your satisfaction.

With regard to the moviolas, something should be worked out whereby we will not be compelled to purchase new equipment.

With foreign markets gone, even Walt was focused on cutbacks.

THE STRIKE

THE OUTBREAK OF WAR IN EUROPE caught the studio during a financially vulnerable period of growth. Walt's willingness to risk all the profits from *Snow White* on *Fantasia, Pinocchio, Bambi*, and the new Burbank studio—and to go into debt as well—was predicated on receiving income not just from the United States but from the rest of the world. There could hardly have been a worse time to lose that income.

With the studio struggling, Walt and Roy decided to sell stock in the company. This helped ease the cash-flow crisis, but it was a stopgap measure. It was clear to everyone working for Walt that hard times had hit. But the studio was large now, and Walt had lost direct contact with many of his writers and artists. They couldn't know that Walt was opposed to making up shortages by getting rid of staff, that he was losing sleep at night worrying about money, that he was fighting to save their jobs.

Walt understood that the company was entering a period in which pay levels weren't going to change much, and he wanted to help his employees weather the crisis. So, he gave them stock in the company and a stake in its future. The gesture had unanticipated consequences. "I gave all my employees stock, according to the time they'd been there," Walt said. "The big thing that disillusioned me was when they sold it on me instead of holding it. Then the stock started going down and down." Walt may have felt that the stock represented the company's future, but to many of his staffers with mortgages to pay and children to raise, the stock was a quick way to raise needed funds. Neither side really understood the other.

By 1940, most of the Hollywood studios had been unionized—with the exception of the animators at the Disney studio. The unions thought that Walt was rolling in money and that his salary was excessive. They reasoned that because he had just built a brand-new, state-of-the-art studio, there was a lot of money to be had. As historian Paul Anderson recounts, with rumors rampant "of the massive layoffs and the major salary cuts that were most assuredly coming," the Disney studio was ripe for unionization.

always hated to fire anybody. I'd think, "Well, gee, he's got five kids."
WALT DISNEY

71

Walt thought his carefully landscaped Burbank Studio would provide an ideal workplace.

There were other reasons for labor problems at the Disney studio. Anderson: "When they moved to the Burbank studio, a lot of the artists complained that it seemed very compartmentalized and that there was a real class system among the various echelons and levels of the artists. And another factor was the New York City animators and artists who had come to work at the Disney studio. They brought an attitude that didn't mesh well with the paternalism of Walt Disney or with his laid-back California artists."

Bill Littlejohn was a union leader at the time. He explains that when *Snow White* was made, artists were promised additional compensation if the film was profitable. "Some people," he says, "did get their due bonuses, and some people didn't. And the complications over how they were to be calculated got to be a sore point."

What's more, Walt's system for giving raises and promotions was subjective—if he thought you deserved it, you got more money. This was anathema to the unions. Littlejohn: "Seniority, which is very important to employees, was not honored, and that created a festering situation. And complaints weren't addressed properly."

Two unions sought to organize the Disney animators. One was the unaffiliated Federation of Screen Cartoonists, a sort of in-house union that wouldn't have given Walt any problems. But the other, the Screen Cartoonists Guild, was affiliated with the American Federation of Labor. It was led by Herbert Sorrell, a tough union organizer skilled in bare knuckles labor-management fights.

Anderson: "When Walt and Sorrell tried to negotiate, Sorrell went in making all sorts of demands, saying that Walt better sign with him or he was going to strike, and he was going to get Walt on the unfair labor lists; at one point, he even threatened to turn the

> ✳ **It was surely a beautiful studio but it [didn't make up for] the treatment of the people in regard to their bonuses. Walt was a patriarch. He thought he was a father for these people, and the children were turning against him. He was, apparently, deeply disturbed.**
>
> Union leader BILL LITTLEJOHN

Disney studio into a dust bowl. 'Well,' Walt said, 'I can't, in good conscience, sign my boys to this union without a vote. I need to know where they stand. The other union has come to me and they've said that you don't have a majority.' "

"Until that moment," says Roy E. Disney, "Walt really thought of everybody as friends working together. But there was a clear and sudden realization that this was a division between the bosses and the workers. I think it hurt both Walt and Dad a lot."

In February 1941, Walt gave a speech to his employees in which he spoke about his philosophy of work. But it was too little, too late. On May 28, Walt arrived at the studio to find a picket line. "The strike was a cataclysmic event in Walt's life and career," says his biographer Bob Thomas. "He had a rather paternalistic view towards the studio and its employees. He thought he treated them well, and he was astonished to see the ingratitude of these people out there on the picket line, yelling names at him as he passed through with his daughters. He just didn't understand it. I think it weighed on him very heavily, and it changed his attitude toward his employees forever."

The antipathy between labor and management grew, and the issues involved became increasingly complicated. Animator Art Babbitt, a senior Disney staffer with little to gain from a union, became one of the leaders of their cause, an act Walt took as a clear betrayal. Anderson: "As the hot summer months went on, the strike situation worsened. Sorrell even tried to shut down the Disney studio but wasn't able to do so because other unions wouldn't honor the picket line. Walt grew really disillusioned and discouraged."

By and large, Walt didn't want to deal with the situation. He turned the negotiations over to a

All of the left-wingers were over picketing my place. I took photographs of the picket line. Half of them I'd never seen before in my life. They'd never been in my studio. And I showed it to the FBI fellows who came in. One said, "These fellows have been at every one of these strikes."

WALT DISNEY

Strikers outside of the Disney studio, 1941

WORLDS TO CONQUER

RIGHT: *Tension between management and employees is reflected in this terse memo from Roy.*

BELOW: *Studio lawyer Gunther Lessing*

WALT DISNEY PRODUCTIONS

INTER-OFFICE COMMUNICATION
P-127 M

To ALL EMPLOYEES   DATE JULY 24, 1941

FROM ROY DISNEY   SUBJECT

Any discussions of union activities or infractions of established company rules on company property during working hours will be considered cause for immediate dismissal.

studio attorney named Gunther Lessing. Lessing was tough, like Sorrell, and his hard-line tactics didn't ease relations at all. Says Thomas, "Roy oversaw the whole negotiation. He tried to keep Walt out of it because he knew that Walt was so volatile and emotional about the whole thing. Lessing was overconfident that he could make a deal, but the deal he finally made wasn't very satisfactory for the studio. When the government, through Nelson Rockefeller, offered Walt a chance to take his animators to South America on a good will mission, Roy was relieved. He felt that Walt needed to get away from the situation, or he might crack up."

The invitation to South America began as a public relations mission—designed to help prevent Latin America from falling into the Axis orbit—but Walt insisted that he would go only if real work could be done there, as well. So, with 18 artists and musicians in tow, Walt set off for South America.

Was Walt Anti-Semitic?

One of the most prevalent myths about Walt Disney is that he was an anti-Semite. It's likely that this idea came out of the strike era, when union leaders may well have made good on Herb Sorrell's threat that he'd "smear" Walt.

In any case, when B'nai B'rith decided to give Walt its Man of the Year Award in 1955, it thoroughly explored the matter and determined to the satisfaction of its leadership that Walt had no anti-Semitic tendencies.

Says his daughter Diane, "My dad was interested in and respected all cultures and religions. His friendships did not know any racial or religious boundaries."

Many Jewish employees of the studio vouch for the idea that Walt showed no negative attitudes to men or women of the Jewish faith. "As far as I'm concerned, there was no evidence of it," says Joe Grant, "and I think that whole idea should be put to rest and buried deep."

INSIDE THE DREAM

"He was mobbed everywhere he went," says historian J. B. Kaufman. "He grew a little tired of always being on display as a gaucho. But public relations was a big part of his function, and he was very good at it. He was always good at entertaining people. In one of the programs they presented while they were in South America, he ran out of things he knew how to say in Spanish, so he just stood on his head. The audience loved it.

"The entertainment that came out of the South America trip was originally supposed to be a series of one-reel cartoons. When they had the first package of four shorts almost completed, they decided to combine them into one feature-length picture, which became *Saludos Amigos*. The other feature that came out of the trip, *The Three Caballeros*, is still a popular favorite many decades later."

The strike was settled while Walt traveled in South America. But Walt was unable to forgive and forget. Bill Melendez was an animator at the Disney studio at the time of the strike (and later the creator of the great *Peanuts* television cartoons). He recalls the strike's effect on Walt: "Other Hollywood producers would face strikes, and we'd come back to work and they'd say, 'By God, you beat me that time, but next time I'm going to beat you.' And then we'd forget it. But Walt was seething with anger at our behavior. He just would not make up. He was very unfriendly. Before that, he would always have a smile for me. Never again. He knew I'd been one of the traitors, that I'd been out on the strike against him."

> **Walt wanted a kind of utopia for the people who worked for him. We were "the chosen people." All of a sudden the strike came. He was furious.**
>
> Artist HERB RYMAN

"I think the strike had another effect on Walt," says Thomas. "It made him a political conservative. He felt that the strike had been communist-inspired. And there certainly is evidence that the leader of the striking union, Herb Sorrell, was a communist. Like a lot of people in those Cold War years, Walt became an outspoken anticommunist."

In fact, in 1947, Walt testified before the House Un-American Activities Committee. The gist of his testimony was that the strike at the Disney studio had been the work of communist-infiltrated unions that had trapped and misrepresented the "good, 100 percent Americans" who worked for him. The communists, he testified, "really ought to be smoked out and shown up for what they are, so that all of the good, free causes in this country, all of the liberalisms that really are American, can go on without the taint of communism."

TOP: *Walt and Lilly bound for South America in 1941 with their brother-in-law, Bill Cottrell (far left) and Ted Sears (second from left).*

ABOVE: *Donald Duck and dancer Aurora Miranda (Carmen's sister) in a frame from* The Three Caballeros

BELOW: *Walt testifies before the House Un-American Activities Committee, October 1947.*

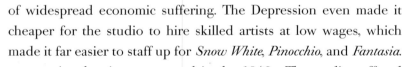

WORLD WAR II

IT'S IRONIC THAT THE DISNEY STUDIO was booming throughout the Depression. "Who's Afraid of the Big Bad Wolf?" struck just the right chord for Americans who feared that the wolf was at their own doors. Mickey, Donald, and Goofy provided laughs in a time of widespread economic suffering. The Depression even made it cheaper for the studio to hire skilled artists at low wages, which made it far easier to staff up for *Snow White*, *Pinocchio*, and *Fantasia*.

Another irony occurred in the 1940s. The studio suffered while the rest of the country was getting back on its feet economically. With the outbreak of war in Europe, Disney lost its European revenues. It was hit by the debilitating strike. And then, when the United States itself entered the war, interest in the Disney films flagged. Explained Walt, "Theaters were just mobbed. They were doing good business with any old piece of cheese they'd put on. But Disney films were a family thing, and theaters didn't want to be bothered with that because they didn't get as much money from them." In fact, *Bambi* was the only Disney feature to remain in production during the early war years. "The whole world was collapsing then," said Walt, "so I practically stopped my feature productions. That was all I could do." *Dumbo*, the last of the pre-war features, was due for release in December 1941. Walt had been somewhat less involved in *Dumbo* than in his other films, because he was deeply distracted by the strike during the initial phases of the film and it was being animated while he was on his long South American excursion.

was the only studio in town that was practically a war plant, because we were so versatile. We could do so many things. We could do live photography. We could do the cartoons. We did anything they wanted.

WALT DISNEY

Joe Grant, the man most responsible for *Dumbo*'s charm and passion, nonetheless gives Walt his due for the flying elephant's success. "Walt's participation might have been a little less in *Dumbo*, but on the whole the spirit of Walt is found throughout the picture. Remember, we were his disciples, and so we certainly weren't going to lose the Walt Disney touch." In fact, the week the Japanese bombed Pearl Harbor, *Dumbo* was scheduled to appear on the cover of *Time* magazine. A drawing for the cover had even been created by Disney artists, but, with the nation at war, other more serious matters took precedence.

Soon after President Franklin D. Roosevelt announced that the nation was at war, the studio itself was drafted. Not just a number of staffers, but the actual studio. As Walt recalled, "I was at home when we heard about Pearl Harbor on the radio. And shortly after that I got a call from the studio manager to say he'd been called by the police. He said, 'Walt, the army is moving in on us. I told them I'd have to call you. And they said, "Go ahead, call him, but we're moving in anyway." ' " Before Walt knew it, hundreds of troops were encamped in his studio, and drawing boards and employee parking sheds had to make way for ammunition and anti-aircraft guns.

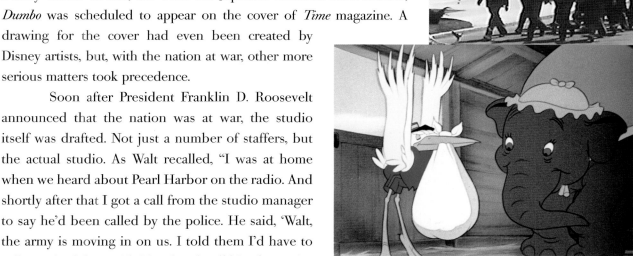

TOP: *500 troops move into the studio.*

ABOVE: *The stork delivers baby Dumbo to his mother.*

BELOW: *An educational film commissioned by the U.S. Government warns viewers about the dangers of malaria.*

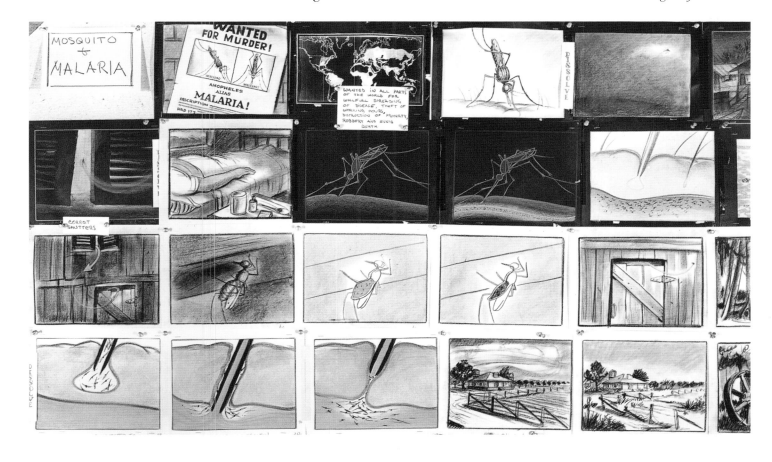

Walt: "The troops were there for eight months, sleeping in every room we could find. I had to double up my artists in rooms so that an officer could have a place to sleep. An officer couldn't sleep with an enlisted man. And they had their sleeping bags down on the floors, and they set up their own mess kitchen." Bill Justice, animator, recalls, "There were guards all around the place, and we had to have passes to get in."

Walt's studio turned to the war effort in a big way. Prior to the war, at its peak, the studio turned out about 37,000 feet of film. In 1942 to 1943, it generated more than five times that amount—204,000 feet—the vast majority of which was for government contracts. Animation, it seemed, was a terrific way to train soldiers, so the studio cranked out films about every conceivable topic, from flush riveting to navigating to avoiding malaria and sexually transmitted diseases.

Turning out these training films was particularly hard because many of Disney's staffers were drafted or enlisted. In fact, nearly one-third of the studio personnel wound up in the military. "They were just leaving by the dozens, every week," said Walt. "which created quite a problem." Occasionally, when an employee was particularly vital to a specific government film, Walt would try to keep him on the payroll, but for the most part, he was proud of his boys overseas. "When I decided to go into the Navy I went to Walt's office to tell him I was going to leave," says studio executive Card Walker. "I knew he'd be disappointed because he needed everybody, but he was really terrific. He told me that at 16, in World War I, he wanted to join up but was too young. But he found out he could go if he joined the Ambulance Corps, which he did. And he said, 'Good luck to you. I wish I could go back myself.' "

In addition to the training films, the studio continued to make cartoon shorts featuring the regular cast of characters. In 1943, the studio released four shorts that combined propaganda with entertainment: *Chicken Little, Reason and Emotion, Education for Death,* and *Der Fuehrer's Face,* in which Donald Duck plays a befuddled Nazi. (The Duck is relieved when he wakes up and discovers that he was only dreaming.) The same year, Walt released a largely animated feature, *Victory Through Air Power,* based on a controversial book by Major Alexander P. de Seversky that explained the potential importance of armed aircraft in the war. In addition, the studio dove into the task of creating hundreds of cartoon-based insignia for various branches of the military.

Working with the government was often a trial for Walt. For example, *The New Spirit* was a film designed to persuade people to pay their income taxes on time. While Walt

TOP: *The Disney studio created hundreds of insignia for military units.*

ABOVE: *Walt donates blood at a studio blood drive.*

Der Fuehrer's Face became a hell of a hit. It was the most popular propaganda film we had. It was put in all languages. The underground were running it into occupied territories, and they were getting a good laugh out of it while they were under the heels of Hitler.

WALT DISNEY

INSIDE THE DREAM

was talking to Secretary of the Treasury Henry Morgenthau, Jr., a secretary questioned Walt's decision to cast Donald Duck in the lead role of Mr. Taxpayer. Walt: "The secretary spoke up and said, 'I don't like Donald Duck.' And Morgenthau didn't say anything. He just stood there. And I began to get a little mad. I said, 'Well, you want to get this message over. I've given you Donald Duck. At our studio, that's the equivalent of giving you Clark Gable out of the MGM

stable. Donald Duck is known by the American public. He'll open the doors to the theaters. They won't be running a cartoon of Mr. Loomis the Taxpayer. They'll be running a Donald Duck cartoon.'" What's more, Walt explained, starring the Duck in this cartoon would ultimately cost him money. "By giving you Donald Duck," he said, "I'll probably be knocking off another Donald Duck that's already booked there." Morgenthau consented, and the cartoon was wildly successful. (A Gallup poll showed that over a third of all taxpayers who saw the film were more willing to pay their taxes.)

But the feds weren't done with Walt. The Treasury Department had asked Congress for $80,000 to pay for the film, half for production costs, half for the prints. Republican congressmen who wanted to attack unreasonable overspending accused Walt of profiteering. The truth was that he lost money on the film. "Here we broke our necks," said Walt, "and then I got postcards calling me unpatriotic, a war profiteer."

Victory Through Air Power was based on a book by Major Alexander P. de Seversky.

As always, Walt prowled the studio at night and on weekends. Says artist John Hench, "Walt was personally involved with everything we did. There was no escaping Walt. I don't know where you'd go if you wanted to hide from Walt, because he visited every corner of the studio." But as much as Walt tried to keep his studio vigorously moving forward, this was a difficult time for him. Says Joe Grant, "Walt, more or less lost control because we had so many of the army brass there at the studio, and all of them considered themselves producers." Recalls animator Ollie Johnston, "I was turned down for the military because I had an ulcer. Walt would stop in the hall and start to talk briefly, leaning against the wall and just standing there for two or three minutes without saying a word. And I didn't want to walk away because I knew he wanted somebody there. He was down because there wasn't anything he really could get involved in. He could talk about *Victory Through Air Power*, the training stuff, but that wasn't where his heart was."

> ✳ **I remember a Navy commander living in Dad's office, who would come up to our house and swim every weekend. He lived in the office, and they couldn't get rid of him.**
>
> DIANE DISNEY MILLER

79

Walt waits on tables at a benefit for the John Tracy Clinic.

"YOU DON'T PAY TO BRING THOSE CHILDREN HERE"

ANYONE WHO WAS CLOSE TO WALT knew how generous he was. When his niece Marjorie was married, he and Lilly gave her a wedding. He put a grand-nephew, Bill Papineau, through college when money was still tight. Young family members and other children close to the family received huge boxes filled with gifts every Christmas. "The box would be so large that they were sent by special parcel post," recalls Walt's niece Dorothy. "The box would come in a big truck and we'd practically scramble to get it in the door." In fact, when Walt first started building trains, he gave one set each to Dorothy's and Marjorie's sons and one to his nephew Ted Beecher, Ruth's son. "He made all the trees, the flowers, and the little cars," says Dorothy.

When he got involved in formal charities—like the John Tracy Clinic, a facility for deaf children and their families—Walt gave money and volunteered his time as well. Recalls actor Kevin Corcoran, who starred in many Disney films, "We would go over to the clinic and put on a show to raise money. After the show there was always a luncheon. After one lunch I remember looking up at a fellow busing the tables. It was Walt."

Toward the end of his life, when he decided it was important to create a new kind of institution for teaching the arts—California Institute of the Arts—he changed his will so that half his estate went to the school (better known as CalArts).

But equally telling are the numbers of stories his staffers tell of Walt's day-to-day kindnesses. A short selection:

Songwriter Robert B. Sherman: "My back was giving me a lot of trouble. One Monday morning, Walt said, 'Bob, come here.' We went to his office, where there was a rocker like the one President Kennedy used. He said, 'Don't tell Lil, but I took it from the house in Palm Springs and we flew it in for you.' "

Secretary Lucille Martin: "Someone must have mentioned to Walt that I had never been in a plane. One day he said to me, 'Let's close the office and you come with me.' And we flew to San Diego. And we sat on a little jump seat. It was my first plane trip."

Actor Fess Parker: "One day, I simply said, 'You know, Walt, I'd like to have a percentage of the profits from the Davy Crockett merchandise.' Much to my surprise I was given 10 percent. That was probably a landmark in the industry."

Camera effects artist Bob Broughton: "When my son Dan was a senior in high school, he was accepted at Princeton. I agreed to let him go if I could get three or four banks to finance it. The next day I asked Walt if he contributed to Princeton University. He told me he didn't. I said, 'Gee, I was hoping you were one of their big benefactors because last night I found out Danny was accepted at Princeton University.' Walt said, 'No, I don't contribute anything to Princeton, but Roy and I have been talking for years about setting up a scholarship fund, and Danny is just the kind of kid we've been thinking of.' Three months later, the Walt Disney Scholarship fund was established and Dan won one of the scholarships. So he went to Princeton for four years."

Imagineer Rolly Crump: "One day back in the '50s Walt was sitting on the steps of City Hall in Disneyland having a sandwich. All of a sudden Walt looks up and here comes a nun with a rope attached to her wrist attached to a kid, attached to a kid, attached to a kid, and then attached to another nun. Here were 15 kids roped together with a nun on each end. Walt got up, put down his sandwich, and introduced himself, asking, 'What is this?' And the nun said, 'These are underprivileged children. We wanted to bring them to Disneyland.' And he asked, 'How much did you pay to come in?' And she told him. He went to the main gate, got the money, came back, and gave her the money back and said, 'You don't pay to bring those children here.' That's the kind of thing you don't hear about Walt."

Mouseketeer Sharon Baird: "Across the street from the studio, at St. Joseph's Hospital, each room in the children's ward had a different Disney character theme. He sent animators and painters across the street. And they didn't just have the characters, but the backgrounds as well."

PART THREE

NEW HORIZONS

After the end of World War II, Walt was eager to launch into brave new ventures, while Roy called for fiscal restraint. A relatively short period of austerity was followed by a frenzy of diversification at the Disney studio.

Like a sculptor who sees art in a slab of stone, Walt saw the potential in the miles of film he had commissioned of Alaskan seals. Overcoming the doubts of the distributor, he produced the Academy Award–winning Seal Island, *which led to the hugely successful* True-Life Adventures *series. Meanwhile, starting with* Cinderella *in 1950, he again began to produce feature-length cartoons, including* Sleeping Beauty *(released in 1959), the most expensive of them all.*

In his ambitious effort to expand into live-action features, Walt produced Treasure Island *in 1950, followed up by other films that were to define the concept of family entertainment, including* 20,000 Leagues Under the Sea, Old Yeller, *and the first of the broad comedies that were a hallmark of his 1960s output,* The Shaggy Dog.

At home, Walt indulged his lifelong love of trains as his daughters emerged from their childhoods.

During this period, Walt's work in television—including the "Disneyland" TV show, "The Mickey Mouse Club," "Zorro", and other programs—was initiated in large part to help finance yet another astonishing project. Walt's ambitious dream: Disneyland.

ENTERING LIVE ACTION: "ACTORS ARE GREAT!"

"RIGHT AFTER THE WAR," Walt said, "a big period of indecision followed. You can't run an organization with indecision."

Walt and Roy both faced the same set of facts: The last major animated film the Disney studio had made, *Bambi,* was released in 1942. For four years the studio had primarily been cranking out material for the government. The studio lacked the funds to tackle a major animated feature; it would take a few years before it was ready to embark on *Cinderella.*

Roy O. Disney

Meanwhile, Walt wanted to forge ahead at all costs, but Roy argued that the studio had to take a more cautious approach. "I've always maintained that you can't just coast," Walt later remarked. "If you do, you go backwards. It's just a slow way of liquidating. And I said we were going to move forward, get back in business, or liquidate. Let's do anything to get some action, you see?

"I felt very sorry for Roy. I'm always sympathetic to him because he has to sit with the bankers. He has to sit with the money men. He has to sit and fight with these stockholders who come in and harass you."

The two brothers fought. As Roy said in a 1968 interview, "All of a sudden we were like a bear coming out of hibernation, with no fat on us. I wanted to shelve the major animated features because they'd be too expensive. But Walt wouldn't shelve them. I remember one night he came down to my office. We sat there from quitting time to eight or so, and I finally said, 'Look, you're letting this place drive you nuts. That's one place I'm not going with you.'

"I walked out on him. I didn't sleep that night and he didn't, either. The next morning, I'm at my desk, wondering what the hell to do. We were in a hell of a tight fix, big payroll on our hands and everything. You don't worry about yourself. You worry about your commitments, your involvements. And I felt awfully low. Then I heard his cough and footsteps coming down the hall. He came in and he was filled up. He could hardly talk. He says, 'Isn't it amazing what a horse's ass a fella can be sometimes?' And he walked out. That's how we settled our differences."

> ✳ **I think you have to remember that when Walt first came to California he wanted to be a director of live-action films, but he wasn't able to get anybody to hire him. When he finally began to do live action, he found it very satisfying, because it was what he wanted to do initially.**
>
> MARC DAVIS

As a compromise, the two brothers made several patchwork films between 1946 and 1948: *Make Mine Music, Fun and Fancy Free,* and *Melody Time.* These were compilations of animated pieces, often set to music. Although they didn't satisfy Walt artistically, he admitted, "The payoff was that I got going, and by getting going I could make decisions."

The one big feature made during these years was *Song of the South*, which used more live-action footage than any major film Walt had made in the past. The enchanting performer James Baskett played Uncle Remus, who lived in a live-action world and told stories of Brer Rabbit and his friends, who were animated. For *Song of the South*, Walt brought together the best crew he possibly could.

"One of the interesting things about Walt's gradual involvement in live action was that he wanted his films to have the same quality of his animated films," says film critic and author of *The Disney Films* Leonard Maltin. "In some cases that meant getting the best people he could find or developing talent the way he did in the animation field. For *Song of the South*, he hired Gregg Toland to do the cinematography. This was the legendary cinematographer who shot *Citizen Kane* with Orson Welles and scores of other incredible-looking movies."

Unfortunately, though the critics seemed to greatly admire the animation in *Song of the South*, they panned the live-action sequences. As one critic wrote, "The ratio of 'live' to cartoon action is approximately two to one, and that is approximately the ratio of its mediocrity to its charm."

Worse, some critics felt that Walt's portrayal of Uncle Remus as a happy-go-lucky former slave had racist implications and that it minimized the horrors of slavery. Says Maltin, "*Song of the South* has always been troubling for some people, and in this era of political correctness it's become something that no one wants to touch. Yes, it depicts African Americans in the post–Civil War era in a way that some people refer to as Uncle Toms striving to please their white masters. But I think generalizing is terrible. You have to look at the way they're actually portrayed. Look at the humanity of the characters. Look at their kindness, their caring, their warmth. Not simply Uncle Remus, but the wonderful character played by Hattie McDaniel, who had won an Oscar for playing Mammy in *Gone With the Wind*. These are such loving and warm-hearted characters that it's hard for me to find anything negative about them. I can think of hundreds of films that are perfectly acceptable to most people, films whose images of black Americans are far worse than *Song of the South*, and yet no one thinks twice about them."

ABOVE RIGHT: *James Baskett played Uncle Remus.*

RIGHT: *Brer Fox and Brer Bear in an animated sequence from* Song of the South

Meanwhile, Walt was trying everything he could to break out of animation and move into pure live action. "We need to diversify," he insisted. But it was an uphill battle. "Here was the king of animated films," continues Maltin, "who had pushed the medium to heights no one had ever anticipated. All the movie industry wanted out of him was more of the same. And that's exactly what Walt never wanted to do. He was interested in live action, but they weren't. He had to force it on them." When Walt tried to make a fully live-action film in *So Dear to My Heart*, for example, his distributors at RKO insisted that he add animated footage.

The *True-Life Adventures* series was another effort to break out of animation, but it, too, was met with resistance by RKO. Recalls artist and Imagineer John Hench, "When Walt first got the idea of *True-Life Adventures* and went to RKO, they turned it down. After all, they were our distributors and they represented the exhibitors, so they should know. They said absolutely not. Rather than abandon the idea, Walt promptly sent out a photographer and a team—just as if RKO had said they would be thrilled to take everything Walt produced. We shot miles and miles of the worst stuff you ever saw, seals scratching their sides and their fannies and sniffing and looking at each other, just miles of footage like this. All the while, Walt was building a story in his head, until he had it."

Walt had the seals' footage brilliantly edited and added music and a story line that brought the seals to life with carefully sculpted narration. He called the finished film *Seal Island* and brought it to RKO, but they still demurred. Undaunted, Walt arranged to have *Seal Island* shown in one local theater in order to qualify for an Academy Award. It won. And Walt's *True-Life Adventures* series was launched.

Leonard Maltin: "Long before *National Geographic* came to television, before there were entire channels devoted to wildlife and nature films, before there was IMAX, before there was any of that, Walt Disney started the *True-Life Adventures* series. Eventually the series spawned two very highly praised and Academy Award–winning feature films, *The Living Desert* and *The Vanishing Prairie*. Until then, there had been many documentaries, and some had even been successful with audiences, but it was almost revolutionary for a professional of Walt Disney's stature to put his stamp on documentary films and put his studio to work to popularize and

TOP: *Bobby Driscoll, James Baskett, and Luana Patten with their animated co-stars*

CENTER: *Walt on the set of Granny Kincaid's cabin from* So Dear to My Heart

ABOVE: *Distributor RKO forced animation into* So Dear to My Heart.

make palatable this kind of entertainment." Walt had finally hit on a way to overcome the resistance to his making live-action films.

Another giant step came through the movies the studio began making in England. At the time, American filmmakers could show their productions in the United Kingdom, but they weren't allowed to bring home the profits. British law required them to use the money they made there—the so-called "frozen funds"—in the U.K. Walt searched for a solution. "My first thought was to start a cartoon studio there, but I didn't think I could, because you have to train artists for it or else import them. . . . I had this story of *Treasure Island* that I wanted to do, and I suggested we go over to the U.K. to do it there." *Treasure Island*, Walt's first fully live-action feature film, turned out to be a great success, and Walt made three more pictures in England to follow it up: *The Story of Robin Hood and His Merrie Men*, *The Sword and the Rose*, and *Rob Roy, the Highland Rogue*.

Maltin: "The costume pictures and swashbucklers Walt made in the early '50s were notable for several reasons: The films brought him into association with a talented young director named Ken Annakin, who would go on to direct a number of other films for Walt, most notably *Swiss Family Robinson*. Another reason was the serendipitous hiring of a very talented matte artist named Peter Ellenshaw, who was able to create scenes and settings that looked real but weren't. Ellenshaw's talent was so prodigious that he wound up working for Walt in Hollywood, spending the rest of his film career at the Walt Disney Studio. Finally, those swashbucklers were just great fun. I think the story of *Robin Hood and His Merrie Men* is one of the really unsung Walt Disney movies."

Although Walt would visit England from time to time, he had to produce these films more or less by remote control, which was cumbersome. The solution: to create the same kinds of storyboards he used in animation. "Until Walt, no one had really used the technique for planning out a live-action film," says Maltin. "It was a way for him to conceptualize *Treasure Island* in his studio in Burbank, for instance, and then send off his producer to shoot it in England with the confidence that the film would turn out as he expected. Using this method was a way of maintaining some control and having a pretty sound idea of how it would play out. And Walt was a master of reading a storyboard—sensing where something needed punching up, where it was lagging."

Says Director Annakin, "I had never experienced artists sketching out a whole picture. In *The Sword and the Rose* I was deeply involved in the sketching of every sequence for Walt's approval. As a director, I was not forced into keeping exactly to

BELOW: Seal Island *poster promotes the first* True-Life Adventure.

CENTER: *Title logo for the* True-Life Adventures

BOTTOM: *A frame from* The Living Desert

the storyboard, but to keep exactly its spirit. And if I started to divert too far, Walt would ask why I was doing it this way. On *Sword and the Rose*, I started to edit a sequence, and Walt asked, 'Why didn't you shoot exactly to what we'd agreed?' I replied by telling him that I had heard we were going over budget and I was trying to save a little. He said, 'Have I ever queried the budget? Have I ever asked you to cut? Let's keep to what we agreed.' And we did."

After finishing his fourth picture in the United Kingdom, Walt was ready for his first major American fully live-action feature, *20,000 Leagues Under the Sea*. He brought artist Peter Ellenshaw to America to do the mattes, and their friendship grew over the years. "He certainly was a father figure," says Ellenshaw. "More than a father figure—he was a vibrant human being. Many years later I found that everybody else felt this, too. They all thought they were someone special in Walt's eyes. Actually, we *were* all special in his eyes."

Walt's selection of a director for *20,000 Leagues* was particularly surprising. Walt chose Richard Fleischer, son of his old competitor in animation, Max Fleischer. As the director remembers, "I got a call through my agent that Walt Disney wanted to meet with me. I couldn't believe it. I was a young director. I hadn't made a really big, important picture up to that time. I went to see him in his office at the Disney studio, and I noticed that on the wall was a sketch of a very curious-looking submarine, entangled with an octopus or a squid. Walt asked if I knew what it was and I said, 'Yes, that's Jules Verne. *20,000 Leagues*.' Walt smiled. 'We're going to make a feature film out of that, and it's going to be the biggest picture we've made.' I said, 'Great. Animation?' And he said, 'No, no. Real live action. And we'd like you to direct it.'

"I was completely taken aback. I couldn't understand why he'd selected me. I asked him, 'You do know who I am, don't you?' He said, 'Yes, I know.' I said, 'Well, why would you

ABOVE: *An underwater scene from* 20,000 Leagues Under the Sea

RIGHT: *The interior of the* Nautilus

want me to direct this picture?' And he replied, 'I saw a film you directed called *The Happy Time*, and I figured that anybody who can make an actor out of Bobby Driscoll has to be a great director.' And that was the reason he gave me for wanting me to direct the biggest picture ever made by the Disney company.

"I said, 'I'd love to do this picture, but I feel very uncomfortable about it, knowing the relationship you and my father have had. I'd like to

Happy Ending

In the early days of animation, Walt and Max Fleischer were arch-rivals. Walt and his crew of characters, including Mickey, Donald, Goofy, and Pluto, were regularly going head-to-head with Fleischer's Betty Boop, Popeye, and others. As the years passed, there was no love lost between the two men, particularly when they were competing for the premier animators of the day. But after Walt hired Max's son, a remarkable détente came about. As Richard Fleischer tells the story: "Just about the time that I finished shooting *20,000 Leagues Under the Sea*, my father came out to

Walt with his old competitor Max Fleischer and Max's son Richard

California with my mother for their golden wedding anniversary. When Walt heard my father was in town he called me up and said, 'I'd like to invite you, your father, and all of his ex-employees to the studio for lunch.' So we had this legendary lunch with all of the ex-Fleischer employees and Walt Disney. And Walt gave my dad a tour of the studio and Disneyland under construction and the two men became friends.

From then on, whenever Walt came to New York he would call my dad and take him to lunch. So the whole thing ended up happily."

A Tall Tale

✳ **Peter Ellenshaw recalls the day Walt told coworkers how the two of them had met. Said Walt, "I was in Trafalgar Square, passing by somebody who was painting a loaf of bread on the sidewalk. He'd written on the bread, 'Easy to draw, hard to earn.' I told him I thought the drawing was quite well done, and the guy looked up at me and said, 'Oh, thanks, Guvner.' And I asked him, 'Would you like to come and work for me?' And he said, 'Well, yes, I would.'**

"And so that's how Peter came to work here."

Of course, the story was complete myth. But, laments Ellenshaw, "The guys believed him!"

Walt and Peter Ellenshaw

call him in New York and talk it over with him to see if he feels I might in some way be disloyal to him by taking on this job.'

"Walt agreed and told me to call him the following morning with my decision. I called my father that night, told him the story, and he said, 'Of course you must take that job, without any question. You didn't have to call me. That's an opportunity you cannot miss.' Naturally, I was very relieved. He said, 'Just do one thing. Give a message to Walt for me. Tell Walt that he's got great taste in directors.' "

The film featured a stellar cast, including Kirk Douglas, James Mason, and Peter Lorre—and, of course, the unforgettable squid. The story of filming the squid fight is legendary. As Richard Fleischer tells it, "The squid that had been constructed for the sequence was totally inadequate, a great big blob covered with some kind of material, with tentacles, some of which weren't even

ABOVE: *The giant squid in a peaceful sunset*

RIGHT: *A storm was added to* 20,000 Leagues *to make the squid attack scene more dramatic (and to hide the squid's flaws).*

connected to the body. What little movement there was required heavy cables to lift its arms and tentacles. The stuntmen had to look like they were fighting something that was alive, but the squid was completely phony. Pieces were even falling off of it.

"What's more, the scene was supposed to take place on a flat, calm sea at sunset. The light from the sunset exposed the cables. No matter what we did we couldn't hide those damn cables. There was no excitement in it. The sub was flat, the lighting was flat, the squid wasn't working. I was going crazy with it and the stuntmen were fighting a big hunk of blubber.

"After a day or two of shooting, I felt a tap on my shoulder and it was Walt. 'I just saw the dailies,' he said. 'What are you shooting here, a Keystone Cops comedy?' I explained the situation and he understood immediately. He told me to stop working on this sequence and to go on to another 'to give me time to talk to my geniuses out at WED and see if we can't come up with a squid that works for you.' "

The result, of course, was that Walt's mechanics came up with a superior squid, and the scene was set during a storm, complete with lightning, thunder, and waves. The cables were hidden in the spray and the waves, and lightning flashes dramatically illuminated the squid. "The effects added a lot more money to the production," says Fleischer, "very nearly closing down the production."

Adds John Hench, who helped with the special effects, "The rain was blown in through the air-conditioning system and the insulation. I don't think Stage 3 dried out for three years."

Walt loved live action. "Actors are great," he once told his animators. "You give 'em the lines, they rehearse a couple of times, and you've got it on film—it's finished. You guys take six months to draw a scene!" Walt was only needling them, of course, but there was some truth to his words. One animator lamented, "As soon as Walt rode on a camera crane, we knew we were going to lose him."

TOP: *Walt and director Richard Fleischer*
ABOVE: *On location for* 20,000 Leagues

WALT & ANIMALS: "I RESPECT NATURE"

ABOVE: *At a zoo in Europe*

BELOW: *From childhood on, Walt was fond of all farm animals, including hogs.*

BOTTOM: *Walt and one of the studio's miniature horses*

WALT'S FIRST PET was a Maltese terrier on the farm in Marceline, Missouri. "He was my pal," Walt said. "He'd always come up and grab you at the heel. We wore stockings, and my mother was always having to repair the stockings because he'd tear them out. Then, one day, my brother Roy went into town in the buggy and he let the dog follow him. When he got into town he lost the dog. We never saw him again. That was a big tragedy."

Fortunately for Walt, there were a number of other animals to play with on the farm. He learned how to ride the large hogs the family kept. And he became close to Charlie, a sway-backed, gray-dappled horse that pulled their buggy. When, on one occasion, Walt accidentally killed an owl, he had bad dreams about the creature for years.

Although it would be a long time before Walt would have another pet—there was hardly room for one in the Disney house in Kansas City—his love of animals was a lifelong affair. After he was married, Walt discovered to his dismay that Lilly didn't share his affection for animals. "I wanted a dog," he said. "And my wife would have nothing to do with dogs. She said, 'Oh, they get hair on everything. They're dirty. And there's dog odor.' So I got a book about dogs and read a story on the chow. The chow does not shed hair. The chow does not have fleas. The chow has very little dog odor. . . . The next day, I went out and bought a chow, and I kept it under wraps until Christmas. I got a big hatbox and put a big ribbon on it. When the time came, I put the little puppy in the hatbox and tied it up with a ribbon."

But when Walt presented Lilly with the hatbox, she was dismayed; Lilly liked buying her own hats and didn't want one as a present. "When she opened it," Walt said, "the little chow stuck its head out. From that time on, that was her baby. I've never seen anybody so crazy over an animal. And, my gosh, she wouldn't let it out of her sight."

One of the few fights between her parents that stands out in Diane's mind concerns an animal—in this case a goat. In the early years of the new studio in Burbank, every Fourth of July was the occasion for a company picnic on the studio lot. There was always a softball game or maybe some badminton on a sound stage. On one of these occasions animator T. Hee, who raised goats, gave Walt a small female goat with a ribbon and a bell around her neck. It was ostensibly for his daughters, but Walt was delighted with the gift. As Diane recalls, "When it came time to go home, Dad put the goat in the car and Mother said, 'We're not taking this goat home.' And Dad said, 'Well, what do you mean?' She said, 'I won't have it.' Dad said, 'Well, of course you will. It was a gift to the kids and we're going to take it home.' So we put the goat in the car and we were on the road home when all of a sudden I heard this sobbing in the back seat, and mother was sitting there crying. These furious tears were coming down her cheeks. It was really quite a tense situation. Anyway, Dad got furious, and said, 'OK, we won't keep the goat.' "

Walt may not have gotten his goat, but he found plenty of opportunities to be in the company of animals. His affection for the miniature horses at Disneyland was legendary. When one of them had a colt, Walt was smitten. He spent hours petting the little horse, and the young animal would crawl right into his lap.

Walt's loyalty to creatures, whether domestic or wild, is part of Disney family lore. "I remember Daddy coming home at night and going out and feeding nuts to the blue jays," his daughter Sharon once recalled. "They're mean birds. But Daddy would sit out there and feed those things." Walt's niece Marjorie remembered a similar, typical incident: "One time, the gardener was complaining because the squirrels were eating all the fruit. He had planted all these beautiful fruit trees down in the canyon by the house." Apparently, the gardener planned on poisoning the squirrels. But Walt wouldn't hear of it. As Marjorie recalled, "He just said, 'Plant some more. Plant enough for everybody.' " He told Lilly, "Look, you can go to the market to buy fruit. They can't."

7. ISN'T THERE A LITTLE BIT OF "BAMBI" IN WALT DISNEY, OR FOR THAT MATTER, IN EVERYTHING YOU TRY TO DO?

I RESPECT NATURE + THE CREATURES OF NATURE — MAN CAN LEARN A WAY OF LIFE FROM IT — MAN IS THE MOST HELPLESS + OF ALL ANIMALS — PATHETIC

DICK STROUT, INC. — Box 907 • Beverly Hills, Ca
Phone CRestview 4-1330

TOP: *Walt and his poodle Dee-Dee*

ABOVE: *Walt expresses his philosophy on nature in a handwritten note to a reporter.*

RIGHT: *A coyote from* The Vanishing Prairie

Walt's affection and respect for animals comes through in many of his television shows and films. Says director Ken Annakin, "I think Walt felt that if he observed animals well they could be wonderful instruments for him to make entertainment." Indeed, movies like *Old Yeller, Savage Sam,* and *The Incredible Journey* feature animals as their stars. And the lead-ins to Walt's television shows repeatedly showed him enjoying the company of all manner of creatures—dogs, cats, monkeys, even tigers.

The *True-Life Adventures* pioneered the dramatic use of animals in their natural environments. "I think he rather admired the coyote," said James Algar, director of several of the *True-Life Adventures.* "I think Walt was always on the side of the creature who was doing something for himself and was fending off whatever was threatening him and outsmarting his enemies. The coyote is a very intelligent animal, capable of pulling tricks on people. And I think Walt always admired that in a creature, because he read himself into it. That's what he would have done, if he were a coyote."

Bambi was the first of Walt's films to dramatize the lives of animals (animals, that is, that don't wear white gloves or hats). The film is a heartfelt expression of his great love for animals and his sense of their inherent nobility. It is telling that the only real villains in the story are the human characters. "I respect nature, and the creatures of nature," Walt once wrote in regard to *Bambi.* "Man can learn a way of life from it—man is the most helpless and pathetic of all animals."

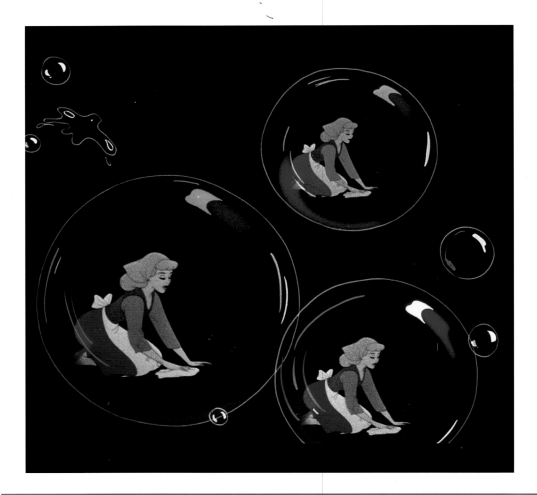

RIGHT: *"I can see it,"
Walt said of the
bubbles that would
represent the three-
part harmony in*
Cinderella.

BELOW: *Walt's "nine
old men"—the studio's
master animators:
(from left to right)
Ward Kimball,
Eric Larson, Frank
Thomas, Marc Davis,
Ollie Johnston, Les
Clark, Milt Kahl,
John Lounsbery,
and Wolfgang
"Woolie" Reitherman*

"WITH EVERY LAUGH . . ."

PRIOR TO WORLD WAR II, Walt had considered producing a number of animated features. But in 1941 Walt wrote, "Due to the present world market, we have suspended production, temporarily at least, on all such pictures as *Cinderella, Peter Pan, Alice in Wonderland,* and others. The cost to properly produce these classics we do not feel is warranted under existing conditions, but instead we believe it is the better part of wisdom to turn out a type of production that can be brought to the screen for considerably less money."

As it happened, Walt wouldn't have the resources to return to feature-length animation until the late 1940s. Even then there was some debate about whether *Cinderella* or *Alice in Wonderland* should be released first. As studio executive Card Walker remembers the story, "Walt had two crews—one working on *Cinderella* and the other on *Alice in Wonderland.* In a way, they were competing with one another, not only to see who would finish first, but who did the best job. Walt would be the ultimate judge of which one worked better. It turned out that *Cinderella* was released in 1950 and *Alice* came out later."

Cinderella bore some resemblance to Walt's biggest hit to date, *Snow White*. But, similarities aside, *Cinderella* "was a gamble for Disney," according to Dave Smith's *Disney A to Z*, "and if it had been unsuccessful it probably would have sounded the death knell for animation at the Studio." Knowing this, Walt didn't want to take any chances. Explains animator Frank Thomas, "Walt insisted we plan *Cinderella* more carefully than prior films. We shot it all in live action first, so that we could evaluate it, because we couldn't afford to make changes in the animation. The animation had to be right the first time. The live action was done without costumes or set. We'd work on a lonely soundstage to see whether the scenes were going to work. Would they be too long? Too short? Will it hold your interest?"

Even though Walt desperately needed *Cinderella* to be successful, his attitude was very different from the days of *Snow White* and *Bambi*. Continues Frank Thomas, "When he came back to animation after the war, Walt never had that same enthusiasm for animation. He was more enthusiastic about the nature pictures and live action. It was never like it was on the early pictures, where he knew every frame of film."

Walt may not have known every cel like the back of his hand, but he was still involved. Ilene Woods, who did the voice of Cinderella, has fond memories of the experience. "To me, he was a true visionary. Others would say, 'Can we?' And Walt would always say, 'We can.' And you'd believe him, because every time he said, 'We can,' he did. When we were recording 'Sing Sweet Nightingale,' for example, he was in the studio listening. He looked up and he asked, 'Ilene, can you sing harmony with yourself?' I said, 'Gee, Mr. Disney, I don't know. I can't hum and whistle at the same time, but what did you have in mind?' He replied, 'I can see it.' And he turned to the engineer and said, 'We'll put the earphones on her, and she'll sing second-part harmony. I see her scrubbing the floor when another bubble comes up and she sings third-part harmony.' The engineer sat there and said, 'If you say so Walt, we can do it.' It was really beautiful. The blend is unbelievable when the same person is doing all the parts. At the end he said, 'You know, all these years I've been paying three Andrews Sisters three salaries and I could have had you for one!' "

Cinderella turned out to be a huge success, one of the highest-grossing films of the year, ensuring the future of feature-length animation in the Disney organization. The next effort was *Alice in Wonderland*, a movie that turned out to be rather problematic for Walt. He felt the film didn't work because "millions of people just didn't care about Alice." Animator Frank Thomas agrees. "The film didn't have emotions; it was in segments. Alice would be disturbed in one sequence and she'd stomp out and go on to another. There was no place where you really cared or worried about Alice." Author John

Ilene Woods sings harmony with herself.

I was enthralled with Ilene's account of the "Sing Sweet Nightingale" sequence. That exchange sums up a lot of Dad's magic. He would throw a suggestion or a challenge to someone in a manner that did not make it seem impossible, but reasonable and doable. Dad surrounded himself with many fine craftsmen and talented technicians, and he himself had sufficient understanding of technical matters to envision the possibilities, to know that he was not asking for the impossible.

DIANE DISNEY MILLER

NEW HORIZONS

Culhane has written extensively about Walt Disney and his creations. When he was 17, he had the opportunity to spend one remarkable afternoon with Walt, who had just returned from *Alice*'s opening in England. "*Alice* has no heart," Walt told Culhane. "That's the problem. You know, I never really wanted to make it. I never warmed to it, but my associates assured me it was the perfect picture for our medium. I was right. The humor is too intellectual. I like a picture that hits you over the heart. Without heart, I don't think anything's good or can last. And with every laugh there should be a tear. I believe in that."

Next was *Peter Pan*. For years Walt had thought the story of the boy who never grows old would make a terrific animated film. In fact, he had arranged for rights to the James M. Barrie play back in 1939. But he didn't actually begin work on the film until a decade later, and it wasn't released until 1953. Says Ollie Johnston, "Walt just

TOP: *Actress Kathryn Beaumont provides animators with a model for Alice.*

CENTER: *Alice falls down the rabbit hole.*

LEFT: *A frame from* Alice in Wonderland

could not make up his mind about what type of picture to make out of it. He kept bringing it up and then dropping it, until finally he got it. I think he wanted something that had a certain amount of heart in the relationship between Wendy and the boys and Peter, and I'm not so sure that we ever got just that. The strongest stuff came in the Captain Hook character. It was a darned good picture, but not really in the way he had started out to do it."

Developing the Captain Hook character wasn't easy. The task fell to animator Frank Thomas, who clearly recalls the episode: "Walt gave us seven or so weeks to work out the new characters in *Peter Pan*, and each of us worked on a different character. The director of the picture felt that Captain Hook should be a real mean guy. The storyman, who'd developed the character, thought he ought to be a fop. "So I said, 'Hey, fellas, can't you get together? What am I supposed to animate here?' And it didn't all work out. I did a scene, and one of the other animators said, 'I wouldn't show that one to Walt.' And I continued to have problems until the day for showing finally came. The story guys sat around and waited to see how Walt reacted to what we'd done. And Walt looked like he didn't think too much of it, so they started saying things like, 'Walt, I think his head's too flat on the top; I think his feet are too small,' picking on all these things that don't mean a thing when you're trying to develop a character with a personality. Walt was saying, 'Yeah, yeah,' as if he agreed, and then he said, 'Well, I think he's a hard character to get hold of.' I thought, 'Bless you, Walt.' And Walt continued, 'Frank's getting close to it now. Let's let him go for another stretch of time and see what he comes up with.' With his blessing on it, the storymen had to shut up. Let's face it, you always had a certain conflict between the storymen, the animators, the directors, the layout men, and the background painters. We all had our different concerns."

Peter Pan was followed in 1955 by *Lady and the Tramp*. (The arrival of the puppy, Lady, in a hatbox was, of course, inspired by Walt's gift of Sunnee the chow to Lilly nearly thirty years before.)

In 1959 Walt released *Sleeping Beauty*, a film that had been in the works for about ten years—and whose costs had run up to an astonishing $6 million, the most the studio had ever spent on an animated feature. According to Ollie Johnston: "We were on *Sleeping Beauty* longer than any other picture. And that's because Walt was distracted by the park and the television shows. He just couldn't get into the film." Frank Thomas agrees. "We'd call him to say, 'Walt, we got a problem here with *Sleeping Beauty*. Could you come in?' 'Well, all right, just for a little

TOP: *Ward Kimball draws the Mad Hatter.*

ABOVE: *Captain Hook encounters the dreaded crocodile.*

LEFT: *This scene from* Lady and the Tramp *was inspired by Walt's gift to Lilly of a puppy in a hatbox.*

RIGHT: *Walt shows off Eyvind Earle's stylized artwork for* Sleeping Beauty.

BELOW: *Mary Costa, the voice of Sleeping Beauty*

I agree with Mary Costa that Dad was "innately musical," and it pleases me to hear that from someone who is so thoroughly, beautifully musical. I'm impressed with his words to her about color and the colors in her voice.

DIANE DISNEY MILLER

while." Then he'd come to look at the sequence and he'd say, 'You're not in any trouble.' And he'd walk out. You couldn't believe Walt would just walk out, but obviously *Sleeping Beauty* wasn't on his mind. He had all these other things going on." Johnston conjectures that "Walt was afraid *Sleeping Beauty* was going to be too much like *Cinderella* and *Snow White*. He worried about that a lot. But he didn't have any solutions, and he just didn't seem to click on it the way he ordinarily did."

Although Walt may not have been giving the animators the time they wanted, he was helpful to Mary Costa, the young singer who voiced the character of Princess Aurora in *Sleeping Beauty*. "He was so musical," she says. "He couldn't have done the voice of Mickey Mouse without knowing how to clip off the end of phrases and to think things through about how to make it funny. He had an innate sense of timing. He once told me, 'God gives everyone a special talent. He gives everyone a set of colors. I want you to drop those colors to your vocal palette and paint with your voice.' I asked what he meant, and he said, 'Everyone is unique. I don't want you to be a copy of anyone else because you have your own set of colors. You must think it out for yourself, not have anyone read a line for you, and you must visualize the character, know what she's about, know her personality, know what colors you would use for her—warm, cool, or whatever—and you must make those images in your mind, drop them to your vocal palette, and paint.' This advice was very important to me. It established a work ethic that followed me all through my career."

Think of the Happiest Things

Mr. Snoops

✳ **When Walt Disney's daughter Diane was 17, she arranged for John Culhane—who was the same age—to meet her father. Culhane became a well-known journalist and author of several books about Disney's films. He also inspired the character Mr. Snoops in the 1977 film *The Rescuers*. The day Culhane met Walt represents one of the highlights of his life. Says Culhane: "He talked to me all afternoon long, walking around in the backyard of his home in Holmby Hills. We talked about a lot of things but the key thing was emotion. He said, 'the primary object of any of the fine arts is to get a purely emotional reaction from the beholder.'**

"Walt also said, 'Think of the happiest things; it's the same as having wings.' I didn't know until the following Tuesday, when I went at his invitation to his studio, that this was a line he was preparing for *Peter Pan*. But he said it not as a line from *Peter Pan* but as advice to me. Now that I think of it, the entire conversation was about the pursuit of happiness."

Walt nicknamed Mary Costa "Happy Bird." As she tells the story, "He was very concerned when we started the voice work for the scene in the woods. He cautioned me about catching cold, and I reassured him that I would be very careful. I said, 'I know how important this is, and I'm certainly not going to catch a cold.' I thought he was very nervous because this was the big scene, and again I reassured him, 'When I was a little girl my father told me that a bird doesn't sing because it's happy; it's happy because it sings. And so I'm not going to get a cold and be unable to sing.' Walt said, 'Then be sure you don't, Happy Bird.' "

Walt did three more animated features in his life. He was displeased with the look of *101 Dalmatians*, because a new advance in animation—Xerography—required relatively sharp lines between the shapes on the screen. Those sharp lines were toned down for the next film, *The Sword in the Stone*. But "it was not really until *Jungle Book* that Walt came back and gave us the heart of the picture," says Johnston. "In about three meetings, Walt made that picture. He told us just what to do. At first, Baloo was

Cruella De Vil, the evil dognapper from 101 Dalmatians

99

Walt and Roy in front of story-boards for The Jungle Book

supposed to be a cameo, but Walt felt he should be the star of the picture. And it was wonderful. We loved doing it this way. When it came to the end, we didn't know how to get Mowgli back into the man village. And Walt was sitting there in a meeting, scratching his head, and he said, 'You know, Mowgli's never seen another human. What if you had a little girl come down out of the village to fill her jug with water. Then she puts it on her head. She sees Mowgli but pretends she doesn't. Then she starts up the hill, tips over the jug, which rolls backwards, and he follows her up.' And Walt said, 'That's the way to get him in!' And that was great for me, because I got to animate it."

Walt didn't live to see *The Jungle Book* on the screen. "But," says Johnston, "He got wrapped up in it. We knew he liked the music. He never got to see the ending, where Baloo walks out into the sunset. I was talking with Hazel George, the studio nurse, who said, "You know, that's just the way Walt went out—into the sunset."

Walt's red barn in Holmby Hills and the Lilly Belle

WALT AND TRAINS: "MY PRIDE AND JOY"

WALT'S FASCINATION WITH TRAINS probably began back in Marceline, Missouri, when he was just four or five. His uncle Mike Martin was an operating engineer on the Santa Fe Railroad. The line ran right through the town, and when Uncle Mike would visit—generally armed with a bag of striped candy for the children—Walt would hear stories about the adventures of the railroaders.

Walt's Uncle Mike (left) with friends

Walt's father, Elias, had worked as an apprentice carpenter on the Union Pacific Line when it was laying track from Kansas City to Denver. And Elias would add his stories to Uncle Mike's—tales of men and machines dynamiting and bridging a path through the Rockies. At a very early age, trains came to mean excitement and adventure to Walt.

In 1917, Walt actually got to work on the Santa Fe Line himself, as a "news butcher"—a young fellow who sold apples, soda, newspapers, and cigars to railroad passengers. According to his brother Roy, who got him the job, Walt was a terrible businessman. "He'd leave his locker unlocked and come back and find a lot of empty Coke bottles and some of the candy gone," said Roy. "He just wasn't attending to business. So he ran a loss. And who do you think paid for his losses?"

But that didn't matter to Walt. He got to wear a uniform with shiny brass buttons, which impressed the young ladies. He got to see the country and to learn how to work the levers and valves for the giant engine. That was enough for him.

Walt carried his affection for trains with him into adulthood, as his wife Lilly quickly learned. "We'd stand and watch the trains come in," she recalled. "And after they'd go by, he'd watch the vibrations on the tracks. I wondered why he did that. That was recreation."

101

Chicago
Railroad Fair

STIRRING CELEBRATION
1848   OF 100 YEARS   1948
OF RAILROAD PROGRESS

OPENING JULY 20th

GREATEST EVENT OF THE 1948 VACATION SEASON
In a setting of World's Fair proportions on the
shores of Lake Michigan, U. S. railroads portray
the growth of a nation—the spectacular miracle
of America on rails setting a pace for the world.

MAKE RESERVATIONS NOW!
See Your Local Ticket
Agent or Travel Bureau

TOP: *Walt at Ward Kimball's*

CENTER: *One of the train sets Walt
put together for his nephews*

ABOVE: *A flyer for the Chicago
Railroad Fair, which Walt attended
with Ward Kimball*

In 1945, Walt had an eye-opening experience
when he visited animator Ward Kimball's house.
Kimball and his wife, Betty, had restored an 1881
Baldwin Mogul Locomotive, and the grand machine
rested on a half-mile of track in their backyard. "I was
living out here in San Gabriel," Kimball recalls. "I had
a party one night and Walt came to it. I asked him if
he would like to run the locomotive. He refused. I
said, 'It's simple, Walt. You take the Johnson bar and
shove it forward, that means it's going forward; you
pull it back, it's gonna back up.' I talked him into it. And he ran
it and I can remember how his mouth dropped open."

Walt got his own train in December 1947, though it
was somewhat smaller than Kimball's. He wrote to his sister
Ruth, "I bought myself a birthday/Christmas present, something I've wanted all my life—an electric train. Being a girl, you
probably can't understand how much I wanted one when I
was a kid, but I've got one now, and what fun I'm having.
I have it set up in one of the outer rooms adjoining my office,
so I can play with it in my spare moments. It's a freight train
with a whistle, and real smoke comes out of the smokestack. There are switches,
semaphores, a station, and everything. It's just wonderful!"

The next year, Walt and Kimball paid a memorable visit to the Chicago
Railroad Fair. According to Michael Broggie, author of *Walt Disney's Railroad
Story*, the two enthusiasts were treated as honored guests. "They were allowed
to go backstage, where the railroad companies had restored these wonderful
old historical locomotives. Ward said later that to run some of those great old
engines, like the 999 and the Clinton, was like shaking hands with Thomas
Jefferson. It was like reconnecting with American history. And so Walt and
Ward had a wonderful time taking motion pictures of each other running
the equipment."

Walt returned from the Chicago Railroad Fair flushed with excitement.
He set out to build model railroads as Christmas presents for his grand-
nephews. He visited others who had trains of their own, and his enthusiasm for
the hobby grew. Before long, Walt decided to create a large-scale miniature
steam-driven train layout for himself.

Unfortunately, Walt's house at the time didn't have the space. So he
and Lilly went looking for a site for a new house. They discovered a spot in
Holmby Hills, an area in Los Angeles between Bel Air and Beverly Hills,
that seemed perfect. "It had sufficient area for Walt to have his miniature
railroad," says Broggie, "and for Lillian to have her gardens. She loved landscaping and flowers. It was an ideal setting, five acres—enough to do it all."

Walt had a design for the track's layout made and brought it home to
show to Lilly. According to Broggie, whose father, Roger Broggie, helped Walt

create his train, "He rolled it out on the kitchen table, and she looked at it and realized the track went all the way around the house. There was a lively discussion, because her understanding was that she would have her gardens around the house and he would have his railroad down in the lower portion of the property." The solution? Walt would build a tunnel underneath Lilly's flower beds.

But it would be no ordinary tunnel. Instead of building a straight path, Walt thought it would make for a more interesting ride if it were an S-shaped curve. Anyone entering would be in total darkness until the curve had been traveled and the sunlight at the other end could be seen. "Walt liked the mystery," recalled Herb Ryman, an artist and a family friend. "The foreman on the job suggested it was cheaper to build it straight. And Walt said, 'It's cheaper not to do it at all.' "

After construction on Walt's railroad was completed, he spent many evenings working on his train in a little red barn—modeled after the barn on the Marceline farm, as he remembered it from childhood—that he had built in his yard. Though many of the train cars were constructed at the studio's machine shop, Walt built the yellow caboose by himself.

Walt loved driving the train around his property, often with friends and children in tow. He even let Sharon sit behind the controls from time to time. "He taught me how to run the thing," she recalled. "I knew how to fire it up—get the engine going. I thought it was great fun." Walt certainly agreed. "It's my pride and joy, and I simply love it," he said.

TOP TO BOTTOM:

Walt gives his daughters Sharon (left) and Diane (center) a ride on his train.

Studio Head Carpenter Ray Fox helps Walt carry his yellow caboose to the tracks.

The Carolwood Pacific passes by the Disney house.

Even after Walt stopped running his backyard train, he had a bigger one to play with—at Disneyland.

Diane and her aunt Hazel, Lilly's sister, at the Griffith Park merry-go-round

DREAMING OF DISNEYLAND

"When we were very young, we had a Sunday routine," recalls Diane Miller. "Dad would drop us off at church, we'd go to our Sunday school classes and then to Griffith Park, where there was a beautiful carousel. It's still there, a wonderful, beautiful thing. I'd ride the carousel over and over and over. There was some apparatus that had rings sticking out from a slot, and you'd grab a ring as you went by. If you got the gold ring, you got a free ride. One day I kept getting that gold ring and I felt so clever and I got all those free rides. Years later, I asked Dad, 'How'd I keep getting that gold ring?' 'Oh, I gave the kid a few dollars and he kept putting in the gold rings where you could get them.'"

While Diane and her sister, Sharon, were whirling around on the carousel, Walt's mind was elsewhere. He was dreaming of a place where children and their parents could enjoy a safe, clean, entertaining experience together; where parents wouldn't be relegated to uncomfortable park benches, trying to make the time pass with a bag of peanuts. As Walt recalled, "The idea for Disneyland lay dormant for years, but it came along when I was taking my kids around to these kiddie parks. I'd take them out . . . every Saturday and Sunday. Those were some of the happiest days of my life. They were in love with their dad. . . . And while they were on the merry-go-round riding around 40 times or something, I'd be sitting there trying to figure out what you could do."

In its earliest iterations, Walt conceived of his new kind of amusement park as a small park on land adjoining the studio lot. Animator Ward Kimball recalls, "Walt was going to have a little ride from the studio across Riverside Drive. You'd get on his one-and-a-half-scale steamer and go onto Riverside Drive to the soundstages. He figured that riding those little cars from one picture to another would be a great way for showing tourists how Hollywood works."

BELOW: *Walt initially envisioned a small park across from the studio.*

CENTER: *A map lays out Tomorrowland.*

BOTTOM: *An artist's portrayal of Main Street*

Walt had designers work up plans for a Burbank park, and his thoughts got pretty far along. Several layouts show that it would have had a train running on a track around the park, a river, and a little Western street. But the more Walt thought about the park, the more he became convinced that the little piece of property across from the studio wasn't going to be nearly big enough to contain all his dreams.

As Walt's thinking progressed, he began to visit amusement parks around the country to get a feel for what worked and what didn't. One of his favorite places during this period was Beverly Park, owned and operated by Bernice and Dave Bradley.

As Bernice Bradley remembers, "Our park was very tiny. There was a carousel, a little train ride, and another little boat ride for children. The boats didn't actually go on water, they simply moved around on the grounds of the park areas. Walt was out there almost every day, sitting on the end of the bench, watching how children enjoyed the

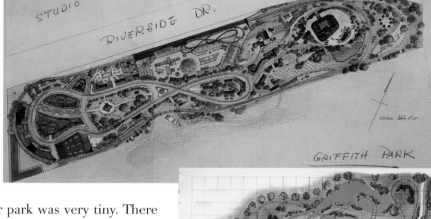

rides. He also talked to a lot of children, which is what he enjoyed most. He challenged them. 'How was that horse you were riding? What color was it painted? Did you like it?' If the children were on the boat he'd ask, 'Did you drive the boat?' "

Bruce Gordon, currently an Imagineer with the Disney company, has done a vast amount of research about Disneyland. Gordon, who co-authored *Disneyland: The Nickel Tour*, explains, "At the time Walt was thinking about building a park, most amusement parks were not in a place you'd want to let your kids go on their own. The parks were kind of dirty, in seedy neighborhoods. You wouldn't want to drop off your kids there and meet them three or four hours later, the way you can in a Disney park today. There was one notable exception: The park in Copenhagen called Tivoli Gardens struck Walt as being very clean, well-run, festive, and he loved the little popcorn lights on all the buildings. A lot of the things that showed up in Disneyland came from Tivoli. And it was an adult park as well as a kid's park."

As it happens, television celebrity Art Linkletter was with Walt on his first visit to Tivoli. Later, Linkletter was to host the television show celebrating the opening ceremonies at Disneyland. Said Linkletter, "Tivoli Gardens is the most famous of all the playground resort areas in Copenhagen. As we walked through it, I had my first experience of Walt Disney's childlike delight in the enjoyment of seeing families and in the cleanliness and the orderliness of everything. He was making notes all the time—about the lights, the chairs, the seats, and the food. I asked him what he was doing, and he replied, 'I'm just making notes about something that I've always dreamed of, a great, great playground for the children and the families of America.' "

But where was the park to be? Walt hired a consultant, Harrison (Buzz) Price from Stanford Research, to look into the situation. Price remembers, "Walt knew he needed a major piece of land. He had studied enough to know that it wasn't going to be a tiny park any more. It had to be big. Finding where to put it in southern California was the first assignment. I asked

Tivoli Gardens in Denmark

him if he had his own thoughts about where it ought to go, and he assured me that he had no idea. It would be up to me to suggest the best location. We studied different variables—freeways, smog, population growth, temperature differences—and we finally came to a shape of land (we called it the amoeba) which was five miles on either side of the Santa Ana Freeway, south from the L.A. County line to Santa Ana. That was the 'amoeba' where we did specific site-location work. In our report we described ten sites that we'd considered and the three we preferred. He actually went for the first site, moving it down a quarter of a section to get farther away from the freeway."

In the earliest days of Disneyland's development—prior to actually purchasing any land—Walt didn't have the support of the Disney Corporation itself. The company, by this time, was publicly held, and Roy was concerned that stockholders would rebel if they heard that their company was embarking on something as risky as Walt proposed, "But I kept working on it," said Walt, "and I worked on it with my own money. Not the studio's money. My own money."

Using the initials of his name, Walt incorporated WED Enterprises to funnel his own money into his new dreams. Mickey Clark was president. "In fact," Clark recalls, "he hocked his life insurance and a few other things to get the money for starting up the Disneyland project."

But while Walt was able to raise enough money to begin work, he needed far more once it got rolling. By this point, his brother Roy was also convinced it was a reasonable idea and was ready to commit Disney corporate money to it. Even so, the company needed financing, too. According to Gordon, "Walt got some money from Western Publishing, the company that was publishing the Little Golden Books at the time. The third big source of money was the American Broadcasting Corporation. The newest of the TV networks was eagerly looking for something to make a big score in television. They thought it would be fabulous if they could get Walt Disney, so they put up a chunk of the money in return for Walt's guarantee of a TV show for ABC. Most movie studios were very afraid of television at the time, but Walt was smart enough to see that television was the mark of the future and a great way to promote films and the park, too.

"Walt called the program "Disneyland" and showed the four 'lands' of the park so that, by the time Disneyland opened, every person in America knew all about it. They already knew the land, how it worked. And they could find their way around the park the first time they went there, because they had learned about it from television the year before. I also think it's amusing that ABC put up a big part of the money for Disneyland and now Disney owns ABC."

With the finances in place, the big effort to bring Disneyland into reality could begin. "The construction of Disneyland took just about a year," says Gordon. "And what a year it was! Like when they had to remove a lot of trees from the building site. Some of the trees were a great asset, and they didn't want to lose them, so they carefully tagged the trees. They put red tags on the trees to be removed and green tags for the ones to be saved. Who would have guessed that the bulldozer operator was color-blind? Until they realized what was happening, the bulldozer was pulling down everything in sight!"

Morgan ("Bill") Evans, Disneyland's landscape designer, described the process: "Walt's approach was to say, 'I need a jungle,' or 'I need a touch of Alpine flavor for the sky ride.' He didn't know which trees would work, but he knew what he wanted. He made specific comments only if something didn't exactly suit his idea. For example, I planted a Brazilian pepper tree near the walk just past Adventureland. It had a big heavy trunk, and its spread was about 30 feet. As we were parading through the park one Saturday morning, Walt stopped and looked back at the tree and said he thought it was too close to the walk.

Landscaper Bill Evans

Bill Evans and his older brother, Jack, were the nurserymen who did the landscaping for our home on Carolwood Drive in Holmby Hills. Their nursery filled a huge canyon off of Sunset Boulevard. Jack usually dressed in English country attire and favored the English garden approach to landscape design. Bill looked like a jungle explorer. He wore Hawaiian shirts and a straw hat and specialized in tropicals and trees of all kinds. Dad recruited Bill to design Disneyland. . . . Today, Bill's health is not the best. It was wonderful that he came to be interviewed for the documentary. It was a rather heroic effort on his part, one that a lesser man wouldn't have attempted—and he did it for my dad.

DIANE DISNEY MILLER

Disneyland is a work of love. We didn't go into Disneyland just with the idea of making money.

WALT DISNEY

Walt shows off his plans for Disneyland.

The next morning we put in another crew, boxed up the six-ton root system, and moved the tree about six feet. The next Saturday morning, Walt walked right past it. No comment. That was characteristic of him. Another time, we had planted a number of trees around the Frontierland station. They were all appropriate for the purpose, with the exception of one tree that had multiple trunks close to the ground. You wouldn't think Walt would pay attention to that kind of detail, but when he looked at it he remarked, 'I don't think that one

"It's a deep secret"

One day, Walt invited me to join him for a ride down to Orange County to see where Disneyland was going to be. "It's a deep secret," Walt said. "You can't tell anybody anything you see or hear." I agreed because I loved adventure and Walt was a good friend, but I couldn't believe my eyes. We were

The orange groves of Anaheim — before Disneyland

driving through little villages I'd never heard of. We were driving through orange groves and dirt roads, when Walt finally announced that we had arrived at the site. I've never been one to discourage a friend, so I didn't tell him what I really thought—that he was out of his mind. After all, it was 45 minutes from where people lived, and there was nothing there! Without offending him, I just wished him luck. Years later, when I told him about my reaction, after Disneyland was already a big success, he said, "I didn't think you were as enthusiastic as I had ordinarily seen you, but you didn't have the vision of what I had in my mind when I looked at those orange groves and saw the beautiful things we were going to build."

ART LINKLETTER

belongs in here. The others are all standard, with a single trunk and an umbrella top.' So the next day, that tree came out and another that suited Walt's fancy went in. And a week later, he took a look. No comment."

By and large, the attractions were new ideas, designed by people who had never worked on an amusement park before but were able to utilize their skills in filmmaking and animation. John Hench was one of these designers. "Disneyland wasn't really a radical step for Walt," says Hench, "because even in the two-dimensional world of motion pictures space is implied. In fact, we used many of the techniques we had learned from the films and applied them to the third dimension. And when we set up a kind of story in our own mind, we would establish an imaginary long shot as if we were taking it with motion pictures."

Imagineer Bruce Gordon expands on this idea of translating one medium into another. "The attractions for Disneyland consisted of a lot of things that had never been done before. They were basically improved, expanded versions of existing types of carnival rides done by people who had never done these before. These were Walt's movie art directors, his artists, his background artists—people who had spent their careers painting backgrounds were now designing amusement park rides. So they did all kinds of things they didn't know were impossible. It was the old classic story: they did it because they didn't know they couldn't.

"Many of the attractions were actually built at Walt's studio in Burbank. These cavernous soundstages were a lot like the big buildings that were going to be built at Disneyland. So they would actually build the entire ride—the scenery, ride system, and track, in the movie soundstage. Then they'd ride the vehicles around to check for problems. The heat from all the lighting in the Snow White ride made the room so hot that they were starting to call it Snow White's Trip to Hell.

"One of the lands in the park was originally called True-Life Adventureland, based on the *True-Life Adventure* films that Walt was creating at the time. This land would have the least fantasy, designed to be a real look at the real world. Here the Jungle Cruise was the big attraction. You would actually take a boat—a real boat in a river— sail it through a real jungle and see real live

TOP: *Frontierland construction*

CENTER and RIGHT: *Main Street U.S.A. construction*

Meeting Walt

This friend of mine and I were sitting in the studio during the lunch hour and we hear footsteps coming down the hall. We glance up, and there's a face with a mustache on it, looking around the corner. He says, "Hi, I'm Walt Disney. Who are you?"

And my friend introduced himself, and I introduced myself and said I came from 20th Century Fox. And he said, "You know, I'm happy that you guys from the studios are coming over here and helping me build my park. See ya."

And he took off. The next week I was walking through a crowded hall of the animation building. Walt was coming the other way; he glanced over at me, smiled and said, "Hiya, Sam." What a memory. To remember a new man that quickly was amazing.

SAM McKIM

animals. Well, that idea was short-lived. As all the experts told Walt, real animals aren't going to work. The big problem is that animals tend to sleep all day, which meant that guests would not get to see them in action. The animals would only come out at night, when it was cool. And Walt was cautioned against putting his exotic birds over the heads of the guests. So he quickly realized that they needed artificial animals. That way you could have hippos and a gorilla in front of you all the time on the boat trip. The special-effects folks at the studio, who had been doing the mechanical effects for motion pictures, were recruited to create animals for the Jungle Cruise.

"Walt was hands-on with everything at Disney-land. This was his park, his dream. I always believed the reason Walt built Disneyland was that he wanted one. He wanted the biggest train layout; he wanted a place for all his toys. In the park he had an apartment above the fire station. Walt would get up early in the morning, before the park opened, and he'd drive his fire truck around Disneyland. People would think he was crazy, but he was only playing with his toy."

TOP: *The Jungle Cruise, before the waters flowed*
ABOVE: *Sleeping Beauty Castle, under construction*

Walt is readied for a television lead-in.

TELEVISION

"In 1945, RCA knew that people coming back from the war would want entertainment. RCA also knew people would be buying television sets," explains Bill Cotter, author of *The Wonderful World of Disney Television.* "Walt started to plan a series called "Your Window on the World," which was going to explain all the wonderful things TV could do. But he pulled the plug on the series when he realized the market wasn't quite there yet. Walt didn't want to jump into television before the time was right, but he really learned a lot."

Walt never forgot something he had learned that might be of use to him in the future. In the early 1950s, he was ready to begin experimenting with television. At the time, other film producers thought television was a monster on the horizon, ready to gorge itself on their markets. Says Cotter, "While the other producers were fighting television tooth and nail—mostly through the unions and legislation—Walt started to embrace it. He was the first producer to break ranks with the others and go into television."

On Christmas Day 1950, Walt ran "One Hour in Wonderland," a special, "which was basically a one-hour commercial for *Alice in Wonderland,*" continues Cotter. "There was a lot of footage of things the studio was doing, clips from different cartoons, but it

ABOVE RIGHT: *Walt addresses the magic mirror in "One Hour in Wonderland."*

RIGHT: *"Operation Undersea" took viewers behind the scenes of* 20,000 Leagues Under the Sea.

"There might be a big angle on television"

Interoffice memo from Walt Disney to Roy Disney and Gunther Lessing, dated October 21, 1939:

"Everything we do in the future should include television rights. There might be a big angle on television for the shorts we have already produced."

was basically a well-planned infomercial, another way in which Walt was ahead of his time. After the first show came out, there was instant clamoring for a weekly series, but Walt just didn't feel the timing was right. He didn't have enough studio staff and infrastructure to produce a series, and he was distracted by a lot of other concerns as he was trying to rebuild the theatrical market from the slump of World War II. So he waited. He did one more show the next Christmas, which was as big a hit as the first one, but he still held off on a series."

Several years later, when Walt needed money to finance his new theme park, he decided that television was the best source. He could get the money he needed and, through the anthology format called "Disneyland," could promote his new Anaheim dream on the show. "In fact," says author and historian Leonard Maltin, "he saw many benefits to working in TV, not the least of which was a means of promoting his own movies. Walt's concept became the greatest promotional vehicle ever devised. The Disney studio won an Emmy for outstanding program of the year for a one-hour show on the making of *20,000 Leagues Under the Sea*. It stood on its own as an interesting, behind-the-scenes featurette on the making of a major motion picture. It just happened to be promoting the motion picture, too."

Recalls Cotter, "With the Disneyland series you could be with Davy Crockett one week—his adventures fighting at the Alamo—and the next week you'd be watching polar bears in one of his animal shows. Next week Donald Duck would be entertaining you, and the week after that you'd see the latest things being built at Disneyland. It was always something new, something different. The unpredictability of the programming was a real plus, especially since TV was in its infancy and people didn't know what to expect anyway. It was also a plus that if you missed a week, you could pick up where you left off for a good, easy viewing experience, without feeling you'd missed an episode of a dramatic plot."

Walt needed a master of ceremonies for his show. At first he refused to be the host. "Walt was very concerned about what he felt was a very nasal twang in his voice, and did not think that it would come across well on television," says Cotter. "So they put out a search for celebrities to host the show. After trotting out several well-known movie actors for screen tests, they realized that a certain spark was missing in every case. That spark, that enthusiasm, really set Walt apart. When he was talking about the show he was not a paid pitchman. He was talking about what he had created, what he believed, something he knew intimately and truly loved."

Not that hosting the show was always easy. Walt was extremely busy, and filming the lead-ins was time-consuming. "Directing Walt on his lead-ins made you about as nervous as you can get," recalls his son-in-law Ron Miller, who filled that job frequently. "After a while,

Walt's voice would get dry and scratchy, so you'd just keep pouring water down his throat to clear his voice."

Bob Broughton, a camera-effects artist, recalls: "For the show's lead-in Walt would come down the aisle in a library. Usually he'd pause at about the middle of the aisle and pull out a book that would contain the topic for that evening's show. Generally Walt would memorize his lines for the entrance and then he'd read the rest of his lines from the book. At one session we got the shot of his entrance. Then he pulls out the book and opens it. His lines are there, but upside down. Walt says, 'Oh, shit.' He goes back and we do another take. This time he comes down, pulls out the book, and when he opens it the page falls out on the floor. So he says, 'Oh, shit.' By now the stage is really quiet, because when the head man is having a problem nobody moves. He comes down a third time, and this time he pulls out the book and drops it. He says, 'Oh, shit. . . . At this rate, I'm gonna start flubbing the words, 'Oh shit.' And then we all had a good laugh."

ABOVE: *Walt in a lead-in for the television episode "Man in Space" (1955)*

BELOW: *TV's Davy Crockett, played by Fess Parker, joins Walt (left) on a ride down Main Street.*

Jack Spiers became Walt's primary writer for the introductory segments. According to Cotter, "They had a lot of common interests in the sorts of shows they thought were good. Jack started writing the way he thought Walt would like, and Walt would tell him what he liked or didn't like. Doing it this way meant that Walt didn't just come out on the stage and parrot some words, then leave. He was actively involved in what he said on camera." Sometimes "Walt's Midwestern tongue had difficulties getting around certain words," Spiers recalls.

Wrangling with Walt

Walt and Fess Parker at the studio

When the first *Davy Crockett* film came out, the Disney studio had no record label. We recorded the sound track on the Columbia label, I think. Shortly thereafter, Disney's Buena Vista label came into being. Meanwhile, Buddy Ebsen and I had formed a little company called Music Land. When we were shooting *Westward Ho the Wagons!* I went to Walt and said, "Here's a cute little song called 'Wringle Wrangle' I think might fit in the picture," and we used it. And a little later I asked, "Is there any chance that Music Land, this little company Buddy and I have started, could possibly have half of the music publishing rights?" Walt replied, "No, I don't think so." I said, "Why not?" He said, "Company policy." I said, "Who makes company policy?" And he said, "I do."

FESS PARKER

"There were some words that I realized I shouldn't ask him to say on screen. Like aluminum—which came up because Alcoa was one of the sponsors of the show. But he just couldn't say it. Somehow I'd have to write around it."

No one but Fess Parker could have been Dad's Davy Crockett. Fess projected a combination of strength and gentleness, and his voice was perfect for the wonderful tunes that were written for the show. I used to sing "The Ballad of Davy Crockett" to my children instead of a lullaby.

DIANE DISNEY MILLER

Walt made the startling decision to shoot episodes of "Disneyland" in color. This was particularly notable because, as Leonard Maltin explains, "Color television didn't exist then, but Walt was smart enough to recognize that filming in color was a good investment." Ron Miller agrees: "I think that Walt probably said, 'Sure, we're losing money now, but let's think of it for the long term. We're building a library for this company that's going to be very important some day.' And it certainly has been. Those films are run over and over." The payback began to come pretty quickly. Maltin: "When "Davy Crockett" took off and became a nationwide sensation, Walt was able to splice the first three episodes into a feature film that was released to theaters. Because "Davy Crockett" had been filmed in color, it didn't look like a cheesy little TV show."

In fact, "Davy Crockett"—as originally seen on the "Disneyland" TV show—turned out to be one of the most outstanding television successes of all time, selling hundreds of millions of dollars' worth of merchandise as well. Its three episodes represent television's first miniseries. The show's star, Fess Parker, became the idol of millions. As Parker recalls, "The show completely changed my life. When I was first sent out by the studio, I could never leave my hotel room, I couldn't eat in a restaurant. I had a promotional schedule that was incredible. I was in another city every day. I actually went to 42 cities, some by myself, some with Buddy Ebsen, and then later I traveled to about 13 countries. That was very hard physical work, and if I hadn't been a fairly strong young man in those days, I don't think I could have done it."

For the title role the studio had been leaning toward actor James Arness, but when Walt saw Fess Parker playing a small part in a James Arness movie, he suddenly exclaimed, "That's him. That's Davy."

Parker remembered being comfortable with Walt the first time they met. "Walt said, 'I see you brought your guitar.' And I said, 'Yes, sir. I wrote this little song. I'll play it for you.' So I did, and we had a nice visit. I don't know what I expected, but he put me completely at ease. He was like someone I could have encountered in my hometown, perhaps. Very low-key. A few days later I got word from the studio that they were going to assign me the role of Davy Crockett."

"Buddy Ebsen was a late addition to the cast," explains Bill Cotter. "They started with another actor who didn't work out, and they rushed Buddy out there at the last minute. At one point Buddy had been considered for the role of Davy Crockett, so it's interesting to see how well he did as Davy's sidekick. It's hard to imagine Buddy as Davy himself."

Ebsen, who went on to star in TV's "The Beverly Hillbillies" and "Barnaby Jones," recalls his work with Walt with great affection. The show was shot on location in Tennessee, differentiating it from most other programs at the time, which were shot on studio backlots. One day Walt was having lunch with Tennessee's governor, Frank Clement. "I happened to be invited to join them," remembers Ebsen. "There's Walt, Governor Clement and his wife,

Walt's television shows helped propel the country's space program.

and me. Governor Clement inherited his style from his father, who was an old-time Southern politician. And he asks Walt, 'Tell me, Mr. Disney, did you have any ideaaaaaaaa when this show "Davy Crockett" opened all over the world that it would be such a sensational success?' Everybody in the room was looking at us. Walt winked at me and said, 'Well, I have to admit, I'm kind of disappointed. I thought it would be really big.' "

Naturally, shooting on location could present difficulties. Ebsen: "Fess and I rode a couple of fifty-dollar horses because the unit manager wanted to save money. To make the horses go, we had to put tacks in our moccasins for spurs. Of course, you were never quite sure where you were going to land if you spurred them too much. Anyway, we were four weeks behind on a one-week picture when the director, Norman Foster, heard that Walt was coming out from California to visit. Norman predicted that this was a sign that Walt was bringing in another director. So he said good-bye to everybody and was on the set the next morning, directing, when a long black limousine pulled up. Walt and his wife stepped out of the limo, and Walt—as was his manner—was shaking hands with the whole company on the way to Norman Foster. Norman was preparing the next scene, pretending that fate was not approaching him from over his shoulder. Finally, Walt came right up next to him, and Norm looked up and said casually, 'Oh, hello, Walt.' And Walt said, 'Hello, Norm.' And then there was a little pause, and Norman asked, 'How'd the stuff look?' Walt says, 'Oh, looked okay. Except for one thing.' And Norm thought, 'Uh-oh, here it goes.' He says, 'What's that?' And Walt says, 'You know that scene where Fess wrestles with the bear? I want you to shoot it over because that bear's zipper was showing.' Then Walt got in the car and drove away. Norm breathed a huge sigh of relief, looked up, and said, 'Thank you, God.' "

Walt's next big move in television had been anticipated for some time. He was committed to creating a children's show for ABC but wasn't sure exactly what form the show should take. After considering several options, he hit on the format for the "Mickey Mouse Club." Walt emphasized that he didn't want a bunch of what he called "Hollywood kids" on the air. Mouseketeer Bobby Burgess recalls, "They had over a thousand kids who were auditioning for the "Mickey Mouse Club." I understand that he would take his producers around the neighborhood and go to the playgrounds and school areas and say, 'See those kids over there? That's what I want for Mouseketeers.' He meant the kids next door, not slick professionals. We had to know how to sing and dance, of course, but he didn't want us to be precocious in any way. He wanted the kids in the audience to relate to us."

Sharon Baird was another of the original Mouseketeers. Her childhood memories of working with Walt are affectionate. "The first time I met him," she says, "we were in the studio taking a break from the shooting. All the kids were running around making noise, until

BOBBY

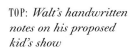

SHARON

TOP: *Walt's handwritten notes on his proposed kid's show*

ABOVE: *Mouseketeer Bobby Burgess*

LEFT: *Mouseketeer Sharon Baird*

somebody said, 'You better cool it. Walt Disney's back there.' And we all stopped in our tracks and looked around. There he was, just like one of the guys, in his workman's pants and shirt. He'd been working with the animators in the paint department, mixing paint with the paint guys, and he was just a regular man. He was very gentle, soft-spoken. He had a twinkle in his eye and loved to laugh. He made sure the crew didn't swear around us. He wanted us to call him Uncle Walt. We all admired him and respected him so much that we called him Mr. Disney. Even when I talk about him today I refer to him as Mr. Disney."

Though all the Mouseketeers were becoming famous, Annette Funicello stood out from the pack. Her piles of fan mail were enormous. "Mr. Disney was a mentor to her," says Baird, "almost like a second father. She said many times how much she wished Mr. Disney were still alive because all the advice he gave her throughout her life was very important to her. At one time, for example, she thought of changing her name, and he advised her against it. 'Then you wouldn't be you,' he said."

Adds Bobby Burgess, "Annette was selected by Walt Disney himself. She was the last Mouseketeer signed. She always had charisma, a special appeal to kids watching the show. And she got many marriage proposals. I think everybody on that show was secretly in love with her."

"The Adventures of Spin and Marty" was one of the most successful segments of the "Mickey Mouse Club." Cotter: "It was a huge hit. Letters started to come in asking for more. At times we received more fan mail than some of Walt's big theatrical hits." Tim Considine and David Stollery starred in "Spin and Marty." "Was I awed by Mr. Disney?" asks Stollery. "Although we were very much aware of Mr. Disney and what he had accomplished, he set everybody at ease. That's very unusual for a man of his prestige. We respected him, but he made us feel perfectly at ease." Tim Considine adds, "We made 'Spin and Marty' at the Golden Oak Ranch. We weren't in the studio, so we never really knew much about the 'Mickey Mouse Club.' Once, when I went to the studio for lunch, I noticed these little kids who were dressed the same way, with these little funny hats on with little round ears. In an interview I described the Mouseketeer hats as yarmulkes with wings. After lunch, they all went out in a pack, and I followed, just to see where they were going. What were they doing? I followed them into their little stage, where they were singing and dancing and carrying on. It was the first time I ever saw a Mouseketeer. I thought, 'I'm sure glad I don't have to do that singing and dancing.' These kids were talented."

As time went on, ABC kept asking Walt to produce more for them, while Walt kept asking for more money for Disneyland. Walt finally offered the "Zorro" series, which became another big hit. Cotter: "Walt had started on 'Zorro' several years before, as a pet project. By the time they proposed the series to ABC he already

A prop poster from "Zorro"

Animals were used in many lead-ins.

When you get it in color, you get that full depth. I mean, it's like a gray day, say, compared to a nice sunny day. . . . I mean, what would the world be without color?

WALT DISNEY

had the rights and had done some of the research. The show was a classic Disney operation from A to Z. Walt spent a fortune to build the sets on the studio lot, sparing no expense for even the smallest props, like the real wrought-iron antique chandelier. He spent more on the sets for 'Zorro' than most TV shows spent for their entire season of production at that time."

As ABC continued to drum away at Walt for more programming, however, problems began to emerge. The network especially wanted more westerns, but Walt refused to be pushed. Worse yet, ABC started to try to influence Walt's decisions on story direction and casting, something Walt wasn't about to put up with. So, Walt and ABC eventually parted ways over what Hollywood types generally call "creative differences." Walt considered where he would go next. Card Walker, one of Walt's closest executives, remembers the decision. "CBS and NBC-RCA were in a fierce competition over their color systems. The CBS system was like tying a washing machine down in the den because the picture would shake, rattle, and roll. We thought the RCA system was better, and we had a meeting with Bob Sarnoff, who was then the chairman of RCA in New York City. Walt really wanted it to go well. He said, 'Come on, you guys, let's get this deal. It's important for me; it's important for the studio. I'll stand on my head in Macy's window if that will make the deal.'" Walt was successful, and that was the beginning of "Walt Disney's Wonderful World of Color," which premiered on September 24, 1961, and ran under that title until 1969.

"After Walt passed away," says Cotter, "there were about three years' worth of projects already in the can, ready to air. Unfortunately, after Walt, the studio didn't know what to do. Without Walt's guidance, leadership, and inspiration, the folks at the studio lost their direction. A certain complacency set in, and after a while other programs took over the limelight and Disney's TV shows began to be of less interest to executives at the studios. The Walt-driven material started to dry up."

BELOW: *Walt and his daughters with the family's first TV set*

RIGHT: *The soda fountain at Holmby Hills*

FAR RIGHT: *At pub at Norton Disney in Lincolnshire*

A GROWING FAMILY

As his two daughters grew older, Walt was discouraged to find himself without playmates at his beck and call. "My daughters reached an age where they fell in love with horses," he said, "and their dad didn't count for much except to pay for the horses and things. Instead of getting them back after the horses, I saw them fall in love with parties and all of the things that come when you hit that teenage period. For a while I was feeling rather frustrated. I didn't know what was the matter with me. I'd say to the kids, 'Come on. Let's go somewhere,' and they'd say, 'No, Daddy, we've got to stay home,' or 'there's a prom on,' and they had to go get their hair done or something."

In spite of his disappointment, Walt continued to take every opportunity to remain involved in the lives of his daughters. "He came to every father-daughter event on the calendar," says Diane. "Once my friend Susie Zanuck and I created a little skit for the upcoming talent show that somehow involved cannibals. We needed some warrior shields and spears. So Dad took us out to the machine shop in the studio on a Sunday and, using suitable materials, he cut shields with the power saw and put handles on the backs, and made up some spears, too. As I remember, we painted them at home. He loved doing things like that, even for a little skit."

When Diane entered her later adolescent years, Sharon "became Dad's little companion," says Diane. In August 1947, the two pals went through a particularly harrowing experience, when a friend named Russel Havenstrite invited them on a trip to Alaska. Diane was away in camp, and Lilly didn't want to go, so Walt and Sharon took a small plane to a tiny Alaskan community called Candle. The plane entered thick clouds. The radio went dead. Conditions didn't permit landing. After two hours, the pilot didn't have any choice

ABOVE: *Walt and Sharon in Alaska*

BELOW: *Walt designed the figures on Diane and Ron's wedding cake.*

BOTTOM: *With a bemused expression, Walt shakes hands with his new son-in-law while Sharon, the sister of the bride, takes in the scene from behind.*

but to land. When Walt finally emerged, he tripped coming out of the plane. "I don't know whether I kissed the ground," he said later, "or fell on it."

Walt continued to drive his two daughters to school every morning until Diane was old enough to drive herself; and then he still dropped off Sharon on his way to the studio. "He found the drive a very productive time," recalls Diane. In 1949 the Disneys moved into their new house on Carolwood Drive. It not only had enough land for Walt's beloved train, but it also included a play-room with a soda fountain, where, as Walt wrote, "the girls can entertain their friends without disturbing the rest of the house-hold." Soon enough, the Disney home became a gathering place for Diane's and Sharon's friends, and Walt bemusedly commented that he was "supplying the whole neighborhood with sodas at my expense." Actually, Walt was delighted to know that his daughters and their friends were safe and sound at home, and the cost of a few sodas was a tiny price to pay. What's more, Walt loved the soda fountain, too. "He'd experiment," remembered Sharon, "by making these weird concoctions that nobody, including myself, would eat. He once tried to make a champagne soda. It was the most awful thing. He couldn't get anybody to taste it, and he agreed it was pretty bad."

In 1951, Diane went off to attend the University of Southern California, where she met a football player named Ronald Miller. They began dating, and, as Ron Miller recalls, "Whenever I first arrived at the house for a date, the first thing on my mind was getting Diane out of there, because I could tell that both Walt and Lilly were sizing me up." Ron clearly passed muster. "My parents liked Ron the minute they met him," said Diane. Walt described him in a letter to his brother Herb as "a wonderful boy, a big athlete whom we all love."

It wasn't a big wedding. You know how normally the cake has a bride and groom on top, dressed in tux and wedding dress? On our cake Walt had us in tennis shoes, Bermuda shorts, and sweatshirts.

RON MILLER

In 1954 Diane and Ron were married in a tiny church in Santa Barbara, California. Diane: "I think Dad relished every role he played in his life, and being father of the bride was a very important, tender one. It was a small wedding by design. My sister was my only attendant. Dad brought me up to the altar where Ron was standing, and I heard a sniffle. I turned, and he turned and looked at me. I felt him squeeze my hand."

After a stint in the army, Ron played professional football with the Los Angeles Rams for a few years. He remembers, "One year, Walt took Diane to a preseason game in which I got hit across the nose and was unconscious for a while. Later in the season, I broke my hand during a game. After the season was over, Walt approached me. By then we already had three children, and Walt said, 'If you continue playing football you're going to get killed out there, and I'm going to have the responsibility of raising those three kids, so why don't you come work with me?' That was a great opportunity, and I took it."

Said artist Peter Ellenshaw, "Ron hadn't been in the studio for long when I commented to Walt that I thought his son-in-law was doing very well. Walt said, 'Yeah. I have great ambition for him. He'll run the studio one day.'"

In the late '50s, Sharon also went to work at the studio for a while. "I knew he was keeping track of me," she recalled. "I mean, not where I was, but he knew if I was late. And he called personnel every so often to find out if I was goofing off or not. During the two years I worked there, he was very proud that every morning I arrived on time and never left until the end of the day." In 1957, Sharon began dating a bright architect from Kansas City named Robert Brown. About 18 months later, Sharon and Bob told Walt they wanted to be married. "Well, she's your problem now," joked Walt, by way of giving his blessing. After a while, Brown, too, came to work for his father-in-law, at WED.*

> ✦ **When Ron and I were building our first house, Dad came out one day and was rather appalled that I didn't have a divider in my silver tray. Afterwards, he went to his woodshop and built me a little wooden thing to divide silver with. He could fix anything in the house.**
>
> DIANE DISNEY MILLER

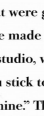

TOP: *Walt, Diane, and Sharon outside his workshop barn*
ABOVE: *Sharon with Walt at her wedding*

> ✦ **When I worked at the studio, rumors circulated that I was in there as a spy, that I was going home and reporting to Daddy all the things that were going on. One night I must have made a comment about someone at the studio, when Daddy said, "You stick to your job and I'll stick to mine." That was it.**
>
> SHARON DISNEY LUND

* Brown died in 1967 and Sharon later remarried.

DISNEYLAND—THE REALITY

ON THE MORNING OF JULY 17, 1955, Disneyland's gates were opened to the public for the very first time. Mouseketeer Sharon Baird was standing beside Walt Disney as the crowds rushed through: "I was only 12 at the time. He had his hands behind his back and was grinning from ear to ear. You could see the lump in his throat and a tear trickling down his cheek. His dream was realized."

The live telecast of the opening-day festivities—featuring Walt and celebrity commentators Art Linkletter, Ronald Reagan, and Bob Cummings—tantalized viewers coast-to-coast with its first look at the wondrous (and now classic) Disneyland attractions. But the magic of television obscured the reality of the day. Linkletter describes the situation gently: "There was a certain amount of disorganization. Disorganized effort, I mean. At one point, with the show about to be transferred to me at any second, I rushed over to one of the places where I was supposed to pick up a microphone, and I couldn't find it. I finally found it under a pile of lumber, just in time to start broadcasting."

Walt himself ran into trouble that day. Linkletter: "Walt tried to go down an alley to his next spot, over at Tomorrowland, and was stopped by a newly hired guard, who said, 'You can't go through here.' Walt laughed and said, 'Do you know who I am? I'm Walt Disney.' The guard said, 'Mr. Disney, I know who you are, but I'm sorry, I have orders. You can't go through here. Nobody can go through here.' And Walt replied, 'Either you let me through here or I'm going to hit you right in the face and walk

LEFT: *Sticky tar, unmanageable crowds, and a shortage of bathrooms marred opening day.*

BELOW: *The opening-day ceremony*

over your body.' The fellow moved over and Walt went on his way."

Linkletter's misplaced mike and an overly zealous employee were the least of the problems. As Disneyland historian and Imagineer Bruce Gordon recounts, "The park was crashed by thousands of people who forged tickets and jumped fences. So it was pretty much chaos. There'd been some trouble with the plumbers' union before the opening, so there weren't as many drinking fountains as there should have been. And because Disneyland was built so fast, a lot of things came together at the very last minute, such as the asphalt in some of the areas, which was still a little bit soft. Women who'd arrived in their high heels for the opening of Disneyland found their heels sinking into the pavement."

There were, of course, newspaper critics present to make note of the opening day hiccups. A few theorized that the absence of water fountains was part of a money-grubbing scheme to sell more soft drinks. "It felt like a giant cash register," one grumbled, "clicking and clanging as creatures of Disney magic came tumbling down from their lofty places in

BELOW: *The first Disneyland ticket*

RIGHT: *The Disneyland ticket book— in use during the park's first year*

ABOVE: *Autopia was among the most popular attractions.*

RIGHT: *Walt devoted his full attention even to small details, such as characters' costumes.*

my daydreams to peddle . . . their charms with the aggressiveness of so many curbside barkers. "But Walt's decades in the movie industry had toughened his attitude toward critics. Newspaper critics, he said are "odd creatures . . . I say, to hell with them."

After opening day, though, Walt set about making sure that all the attractions in the park were running smoothly. Bob Gurr was in charge of the Autopia ride: "By the end of the first day, about half the cars were out of commission, and within a week I think only two out of the 40 cars were still running. I was out alone in the field with my own tools and my own Cadillac, sitting outside the Autopia ride trying to fix the cars as fast as they would fall apart. One day, Walt came by and sat in the shade and watched me work. He wasn't critical. He just observed. I told him where the other mechanics were and mentioned that there wasn't an area designed with the ride where maintenance could be done. So he went away, and about a half-hour later a guy comes down the dirt road on an old tractor dragging a sled. It's carrying this little wooden building. He pulls up and says, 'Where do you want your damn garage? Walt just sent this over here. Tell me where you want it.'"

"Walt knew where every nail in the park was located," said Lilly.

About a week after the park opened, Disney executive Jack Lindquist accompanied a group of journalists through the park. "Walt was pointing the swans out to them in the moat in front of Sleeping Beauty Castle, and one of them said, 'Well, it looks beautiful now, but you've only been open three or four days. Wait until the crowds really come and this moat is filled with cigarette wrappers and paper cups and floating bottles and so forth.'

And Walt said, 'It'll never happen.' 'Why not?' the fellow asked. 'Because,' Walt replied, 'we're going to make it so clean people are going to be embarrassed to throw anything on the ground.' I saw that happen continuously. I'd see people flick cigarette ashes into their hands, or carry cigarette butts until they could find a trash container to put them in. Now, on Rodeo Drive or Fifth Avenue or Regent Street, London, they'd never think twice about throwing a cigarette butt on the ground. At Disneyland, they thought about it. Because there wasn't any litter or dirt on the ground."

Walt enjoyed walking around his park every chance he got, but with the Disneyland television show on the air, he was very easily recognized. He'd often wear sunglasses in hopes of slipping through the crowds unobserved. Inevitably, though, someone would notice him and ask for an autograph. This frustration led to a tiny innovation. Art Linkletter recalls taking a stroll around the park with Walt: "Walt said, 'Art, before we start out, we'll take paper and pencils and we'll autograph about fifty or a hundred sheets each. We'll carry it, and when people ask for an autograph, we'll peel one off and hand it to them.' We did that every time we walked

"Call Me Bob"

Anytime I had any dealings with Walt, he always called me Bob. Now, I was wearing a name tag that said Jack, but it really didn't make any difference. Finally, one day we were at a meeting with Card Walker and Dick Nunis, and Walt asked a question and said, "Bob, what's your opinion on that?" Card turned to him and said, "Walt, his name is Jack." Walt looked at me and the famous eyebrow went way up in the air, and for a couple of seconds he just stared at me. Then he turned back to Card and said, "Looks like a Bob to me." It was fine with me. If Walt wanted to call me Bob, that was my name.

JACK LINDQUIST

A reliable Disney hippo greets Jungle Cruise visitors.

Explosion Inventory

We had dinner on the upstairs patio of the fire station next to the entrance and then we watched the fireworks at ten o'clock. The fireworks were as beautiful and marvelous and interesting as they always are, but I noticed that Walt was making little marks on a pad. Finally, when it was over, he said, "Well, let's see now. We got everything I bought— there were 15 explosions, there were 28 flags, there were 34 rockets." He'd been writing down what he was seeing to check up on whether or not the guy was firing everything he'd been paid for. So he was a mixture of a childlike person, who was not a hard-driving businessman, and yet a perfectionist.

ART LINKLETTER

LEFT: *Tom Sawyer Island was added a year after the opening.*

BELOW: *The Storybook Land Canal Boats were also added in 1956.*

around the grounds. It was a wonderful way of giving a person a real autograph without being stuck in an awkward place."

Every detail was important to Walt. Artist Bill Justice helped design the character costumes for the park: "One day, we were in a big meeting and somebody mentioned a costume. 'Oh, Walt doesn't want to hear about that,' someone said. 'What do you mean I don't want to hear about that?' Walt asked. 'Those are the most important things we've got in the park. Other parks can have parades, they can have bands and thrill rides, and all that kind of stuff. But we have the Disney characters. Don't you realize how much they mean to people? A family comes into the park and they see one of our characters and they immediately have their child run over. They get their camera out and they take pictures of their little kids with Mickey or Minnie or Goofy or whoever happens to be there at the time. This is what people enjoy and this is what is important to us.'"

Dick Nunis started working for Walt in the early 1950s and eventually rose to the position of president of all the Disney theme parks. He recalls Walt's insistence that every guest in his park get his money's worth: "In early 1956, I was promoted to supervisor of Adventureland and Frontierland. My first week, Walt went on a Jungle Cruise boat. Afterwards, he called me over and said, 'Dick, what's the trip time?' Walt knew that, in those days, it was seven and a half minutes. He said, 'Well, I just got a four-minute trip. How would you feel if you went to the movies and they cut the center reel out of the picture? Dick, we've got to establish a terrific show, a consistent show, regardless of how long the line is.' He gave me about three weeks to get things shaped up. When he returned, I had

INSIDE THE DREAM

LEFT: *At the entrance to Disneyland*

BELOW: *Walt and Lilly in front of the real Matterhorn*

> ✳ **In the early days of Disneyland we had pay toilets. Walt went through the restrooms and in the next meeting he said, "I want the pay toilets eliminated." Somebody said, "Walt, people expect to pay for toilets because they're cleaner." He said, "The thing that's going to make Disneyland successful is that our toilets are always going to be clean, and they're always going to be free."**
>
> DICK NUNIS

my best staffer ready to jump on the first boat with him. But after the first ride, he went on three more. He finally got off and gave me a thumbs-up sign. I always wondered what would have happened if his thumb had been down."

Once the park was running smoothly, Walt really began to have fun. As far as he was concerned, Disneyland was an evolving work: "A live picture, once you wrap it up and turn it over to Technicolor . . . it's gone. I can't touch it. In the park, not only can I add things, but even the trees will keep growing. The thing will get more beautiful each year. And, as I find out what the public likes, I can change it." He was true to his word. In the years that followed, Walt added one new attraction after another, including Dumbo Flying Elephants, 20,000 Leagues Under the Sea, Storybook Land, and Tom Sawyer Island. Then, in 1959, he spent over $7 million on the Submarine Voyage, the Monorail, and the Matterhorn Bobsleds.

Walt was determined to make the Matterhorn like no other roller-coaster in the world. Imagineer Harriet Burns remembers the architect and engineer telling Walt, "There's no way you can run two bobsled rides in and out with a sky ride and plummeting waterfalls" and make it look like the Matterhorn. "Walt just smiled. It was done. That was that."

Walt would have brought a monorail to Disneyland sooner, but he couldn't find one that worked for him. Recalls designer Bob Gurr, "Walt and Lilly were driving along a road in Germany when a monorail car drove through

RIGHT: *Shown here with an Audio-Animatronics pirate, Walt died three months before the Pirates of the Caribbean opened.*

BELOW: *Walt loved chatting with Disneyland cast members.*

the trees from one side of the road to the other. Walt stopped and chased the monorail over to a service yard where nobody spoke English. They sent him back across the road to an administration building that housed a monorail company. He'd discovered his monorail. The monorail we built was based on its design. Serendipity really drives the world. Thirty seconds one way or the other and we might not have had a monorail in Disneyland."

Not all of Walt's ideas worked, of course. Harriet Burns reminisces about the story of the Candy Mountain: "After we had completed the Matterhorn, Walt said, 'Now that we can do a mountain, let's do a candy mountain. Every kid loves candy, let's do a whole mountain full of candy.' So we built a huge clay model, and we're about to make artificial candy, when he said, 'Let's have real candy. Let's order every kind of candy we can get and put that on the mountain.' He had a factory custom-make the candy he remembered as a child—little taffies with pictures in them, little wax things filled with liquid, along with fun things like huge candy canes. Finally he said, 'I don't know. I'll bring down John Hench and see what he thinks.' John was his right-hand man. John frowned and said, 'Walt, when you have meat and potatoes and a salad, and then have candy or a sweet for dessert—that's one matter. But when you see piles and piles of candy, that just undoes the whole thing.' Walt agreed and decided to abandon Candy Mountain. It had been built on a huge wheeled platform, and we opened the great doors and pushed

> ✳ **I don't know if I'd heard Bob Gurr's tale of how Dad had found his monorail before and forgotten it, but it is so typical of Dad. He seized opportunities of all kinds, and few if any were wasted.**
>
> DIANE DISNEY MILLER

it outside. The birds came down. The blue jays ate the peanuts out of the peanut brittle and the pecans out of the fudge, and soon we had no more Candy Mountain. That was the end of the whole idea."

Walt continued to tweak and add to Disneyland. After the New York World's Fair ended in 1965, he brought four more attractions to the park—including Great Moments with Mr. Lincoln and the It's a Small World ride. In his last months, Walt busily worked on the Pirates of the Caribbean and the Haunted Mansion. But there was one problem—while he could continuously improve Disneyland, he had less control over the surrounding area.

Jack Lindquist: "Harbor Boulevard, across from Disneyland, frustrated him tremendously. He was very disappointed in the city of Anaheim for not exercising greater control of the development that existed outside the park. Less than 10 years after Disneyland opened, Harbor Boulevard was an example of ugly urban sprawl at its worst."

There was nothing Walt could do to overcome this problem in Anaheim. But it was in the forefront of his mind as he moved on to another project that would eventually become far bigger than Disneyland: his "Florida project."

Walt and Sharon in Disneyland

If you ever wanted a conversation with Mr. Disney, all you had to say at the time I was there was, "How are things at the park, Mr. Disney?" And you had instant conversation. He'd say, "Well, come on up and I'll show you something." He'd turn around and go back into the animation building, where his office was. He'd take you upstairs and he'd show you the neatest thing he was working on.

TIM CONSIDINE

WED: WALT'S SANDBOX

"WHEN WALT WANTED TO BUILD Disneyland, he realized that he had to form his own design company," recalls longtime Imagineer Rolly Crump. So Walt gathered together a small band of prized studio employees and dubbed the new entity with his own initials—WED. Walt financed WED in part by charging the Disney Company for the right to use his name and giving the income to WED. "At the same time," says Mickey Clark, an early WED executive, "Walt arranged for a license agreement with Walt Disney Productions in which WED received royalties from the use and sale of the Disney characters. That was the first form of income that WED Enterprises had."

As time went on and the Disney corporation became the owner of Disneyland, WED continued to design attractions for the park. But Walt wasn't interested in making profits from his little firm. Clark: "He charged labor costs plus his out-of-pocket expenses. He just wanted to get the job done."

Walt with a model for the Red Wagon Inn (now called the Plaza Inn)

Walt loved WED. While the studio had grown large and somewhat bureaucratic, WED was a place where he could have fun. It was a small company doing what it wanted to do. According to Bill Cottrell, Walt's brother-in-law and first president of WED, "Nobody had to ask anyone at the studio for permission. If you wanted to start developing a thing like Audio-Animatronics, you'd do it as long as you had the money to do it. And by this time Walt had the money. He had borrowing power. WED was a wonderful thing for Walt."

He called it his "sandbox." Others called it his "laughing place." "He sort of hung out," remembers model-maker Harriet Burns. "He seemed to like to relax at WED because he didn't have meetings like the ones that were scheduled in the animation building. He could be just one of us, and kick stuff around. When we'd be working on a project he could hardly stand it. If I was soldering something, he'd want to solder it himself. When I was trying to get air into polyester to make permanent bubbles, he said, 'Let me try it.' He was always intrigued."

This hands-on attitude could lead to the occasional problem, as when Burns, who was working on an intricate stained-glass window, left it out for soldering. "I had 358 pieces of lead, and he came in and picked it up." Of course, the window splintered into 358 pieces. Burns: "So finishing that the next day was out."

In assembling his staff for WED, Walt drew on some of the most creative talents at the studio. Crump recalls hearing WED referred to as "Cannibal Island," because it "was gobbling up all the people that were

Priorities

✳ **We were working very hard at the New York World's Fair to complete the four Disney shows. While I was traveling back and forth every week between New York and Los Angeles, some of my colleagues had been away from their homes in Los Angeles for two and three months. About a month before the fair opened, Walt came through to review the shows, and a few of us took him back to his hotel. On the way back he said, "How are your spouses enjoying New York?" Nobody said a word. But we didn't have to because he looked at us and he said, "Oh, I get it." The very next morning, every one of us got a call from somebody in administration at WED, and the question was, "When do you want your spouse to arrive in New York?" Walt had just taken care of it. His concern for us as human beings and as family people was very clear.**

MARTY SKLAR

Some called WED "Walt's Laughing Place."

Meeting Walt

Bob Gurr

✳ **I went over on Saturday mornings to start working on the body for this little Autopia car for Disneyland. This guy walks up, unshaven, and I remember he had a Roy Rogers-type belt on with little silver-painted fake bullets and a funny looking tie, and I thought he was probably a father or one of the night guards, because he just sort of oozed into the conversation. Then I noticed the other guys were calling him Walt, and then when everybody walked away, I thought "Gosh, that's Walt Disney."**

BOB GURR

X Atencio with parrot

in animation"—people like Marc Davis, John Hench, X Atencio, and Bill Justice. "In those days," recalls Bob Gurr, who worked on a number of Disneyland attractions, "Walt was gathering people almost like instruments in an orchestra. He put us all together, but he never passed out the music. Oddly enough, I think he was the only one who knew where he was going to go. He knew the different skills that all the different folks had, and he put them all together. But only he knew what the outcome was going to be."

Once the artists chosen for WED arrived, they were often put to work on projects unlike any they had encountered before. X Atencio tells a typical story. He had been an animator at the studio until the day Walt called him up to his office and asked him to move over to WED. "I went over to WED," Atencio says, "and nobody over there seemed to know what I was supposed to do. About a month later, Walt called over and he says, 'I want you to do the script for the Pirates ride.' I had never done any scripting before, but I had done storyboarding at the animation end of it, so I said, 'OK.' I put on my pirate hat and I researched all the pirate stuff I could get hold of. The first thing I worked on was the auction scene, and when I was finished I sent it over to Walt. 'Fine,' he said, 'go right along.' So, I went with it. And when the scripting was finished, I said to Walt, 'I have an idea for a song—a song would be real good in this.' I had a melody in mind and sang it for him—it started with a 'Yo ho ho ho, a pirate's life for me.' And Walt said, 'Hey, that's fine. Get Joey to do the music for it and we'll put it in the show.' I thought he was going to tell me to get the Sherman brothers to write the words, but he didn't. So after becoming a scriptwriter, I became a songwriter."

Rolly Crump tells a similar story: "When Walt wanted to do the Tiki Room, he asked me to design some of the pre-show Tikis that you stand and listen to before you go in. I did some very crude little pen-and-ink sketches and showed them to Walt, and he said, 'Great. Let's go with those.' We only had one sculptor at that time and his name was Blaine Gibson. 'Blaine,' I said, 'Walt wants us to go ahead and get these sculpted.' I hand him the sketch, and Blaine says, 'I don't have time for that.' I said, 'Well, who's going to do this?' He said, 'You are.' I said, 'I've never sculpted before in my life.' And he said, 'Well, you're going to sculpt now.' I sculpted about 80 percent of the Tikis in the Tiki Room. Other people were brought in to help, and none of us had ever sculpted before. In those days we did a little bit of everything, which was marvelous. I did ticket booths. I did trash barrels. I did Sunkist, on Main Street. I did the Bazaar. Walt had never built a theme park before, so we just made things up as we went along."

Walt and John Hench

Flexibility was a valued requirement in WED staffers. Walt was not particularly patient if his WED employees—who would come to be called Imagineers—hesitated about jumping into something entirely new. John Hench experienced Walt's impatience firsthand: "I came to Walt once when he'd asked me to oversee a change we were making in the restaurants. I tried to explain to him that I was the wrong person for the job because I couldn't understand anything the food people were talking about. He wasn't at all sympathetic. He said, 'Don't expect me to understand that language either—just go and find out about it.' So I took a restaurant management class at UCLA and had no more trouble. I learned the difference between a bain marie and a salamander. But Walt was like that. If you didn't know something that he wanted you to know, you'd go find out about it. He insisted on it."

Scale Tale

✳ I was doing sketches of the Bazaar for Disneyland, and one day the carpenter came up and said, "What scale is this?" I said, "Scale?" And he said, "Yeah, what scale are you using?" I said, "I don't know what you're talking about—what is scale?" He said, "Do you know what a scale ruler is?" I said, "No, I don't know what a scale ruler is, but I know how big these are." So I made my own cardboard scale ruler—I think one foot equaled an inch and three-quarters—and I made copies and gave them to the carpenters. When we finally finished the job, one of the carpenters came up and said, "Do you mind if I keep your scale ruler? We may work together again."

ROLLY CRUMP

A COMFORTABLE MAN

UNLIKE MANY HOLLYWOOD BOSSES, Walt vastly preferred the company of his family to that of slinky starlets or powerful studio heads. "Walt was not a cocktail party man," says family friend Art Linkletter. "In fact, he loved to come to my house for dinner, because it was kind of a family affair and there weren't photographers and reporters or the kind of people who want to grab you and sell you something. He just liked to talk to people he respected."

In fact, Diane can only remember a few instances in which her parents had dinner guests. Sharon recalled that "So many people think that in Hollywood there are big social events and movie stars all over the house. In our home there were never any." Linkletter agreed: "He could just as well have been a very successful plumber somewhere," says Linkletter. "He'd be the best plumber, of course, and the plunger would probably play 'Auld Lang Syne' in the toilet."

According to Dick Van Dyke, "Middle Westerners hate affectation, which you tend to see in southern California. Walt was not in the least

ABOVE: *Walt and his dog Lady share a snack, an evening routine.*

RIGHT: *Walt relaxes in the backyard of his Holmby Hills house.*

134

ABOVE: *Lilly wasn't thrilled with Walt's gift of a petrified tree; it ended up at Disneyland.*

RIGHT: *Walt and Lilly*

affected. He was who he was, one of the most comfortable people you could possibly be around."

For the most part, evenings in the Disney household were relatively simple. Cocktails (often featuring a drink called a scotch mist) were followed by dinner. In the early '50s, Walt would wander into his workshop and spend hours tinkering on his trains and miniatures. In later years, he'd usually retire to a comfortable chair and read scripts. He generally slept well, recalled Lilly, "unless an idea came to him." Then, he'd willingly stay up for hours, sketching out his thoughts.

On Sunday nights in the 1960s, Walt and Lilly would watch the "Wonderful World of Color." Lilly recalled, "We would eat in front of the TV. He wanted my reaction to the show. Every time I would take a mouthful of food he would look over and say, 'You're not looking. You're not looking.'"

The fact that Walt himself was a regular guy did not mean that he didn't enjoy living well. He and Lilly traveled frequently. They enjoyed their vacation home at Smoke Tree Ranch. (They had bought their first "second home" there in around 1950, which they sold several years later to help

Foo Foo

Thelma Howard was, in Diane's words, "housekeeper, cook, sometime nanny, and wonder woman." She worked for Walt and Lilly for many years and had a remarkable relationship with Walt and the family. Usually known as Foo Foo, Thelma was also beloved by the Disney grandchildren. "My grandfather had an incredible rapport with her," remembers Walt's grandson Chris Miller. "They seemed to share everything, from a sense of humor to their notions about what was happening with the kids and what was best for them. Foo Foo was, in many ways, kind of a teacher to us. I think we learned most of what we knew about Hollywood and celebrity-hood from her. She also gave us an idea of how to accomplish tasks, how to make crafts, how to draw." Says Chris' sister, Tamara, "Foo Foo was a dynamite lady and we were all drawn to her, to her kitchen, and to her world."

According to Diane, Walt enjoyed teasing Foo Foo. "He'd come home from the restaurant called Biff's, and say 'Thelma, you ought to go down to Biff's and find out how they make those wonderful little silver dollar-sized pancakes.' Or 'Biff's makes the best hash brown potatoes. You ought to go

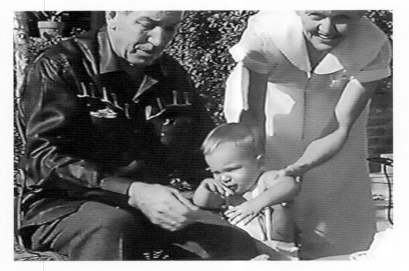

Walt, grandson Chris, and Foo Foo, taken from a home movie

see how they do it.' It was all in fun. Foo Foo was a great cook and he knew it."

Periodically, Walt would give Foo Foo a few shares of Disney stock as a present, generally telling her, "Now, don't you spend this. Hang onto it." She never spent a dime on herself and, thanks to Walt's gifts, by the time Thelma Howard died in 1994, she was a multimillionaire. A foundation that bears her name has given well over $1 million in grants since 1995.

finance Disneyland. When Walt began to recoup the money he had invested in the park, the Disneys built another house with a distinctly contemporary design. Lilly hired a decorator who filled it with bright colors and fabrics.) Walt rode his bicycle everywhere and took up lawn bowling. "He purchased a home in a nearby golf course development that he intended to use for business guests. He would bring his guys down to him instead of his having to return to L.A.," says Diane. Walt also took great pleasure in the private plane the studio provided him. Granddaughter Joanna has fond memories of playing flight attendant. "I think you're thirsty, Grandpa," she'd tell him. "Would you like something to drink?"

In 1964 Walt bought himself a particularly luxurious treat. As he wrote his sister Ruth, "I haven't hit the rocking chair, either. . . . I bought myself a jazzy little sports car this year, a Mercedes 230SL. . . . Anyway, it's a car for the man who thinks young, and I am just the guy for it. I thought for a while I was going to have to fight Sharon for the possession of it. I loaned it to her one week while we were away and she threatened to steal it. It's a little beauty, and almost as good as a blonde on each arm for getting a little envy from my fellow man."

Fred MacMurray, shown here in Son of Flubber, *starred in several of Walt's special-effects-filled comedies.*

"A VERY COMMON TOUCH"

AS YEARS WENT ON, Walt's live-action films became synonymous with reliable and consistent family entertainment. Walt fought the notion that he was making movies for children. He wanted to make films that—not unlike Disneyland—could be enjoyed by the whole family. In 1956, Walt told the *Kansas City Times,* "I remember when I was a kid and some adult would pat me on the head and say, 'Well, little man, how are you?' I always felt like I wanted to kick him right in the teeth. When we put on a show, we try to put the children right in the middle of it. We never discount their intelligence. We don't try to be frenetic and jump all around and say, 'Isn't that funny?'"

> *All right, I'm corny. But I think there's just about a hundred and forty million people in this country who are just as corny as I am.*
>
> WALT DISNEY

Walt understood that the value of his brand name was incalculable. He would have liked to expand his horizons and make films that didn't fit the standard Disney formats. But he was a prisoner of his own success. Even a mildly risqué scene in *Bon Voyage,* which featured a streetwalker, was met with howls of protest by some moviegoers, who claimed to be shocked that Walt would include such material.

Ron Miller, Walt's son-in-law and a producer at the studio, remembers, "Walt invited us to his house, where he had a projection room, to watch *To Kill a Mockingbird.* When the lights came on, Walt's first comment was, 'That's the kind of film I wish I could make.' He was frustrated because he was locked into producing a certain kind of G-rated family film, which limited what he could do.

NEW HORIZONS

ABOVE: *Walt's daughter Sharon on the set of* Johnny Tremain.

BELOW: *A frame from* The Third Man on the Mountain

Walt may have felt shackled by audience expectations, but the handcuffs were golden. Though there were certainly some clinkers along the way, by all standards his output of strong films was prodigious. In the 1950s, Walt focused on outdoor adventure, including *Westward Ho the Wagons!*, *Johnny Tremain* (in which his daugher Sharon had a small part), and *The Third Man on the Mountain*. Between 1959 and his death in 1966, Walt produced such films as *Old Yeller*, *The Shaggy Dog*, *Darby O'Gill and the Little People*, *Pollyanna*, *Swiss Family Robinson*, *The Parent Trap*, *Mary Poppins*, and *The Happiest Milliionaire*.

"While Walt relied heavily on his directors, writers, and co-producers, he always kept a hand in," says director Ken Annakin. "In *Third Man on the Mountain*, for example, he personally found the choir that sings in the picture. He brought them out and arranged that they would work for us."

There's a famous story about Walt Disney describing himself as a bumblebee spreading concepts around from flower to flower, but it was always a mistake to try to replicate Walt's suggestions precisely. "A lot of times the writers would take his words literally," says Ron Miller, "not understanding that Walt was only throwing out an idea for other people to embellish. He would be very disappointed when a writer or a storyboard man would do only what he gave them." On the other hand, once Walt had made up his mind about something, he wasn't easy to budge. "On one of my pictures I tried to pull out a gag I thought was pretty corny," says actor Dean Jones, "but Walt said, 'That gag was funny in 1923 and it'll be funny today.' He didn't listen to me; he kept it in the picture. When that gag came up at the premiere, I laughed along with the rest of the audience. Walt was right; it was still funny."

Adds Imagineer Rolly Crump, "Walt had total recall. Here's an example: While he was looking at the dailies of a scene from *Toby Tyler*, he turned to the director and said, 'I saw seven elephants coming down the road, and in the script there were eleven.' You have to understand, Walt read that script three years before!"

Ron Miller recalls a similar incident in the making of *That Darn Cat!*: "Bill Walsh and I were associate producers. We were watching one scene in which the young boyfriend of Hayley Mills gets up after eating a lot of potato chips and wipes his greasy hands on the curtain before he leaves the room. I urged Bill to edit it out because I found it distasteful. Lo and behold, when we screened the picture, Walt asked, 'What ever happened to the scene where the kid wipes his hands on the drapes?' At that point Bill Walsh, who was a wonderful guy and a dear friend of mine, said 'Ron had it cut out. It was his decision.' So I sat there with egg on my face, while Walt said, 'You're going too far in cutting these things. Let me make some of the decisions.'"

In some of the movies he helped inspire the performers—particularly when they were young. Kevin Corcoran, who starred in a number of Disney films, including *Old Yeller*, recalls, "In between set-ups Walt would chat with me and say, 'Guess what you're going to be doing next?' He had a very childlike enthusiasm, and he would pretty much play out the story. He motivated me. If you looked into his eyes, he was just having a great time because he was telling a story."

According to artist Peter Ellenshaw, when Walt came onto a set, you'd know it, even though there was nothing said. The door would open, he'd go over and chat with an electrician, ask him about his job, and get interested. He'd never come in and just announce his arrival. Adds actor Dean Jones, "*That Darn Cat!* was my first picture for Walt, and I remember him asking the cat trainer, 'How did you train the cat to jump up and hit that button to get the ironing board to fall down?' At the time, he seemed to me more like a tourist from Duluth than the head of a studio. He had a very common touch."

RIGHT: *The hand-wiping scene from* That Darn Cat!

BELOW: *Walt and Kevin Corcoran (left)*

In 1959 Disney released *Darby O'Gill and the Little People.* Says film critic Leonard Maltin, "I think this film is another of the unsung live-action Disney masterpieces. I don't use the word lightly. I think it's a wonderful, wonderful film. I would put *Darby O'Gill* at the very top of the heap for its special effects. It's not an outer space film; it's not an underwater film. It's a film that takes place in the real world and yet has this incredible and convincing fantasy happening right in front of your eyes, and you believe it. I'd put it on a level with *King Kong*, which is one of the all-time great special-effects movies, because it combines reality with make-believe. When Darby is playing his fiddle and the leprechauns are dancing around, you believe there are those little people there.

ABOVE: *A TV lead-in promotes* Darby O'Gill and the Little People.

LEFT: *Remarkable special effects were a hallmark of* Darby O'Gill.

"Paint It"

Dean Jones in That Darn Cat!

✴ In *That Darn Cat!* there's repeatedly a shot of the cat moving away from me down alleys, down streets, and so forth. The cat was dark, and in Panavision the cat's rear end was about ten feet in diameter and very light-colored. When Walt said we needed to do something about the cat's behind, everybody looked around wondering what to do. Walt said, "I don't know. Paint it."

So the next day the set painters mixed up some paint containing kerosene or turpentine that sent the cat up to the top of Stage 2 for about three days. When they finally got the cat back, they changed to a mixture of black licorice that the cat seemed to tolerate just fine.

But when the makeup people heard that the painters were making up the cat's behind, they sent a union representative. They claimed it was really a makeup job and that painting the cat's behind was their responsibility. I asked Walt how he dealt with this and he said, "It's all a part of doing business."

DEAN JONES

A promotional shot for The Absent-Minded Professor

"Actually, when I first saw the movie as a kid, I was confused, because I was just old enough to say, 'Wait, leprechauns don't exist, do they?' But they seemed so real that I wondered if maybe there was this species I hadn't read about. And I was too embarrassed to ask anybody. I felt too foolish."

The Shaggy Dog, which was released in 1959, was of particular significance because it was the first in a long series of whimsical comedies, many of which combined fantasy with special effects and humor. Maltin: "I don't think Walt Disney himself could have predicted the path his studio would take in the live-action movie world. For a while, it looked like they were going to be making outdoor adventure films forever, but then they planned a comedy called *The Shaggy Dog* and, unlike most of the other shows, it was produced in black and white, because they didn't think they could make the special effects convincing enough in color. To everyone's shock and amazement it became a sensational hit—not just successful, but hugely successful.

"When *Shaggy Dog* took off, two things happened. First, the studio decided to make more comedies with fantasy, action, and slapstick. Second, they decided to bring back Fred MacMurray to become sort of the house star at Disney, as Fess Parker was the dominant live-action star in the films of the '50s."

But while comedy was Disney's bread and butter in the '60s, it wasn't all the studio did. Notable was the 1960 hit *Swiss Family Robinson*, based on the book of the same name. Naturally, Walt never hesitated to take liberties with his original source material. According to the film's director, Ken Annakin, "We diverged completely from the book. Walt just said, 'The book tells of a family that leaves Europe and gets shipwrecked on an island, where they can have anything they want. Let's all just think of the things you would like if you were in their shoes.' In the morning Walt would say, 'I just had an idea last night. Why don't we have them finding an elephant or a tiger on the island?' And you would say, 'What country is this?' And he'd say, 'It doesn't matter. We can always say there was a land bridge.'"

Kevin Corcoran, who played one of the sons in *Swiss Family Robinson*, recalls, "And I remember Walt and the art director went through this huge tree house just before the shoot to add little devices that Walt thought would be fun. Of course, this was after it was pretty much built. Frankly, I don't know if they were things Walt had seen before or if he just dreamed them up right there on the set. Eventually the tree house became one of the attractions in Disneyland."

During this period Walt discovered Hayley Mills, the daughter of the popular English actor John Mills. According to Leonard Maltin, "When Walt saw her in *Tiger Bay* he knew then and there that there was something special about this young lady, and he brought her to America to make *Pollyanna*. You couldn't ask for a better marriage of child actress and a role, or a better showcase for an actress of any age than *Pollyanna*. The film made Hayley Mills an overnight sensation in this country—even around the world, I dare say."

Richard M. and Robert B. Sherman—known to all as the Sherman brothers—wrote many of the songs for Walt's pictures in the 1960s. They first met Walt to discuss a television movie called *The Horsemasters*. Walt started off the meeting by asking if they were really brothers, because in vaudeville, he explained, "We did brother acts and we just called ourselves brothers but we weren't." Richard Sherman remembers how the rest of the meeting proceeded, after Walt had established that they actually were brothers: "Walt launched into a big description of a picture that would eventually be called *The Parent Trap*. He talked about these two sisters meeting in a summer camp, and we grew terrified, thinking, 'Here is this icon and he's talking to us about the wrong movie.' So my brother, who is extremely brave, said, 'Mr. Disney, we came with a song for Annette Funicello to sing in *The Horsemasters*.' Walt got sort of peeved at himself and said, 'Well then, why are you letting me go on like this?' He stood up, and we followed him into another room, where a piano was facing the wall. If you're a musician, you don't like to sing to a wall when the person listening to the song is behind you, so I arched my neck to sing to him. It was terrible. Under these conditions I sang 'The Strummin' Song' for the first time for the great man.

TOP: *The shaggy dog*

CENTER: The Shaggy Dog *was the first of Disney's broad comedies.*

RIGHT: *Walt enjoyed all the gadgets in the* Swiss Family Robinson *tree house.*

BELOW: *Hayley Mills stars as each of the sisters in* The Parent Trap.

"After I was finished, he said to Jimmy Johnson [general manager of the Walt Disney Music Company], 'Yeah, that'll work. Since I wasted all this time telling them about the other picture, why don't you give them a script and see if they can come up with a title for it. I don't like the title.' So we left the room thinking the interview was pretty much of a disaster, when Jimmy Johnson congratulated us. 'That was great, you guys. Don't you realize he accepted the song?' We couldn't believe it. Johnson explained that when Walt said, 'That'll work,' it was a good thing. Later we learned it was Walt's highest praise."

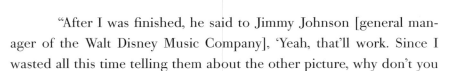

Occupational Hazard

In *Swiss Family* Walt wanted a tiger, and he wanted it to be quite active. When the dogs attack, he insisted that they actually touch the tiger. I just said, "From my experience shooting in South Africa, I say that a tiger is much less trainable than a lion." And Walt suddenly said, "Ken's afraid of the tiger," and he kept it up the whole time. Whenever we came to the tiger, he said, "Of course we know Ken's afraid of the tiger, but do you think you can possibly shoot it this way?" And that became a gag throughout.

KEN ANNAKIN

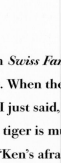

TOP: *Director Ken Annakin*
ABOVE: *"Ken's afraid of the tiger," teased Walt.*

Given his lack of formal training, Walt was uncanny in being able to communicate musical thoughts. Says studio composer Buddy Baker, "He didn't speak in musical terms with us. He had a sense of when it should be a symphonic sound, or a dance-band sound, or a little cute cartoony sound, but he couldn't tell you musically." Says Robert Sherman, "He couldn't write music. He couldn't sing very well, but he knew what he wanted. Once, they were doing a picture called *Bon Voyage*, and Dick and I wrote a lilting French love song for it that everyone loved. Walt called us to say he heard we had written a great song for him. That was the kiss of death. We played it for him in his office. We knew that when Walt didn't like something, he had a habit of very arhythmically tapping on the arm of his chair, and he was tapping pretty resolutely that day. He was clearly unhappy with the song, so when Dick was through singing Walt said, 'Yeah. Well *my* song is "California, Here I Come!" only in French.' And we knew what he meant."

Dick Van Dyke starred in Disney's masterpiece *Mary Poppins*, as well as in one of the last films to come out before Walt's death, *Lt. Robin Crusoe, U.S.N.* "He was such a comfortable man to be around," says Van Dyke. "I liked that he still had the enthusiasm of a ten-year-old about the work."

After Walt died, Dick Van Dyke made a film for another studio called *Chitty Chitty Bang Bang*. "It should have been done by Disney," he says. "Walt had a golden touch when it came to entertainment. He dealt with fantasy and had that wonderful imagination. I loved doing *Chitty Chitty Bang Bang*, and it was moderately successful, but I think it would have had a lot more magic if it had Walt Disney's touch."

✴ **John Canemaker and others have called my dad a natural actor, and as a boy he did begin his entertainment career trying to be a vaudeville actor, doing Chaplin imitations. Dick Van Dyke is probably the kind of actor Dad would have liked to have been. While he can be wildly funny, he can also evoke pathos, and he moves with a wonderful comic grace. There is no one like him. We were thrilled that he accepted our request to narrate the documentary.**

DIANE DISNEY MILLER

TOP: *Composer Buddy Baker*

CENTER: *Songwriters Robert and Richard Sherman*

ABOVE : *Walt on the set of* The Happiest Millionaire, *which was released in 1967 after his death*

PART FOUR

TOMORROW LAND

By the 1960s, although Walt was already considered a giant of 20th-century entertainment, his furious pace grew even more intense. The studio produced dozens of films—live-action and animated—including Pollyanna, Swiss Family Robinson, 101 Dalmatians, The Absent-Minded Professor, and The Parent Trap. His involvement in these films varied, but the one movie that commanded his full attention—Mary Poppins—was proclaimed Walt's masterpiece.

With the studio humming along, Walt had the most fun at WED, where designs for Disneyland attractions were being produced. When he decided to create attractions for the 1964–1965 World's Fair in New York, his WED staff—dubbed Imagineers—were dubious. Walt regarded the fair as an opportunity to spend other people's money on new technological innovations. Equally important, it was a chance to see how Disney entertainment would be received by East-Coast audiences.

Walt was thinking about a second theme park on the eastern seaboard; ultimately he settled on Florida. But the park he visualized was a means to an end. Walt wanted to create a living, breathing laboratory for innovations in urban living, called EPCOT (for the Experimental Prototype Community of Tomorrow). Walt absorbed himself in solutions for better transportation, sanitation, and communication.

Other dreams were nurtured during this time as well, including a new kind of ski resort, called Mineral King (which never came to be) and an exciting new venture in education, the California Institute of the Arts.

When Walt, a lifelong smoker, died of lung cancer in 1966, it struck his family—and the world—as an unfathomable loss. In the words of late TV commentator Eric Sevareid, "We'll never see his like again."

The nannies are whisked away in Mary Poppins.

Julie Andrews: "Practically perfect in every way"

MARY POPPINS

"I THINK OF *MARY POPPINS* as Walt's masterpiece, and I don't use the term lightly," says film critic Leonard Maltin. "I think that, in a way, it had to come when it did. It couldn't have come earlier in his career, because it was the culmination of everything he'd learned.

"He saw Julie Andrews and said, 'She's exactly the right woman to play Mary Poppins.' Now that was not conventional wisdom. She'd been passed over by Jack L. Warner, a pretty canny producer himself, to recreate the role of Eliza Doolittle in *My Fair Lady* for the screen. Warner didn't think Julie Andrews was photogenic enough, and, although she had a name on Broadway, she had no name in the movies, so he hired Audrey Hepburn instead. Walt didn't have any such qualms.

"Dick Van Dyke was already successful on television and had made a success in movies like *Bye Bye Birdie*, but *Mary Poppins* gave him the greatest role of his career. Walt had already hired the Sherman brothers to create delightful songs for TV shows, for records, for some of his earlier feature films, but he inspired them with *Mary Poppins*. He challenged them to rise to new heights and got the very best they had to give. It was as if, in every way, his inspiration and passion to make this film as great as it could be pulled everybody else up with him and made them give their very best."

Many critics agree with Maltin that *Mary Poppins* was the pinnacle of Walt's live-action career. The film was released in 1964, but the road he traveled to its creation was a long one, dating from the time he gave the classic children's book to his daughter Diane. She loved it, and Walt read her copy of the book in the early 1940s. Charmed by the story, he sought out P. L. Travers, *Mary Poppins*'s author, to consider the possibility of turning it into an animated film.

Brian Sibley, a British journalist, interviewed Travers on several occasions and tells the story of the rocky relationship between the Disney brothers and the strong-willed author. "Initially, of course, Walt Disney was visualizing the book in terms of animation, because that's primarily what he did. Mrs. Travers was not keen on the idea. She once said to me that she really didn't like anything about Walt Disney's filmmaking. She didn't like the shorts. She didn't like the *Silly Symphonies* series that he made. She didn't like what he did with fairy tales—she was a great stickler for the way fairy tales were originally presented. There was certainly no way that she was going to agree to an animated film being made of *Mary Poppins*.

"Later, Roy Disney went to meet Mrs. Travers when she was in New York, and he put to her the idea that maybe they could make an animated film which incorporated both animated sequences and live action. But she still said no—it wasn't for her; she just wasn't prepared to let the story go. It's quite remarkable, because Mrs. Travers was

> ✳ **Walt always had his way. . . .**
> **That was the guy. He was just irresistible.**
>
> ROY O. DISNEY

ABOVE: *P. L. Travers, author of* Mary Poppins

BELOW: *Matte artist Peter Ellenshaw created this fantastic London skyline for* Mary Poppins.

"What do you mean, problems?"

Walt did not like negative thinking. The chimney sweeps had gone through their whole routine on the rooftops while Walt and I watched. It may not look very complex, but there are a lot of effects, things like traveling mattes and all kinds of ideas that we didn't know how we were going to do at the time. At the end, I was sitting next to him when he said, "I don't see any problems here, do you Peter?" And like a fool I responded by saying that there were some problems. He questioned me, "What kind of problems?" He was really annoyed that I had made a negative remark, instead of my saying, "There are problems, which we are going to have fun solving. Golly, it's going to be great, Walt. I'm so happy." I guess my being English made me unable to do that. Someone caught a picture of Walt scowling at me, "What do you mean, problems?"

PETER ELLENSHAW

"What kind of problems?" Walt asks artist Peter Ellenshaw.

not a hugely successful British writer. She was not in a position where the money was unimportant to her. But she stuck to her guns and said no.

"But Walt was absolutely determined. He was in Britain, visiting London when one of his films was being made over there, and he went to see her. And, here, the story takes a remarkable and dramatic turn. Mrs. Travers, who may have been a formidable lady, was nevertheless susceptible to the male charms. I knew her well towards the end of her life. She loved flirting with gentlemen—in the nicest possible way, certainly in the only way that a lady of her advanced years would have flirted, but she enjoyed male company. No doubt she warmed to Walt Disney immediately. He clearly worked his charm on Mrs. Travers, because by the time the meeting had come to an end, she was prepared to discuss how the film might be made. But by this time Walt had the confidence to say it would be made only as a live-action film."

As everyone knows, of course, Walt did bring animation back into the movie, creating some of its most unforgettable sequences. Richard Sherman, who along with his brother, Robert, wrote the music for *Mary Poppins*, recalls the unforgettable day when Walt first tipped his hand, indicating to his staff that cartoons were going to find their way into the movie.

"It was like a bombshell," Sherman recalls. "We had no idea that he had any of these little things floating around in his brain. But one day I was in the middle of singing a song Bob and I had just finished called, 'Jolly Holiday.' We came to a section of the song where a quartet of waiters was going to come out and sing, 'Order what you will, there'll be no bill. It's complimentary.' I had just finished that little piece of singing for Walt, when he said, 'Hold it.'

I wondered what he was going to do; I thought he didn't like the tune or something. And then Walt said, 'Waiters always remind me of penguins. I think we should have penguins as the waiters.' That was a weird thing to say. How can you teach penguins to sing? And he replied, 'We'll animate the penguins.' Animate the penguins! That's the first time we heard anything about animation in the film. Bob and I were dumbfounded. We couldn't believe it. But then Walt said, 'We'll mix animation and live action. All the principal players will be live action, and everything else will be animation. It'll work, you'll see.'"

Creating these scenes required the development of new technologies. "Walt was always doing things that were way ahead of his time," says Dick Van Dyke, who reports that he enjoyed cavorting with cartoon characters. "These were effects I don't think anyone had ever done before."

The animated sequences in the film certainly did work, as any one of its millions of fans can attest. But, as Sibley recalls, Mrs. Travers was a bit put off. "It came to her as a rude awakening, when she arrived at the Burbank studio, to discover that the story she had entrusted to Walt Disney was not quite the story that they seemed to be making on film."

The two compromised, Walt agreeing to allow Mrs. Travers to be a consultant on the film. Her relationship with the Disney production team continued to be challenging, however. The men and women who worked with her on Walt's behalf often grew exasperated when she lectured them in schoolmarmish tones about what "her" Mary would and would not do.

ABOVE: *Animators Ollie Johnston and Frank Thomas strike a penguinlike pose.*

RIGHT AND ABOVE RIGHT: *Dick Van Dyke with some animated friends*

The animated sequences were far from the only dramatic effects in *Mary Poppins*. Peter Ellenshaw, matte artist extraordinaire, was called in to produce the backgrounds for the film—and also to work on many of its special effects, including the black smoke staircase climbed by the chimney sweeps.

Ellenshaw also helped in a lower-tech way—he contributed the steps for the chimney sweeps' dance. As he recalls, "Bill Walsh, the producer, wanted to know if I knew any dances that were popular in English pubs. And I did know one, a vulgar dance called 'Knees Up Mother Brown,' that might work. He asked if I would demonstrate, and I showed how you just dance across the floor getting your knees up high, while shouting out the words of this vulgar song. A number of men sitting in the director's room wanted to get Walt in and show him. I was too embarrassed to dance for Walt. After all, I'm an artist, not a dancer! But they insisted I show him because it was my idea.

"In comes Walt. 'Oh, do you think you could do that?' he asked. So, he and I and Don daGradi danced across the room singing 'Knees Up Mother Brown.'

"Walt liked it and got the two Sherman brothers to write the song that turned into the 'Sweeps Dance.'"

From beginning to end, the Sherman brothers seemed to be on a remarkably similar wavelength to Walt in creating their music for *Mary Poppins*. When Walt first got them involved in the project, he gave them a copy of the book and asked them what they thought. The brothers realized they would have to select specific episodes from the novel to use in the film.

Robert Sherman remembers, "Dick and I chose six chapters in the book, and, after two weeks, we went to Walt with our ideas. We pointed out the six chapters that might work, and he smiled, leaned back to get his own copy, and showed us that he had marked the same chapters. That was a wonderful feeling."

Dick Van Dyke as the old banker in Mary Poppins

Part of what makes *Mary Poppins* such a remarkable film is the marriage of story, special effects, music, and powerful performances. From the outset, Dick Van Dyke was eager to be part of the effort: "Walt had rooms of storyboards that he showed me, and his enthusiasm for the film grew as he spoke. He was like a kid, getting so excited about it that by the time I left him I was excited about it, too. He had me sold. I wanted to be a part of that movie so much. Working with Walt was one of the most serendipitous things that ever happened to me."

One role wasn't enough for Van Dyke. In addition to playing Bert, he really wanted to play the role of the senior banker, because he had always enjoyed playing old men. "I told Walt that I wanted to play the old man's part so much that I wouldn't charge him a nickel. Walt liked my screen test, but being the old horse trader that he was, he told me I had to donate $4,000 to CalArts if I wanted to play the old man. I gave him the money happily."

Julie Andrews, of course, was the ideal Mary Poppins, but the author wanted to check her out. According to Sibley, "P. L. Travers rang up Julie when she'd first been cast in the part. She reached Julie in the hospital, where she had just given birth to her daughter Emma. There was this rather abrasive voice at the other end of the receiver saying, 'Are you Julie Andrews? I hear you're going to play Mary Poppins?' 'Oh yes,' said Julie, and she was very pleased to be doing so. 'Well, speak to me,' " Travers said. 'Speak to me. I need to hear what you sound like.' So Julie said, 'Well I don't really know what to say, except that I'm delighted to be doing this and I hope I can do justice to the part.' And Mrs. Travers responded, 'Yes, yes, you'll do. You're too pretty, of course, but you've got the nose for it. You've got the nose for it.' "

Karen Dotrice, who was a child when she played Jane Banks in the film, recalls the experience of its creation as sheer wonderment. "Walt seemed to be on the set all the time. Of course, he couldn't have been, because he had other movies going on, but he was always there with Julie and Dick, making sure that everybody was happy. That was the thing—he wanted everybody to enjoy the experience. I remember his wanting me to stay natural and normal and innocent. I think this was one of the gifts he gave me, that it was okay to be innocent. You didn't have to pretend you were a grown-up. Be a kid, be silly. During the endless filming of the 'Supercalifragilistic' sequence—where we're sitting up on a post waving toffee apples around in the air and watching animated creatures that didn't exist—he suggested that for the duration of filming the sequence, the toffee apples should be different flavors every day. At the end of the day's shooting, Matthew Garber, who played Michael, and I could tell the prop people what flavor we wanted for the next day."

While they were filming, Dotrice celebrated her ninth birthday. "And the biggest cake got wheeled onto the set. Wheeled in by Uncle Walt. Everybody was singing 'Happy Birthday' and brought presents. Walt helped me cut the cake, and he made that famous face, the big beaming smile and the twinkling eyes. He really enjoyed being around the little ones."

"That's what it's all about, isn't it?"

When we were reading various stories written by Mrs. Travers, we came across the bird woman selling bread crumbs, who said, "Feed the birds—tuppence a bag." And we said to each other, "That's the metaphor for the whole film." A little extra bit of kindness—it doesn't take much. After all, a tuppence is no money at all. There's a great statement there that describes the whole picture.

Mary Poppins teaches the family how to stick together and do things for each other. I think that's why Walt loved the song. It has to do with being kind and loving. It's what his life was all about, really.

Usually, after the hectic week, Walt would ask us how we were doing, and we'd tell him what we were working on. Then he'd ask us to play it, and I'd sit down and play, and he'd look out the north window and get wistful. Then he'd turn around and say, "That's what it's all about, isn't it? Well, have a good weekend, boys." I love that memory.

RICHARD SHERMAN

Jane Darwell "feeds the birds."

TOP: *Opening night of* Mary Poppins

ABOVE: *Dick Van Dyke, Walt, and Julie Andrews at the premiere*

M*aybe the employees will now have a feeling that I know what I'm doing. Because this is a great picture.*

WALT ON *MARY POPPINS*

Throughout the filming, Walt was never satisfied. According to Leonard Maltin, nothing was ever good enough for Walt. "A sequence that might seem ready to go, Walt would think about again or an idea would spark him and he'd add on to it." But when the film was finally completed, it was a product he could be proud of. "The night of the premiere at Grauman's Chinese Theatre on Hollywood Boulevard was one of the really triumphant nights of his life. And certainly of his career. It was everything he'd hoped for and everything he'd worked so hard for."

"Yes, the premiere was a grand night," agrees Richard Sherman. "That was my very first world premiere, and it was amazing. They had the entire parking lot right next door to the Grauman's Chinese decorated. And the thing I remember most is the fact that I was so nervous I could hardly sit still when they were running the film. When the film was over, people stood up to applaud. It was an incredible, incredible response. There was cheering and applause, and it was a much deserved tribute to Walt because it was everything he knew. All of his tricks were out of the bag in this film. He did all the magical things he was famous for in one picture. It was a great tribute to Walt."

WALT AND ROY

"WALT AND ROY were about as close as two brothers could be," says Bob Thomas, author of biographies of both men. "Roy was eight and a half years older, but he was sort of Walt's guardian through Walt's early boyhood. He pushed him around the sidewalks of Chicago in a pram, and they were buddies on the farm in Marceline and delivered papers together in Kansas City. And of course, Roy was always there to advise Walt and to help him."

ABOVE: *Walt and Roy, c. 1917*

BELOW: *Lilly and Edna at Roy and Edna's wedding*

BOTTOM: *Roy, Edna, Lilly, and Walt on Waikiki Beach in Honolulu*

Their relationship was the cornerstone of one of the great entertainment empires of the century—with Walt running the creative end, Roy the business side—but at heart it was as simple as two brothers who loved, fought, and, at the end, supported each other in any way they could. "We were great pals," Walt said about their childhood together, "and anything that happened, I'd tell him. I never kept anything from Roy. If Roy had a brand-new tie, I'd wear it that day to school. I'd usually end up with chili and beans on it somewhere. Then I'd sneak home before Roy got back and take the tie off, hang it up, and when Roy'd go to put it on to go out with his girls, he'd see the chili beans on it. He used to get mad at me. But it was funny. We'd argue and fight, but we'd crawl in bed and we'd go to sleep and we'd tell each other the latest stories that we'd heard."

The brothers' closeness only strengthened over the years. Despite all the time they spent together at work, Walt and Roy socialized a great deal, especially in the early years. Their wives Lilly and Edna were good friends, and the families often traveled together. "We used to talk about the Disney disposition—kiddingly," Edna once said.

Of course, the two men were very different. Roy's son, Roy E. Disney, puts it in a nutshell: "Walt was obviously the adventurous one; Dad was the conservative one." This left Roy frequently scrambling to find the money necessary to finance Walt's latest adventure. Roy E.: "I think probably nine times out of ten, Dad's question would be, 'Where am I going to get the money to do it?' Not, 'Is that a good idea or not?' I think he really wanted his little brother to do anything he wanted to do because he recognized the power of his ideas."

Director Ken Annakin recalls Roy's desperate efforts to keep his brother's plans in the affordable range: "Roy would come into a meeting and listen and then say to me afterwards, 'Well, I know he's determined to have this, but, for goodness' sake, try to keep the cost down, because I've got to find the money and I don't want Walt to lead himself into a position where we'll go broke.'"

It helped a great deal that Roy's ego was satisfied by doing his job well. Early on, the company had been called the Disney Brothers Studio, but shortly after its founding in 1923, the company's name was changed to Walt Disney Productions. Roy realized that his brother was the genius of the company, and they both recognized that by selling the name Walt Disney they could create a product people would easily recognize. As Bob Thomas remarks, "It proved to be an extraordinarily brilliant move. Walt Disney is now a trademark known around the world, as much as Coca-Cola. It became a great asset to the company to have Walt's own name on the product."

As the years went on, Walt successfully removed himself almost entirely from the financial side of the studio. In fact, he even refused to have any formal corporate titles and left Roy to deal with shareholders and bankers. "Walt would never go on the board of directors," says Roy E. "So my dad wound up taking the brunt of that. He always conducted the shareholders' meetings, and he was always asked, 'Where is Walt?' And Dad always said, 'Well, he's awfully busy making money for you people, so you ought to be glad he's not here.'"

Of course, the inevitable tensions between the two men's outlooks led to more than one fight. Walt called them "screamers" when they became particularly voluble. The best-known of their arguments were over Roy's hesitancy to start making color cartoons; over his fear that *Snow White* would drive the studio to ruin; over his concern that shareholders wouldn't go along with the company financing Disneyland; and a particularly unpleasant confrontation in which Roy argued that shareholders might think Walt was unfairly taking advantage of his position to make money for his own company, WED.

At the height of the battle over WED—which was only resolved after months of harsh words and periods in which the two brothers barely spoke—Roy overheard his studio attorneys threatening to take legal action against Walt. Despite his personal anger, he wasn't letting anyone talk about his brother like that. "Look," he told them. "You know we are all here right now because of Walt. My God, all of this is because of Walt. Don't treat him as if he's some outsider we don't need around here."

TOP: *Elias and Flora at Roy and Edna's wedding*

CENTER: *Roy and Walt*

ABOVE: *Walt and Roy visit Marceline.*

LEFT: *Many staffers were mystified by Walt's involvement in the World's Fair.*

BELOW: *Imagineer Rolly Crump and Walt at The New York World's Fair*

THE WORLD'S FAIR

ON AUGUST 10, 1959, *The New York Times* ran a long article about the upcoming World's Fair in New York City. Walt immediately saw opportunities for his organization. But, as was often the case, his vision wasn't particularly clear to those around him.

In his journal, *Persistence of Vision*, Paul Anderson has explored Walt's involvement with the World's Fair at great length. "There were a lot of people in Walt Disney's organization and at WED who were very puzzled about why Walt wanted to be involved in a fair that was being set up nearly 3,000 miles away. After all, the staff was relatively small, and their plates were full working on Disneyland."

Marty Sklar, who had worked with Walt from the earliest days of Disneyland, was one of those people. As he now understands, "The World's Fair was, in fact, a great opportunity for Walt. He saw something that none of us realized at the time."

Dick Nunis, also a Disneyland veteran who would go on to run all the Disney company's parks, explains just what that something was: "It was very basic. Walt was testing the East-Coast market. He was also testing our creative people to see if they could compete with the world-class designers. And he was testing to see if our operations people could really run a Disneyland-type attraction on the East Coast. On a scale of 4, The New York World's Fair was 4-plus on all those points, which gave Walt a lot of confidence about going forward with Project X, which today is Walt Disney World."

Buddy Ebsen helps Walt pioneer Audio-Animatronics.

Adds Sklar, "Beyond that, Walt had the idea he could expand Disneyland by using other people's money—namely, money from the big corporations."

Paul Anderson described the process: "Walt organized a task force to solicit nearly 500 of the major companies in America to see if they were interested in having the Disney company set up an exhibit at the fair. He'd already been negotiating with a few of these companies for Disneyland, and they naturally came to see him. But for the most part, Disney sought them out."

Walt and his team ultimately created four major attractions for the World's Fair: Great Moments with Mr. Lincoln, for the state of Illinois; It's a Small World, for Pepsi-Cola; the Carousel of Progress, for General Electric; and Ford's Magic Skyway, which ran through the Ford Wonder Rotunda.

Walt was particularly excited about Audio-Animatronics—creating lifelike figures that could talk and move. He had spent a lifetime creating two-dimensional life with drawings and cameras. Audio-Animatronics represented a natural extension of that work into three dimensions. Although the World's Fair allowed him to advance the work with other people's money, Walt had been thinking in those terms since the mid-1940s, as Buddy Ebsen, a former song-and-dance man who later performed in *Davy Crockett*, remembers.

Ebsen recalls, "After I got out of the service, I needed a job. Out of the blue I got a call from Walt Disney, who invited me to his studio for lunch. He took me to a small workroom, where some folks were fiddling around a little wooden man that had wires coming out of his bottom and was connected to a wheel with cams on it. As the wheel turned, the little man's arms and legs moved. Walt looked at me and said, 'I want you to do a corny soft-shoe dance for us, which we're going to photograph.' So while they photographed me dancing they rigged the cams and wires in such a way that the little man moved as I moved. Meanwhile, Walt was off to the side showing me how he wanted me to move by doing little dance steps and telling me to repeat the steps. This became the beginning of Audio-Animatronics."

Harriet Burns

My husband remembers Harriet Burns as being meticulously groomed and always wearing some sort of apron. I recall a gracious, lovely lady who presided over the model-making workroom at WED Enterprises. My sister and I would walk through that room on our way upstairs to the meeting rooms. It was fascinating to us—like a huge, sophisticated kindergarten, where adults labored at fanciful projects. Harriet's serene loveliness belies the kind of work she's capable of doing—welding, sawing, as well as the more meticulous work, like assembling stained-glass windows.

DIANE DISNEY MILLER

Nearly two decades later, that work was to reach fruition in the form of Mr. Lincoln. Harriet Burns, one of Walt's earliest Imagineers, was given the job of creating the head of the 16th president of the United States. She remembers, "Lincoln had been Walt's childhood favorite, and he used to do imitations of him at school, for which he received some credit. I thought to myself that this project was going to get us in trouble, because people have a good idea of what Lincoln was like, and we'd be in deep stuff if we didn't get it absolutely right. With that in mind, we pulled together enough visual reference for one of our head sculptors to do a model of Lincoln, which sat on my desk as a transparent figure for about a year and a half. Walt would come in to meet with us and he would do his Lincoln imitations, showing us what he wanted Lincoln to do. He'd lift an eyebrow, and we would work on how Lincoln should lift an eyebrow. We finally got it all. The machinist got him down to well over 300 movements, which pleased Walt, even though he knew all the movements wouldn't be used. And, you know, when Lincoln was first in the show, many people thought he was an actor, not an animated character. They thought it was a human."

> **When they were doing the Lincoln show in New York for the World's Fair, I think my Dad cried every time he sat through it. Lincoln's speech was so good, and my father never felt there was anything wrong with crying.**
>
> SHARON DISNEY LUND

Audio-Animatronics figures. It's another door that's opened for us. You see, our whole forty-some-odd years here have been in the world of making inanimate things move—from a rough drawing through all kinds of little props and things. Now we're making human figures move, dimensional figures move, animal figures move through the use of electronics.

WALT DISNEY

RIGHT: *The Illinois attraction at the 1964 World's Fair*

FAR RIGHT: *The original Audio-Animatronics Abe Lincoln*

AS I WOULD NOT BE A
A MASTER THIS EXPR
RACY WHATEVER DIF
EXTENT OF TH DIFFE

TOP: *Ford's Magic Skyway*

CENTER: *"It's a Small World"*

ABOVE: *The Carousel of Progress*

Walt had spent a lifetime working for just one man—himself. Now he occasionally found himself compelled to deal with bureaucrats. He wasn't naive, of course; he was willing to jump through a certain number of hoops to sell his ideas to his corporate sponsors. Robert Sherman worked with his younger brother on the songs for It's a Small World and General Electric rides. As he recalls, "One day, Walt called us into the office and told us put on a tie and come down to Stage 2, where a piano was set up. He asked us to turn around, and he pinned something (we didn't know what) on our backs. Then he asked us to sing 'It's a Great Big Beautiful Tomorrow' for the General Electric people. He sang along with us. And then he said, 'Okay, now do it again, and this time, when you're through, I'll say a few words and then you turn around and walk off.' So we did as he directed, and the camera caught two G.E. slogans pinned on our backs."

Although Walt was willing to sell, he was not willing to sell out. Paul Anderson: "Early on in Disney's working with General Electric for the World's Fair, a vice president, whose previous experience had been in heavy machinery, had assumed the role of liaison with Disney. Walt went into a meeting to present his idea for the Carousel of Progress—the American family through the ages and through the advancement of electricity. Suddenly the vice president stood up and complained, 'What do we need this for? This is all a bunch of nostalgia. General Electric's all about progress.' A frosty silence spread over the room. Walt stood up and told the vice president that he didn't know what he was talking about. Disney had made a living out of telling stories with nostalgia. That was the Disney way. Walt stormed out of the conference and went to his legal people to see if there was any way to get out of the contract with General Electric. When the president of G.E. heard about this he immediately contacted Walt. The vice president was instructed to stay out of Walt's way."

Luckily for all concerned, the Carousel of Progress eventually moved to Disneyland to become an exceedingly popular attraction. Meanwhile, according to Marty Sklar, "General Electric had a good reason to come on strong at the World's Fair. In the late '50s and early '60s, they'd been involved in a price-fixing scandal, which created a real public relations problem. Before the fair they did surveys about the attitude of the public toward General Electric. After the fair they did another survey. The attitude toward General Electric had turned around entirely, going from negative to 85 percent positive."

For Walt's crew, however, the biggest challenge was It's a Small World. As Paul Anderson tells the story, "Less than a year before the opening of the fair, WED received a phone call from the Pepsi-Cola people, who had been searching for several years for someone to design their pavilion. They had decided the exhibit would be a tribute to UNICEF. Admiral Joe Fowler took the phone call and told me in an interview, 'My God, we looked at everything on our plate: three pavilions for the fair and all the work for Disneyland. I didn't think there was any way in the world we could do it. So I told them no.' When word got back to Walt he got really upset and said, 'I make those decisions here. Tell Pepsi I'll do it.' In under a year, Walt and his organization created It's a Small World for Pepsi-Cola, which became the quintessential Disney theme park attraction for all time."

Rolly Crump was one of the Imagineers given the task of turning Walt's confidence into reality. But when he first heard of Walt's newest project, Crump was dubious. "Walt came in one day while we were working on the Ford pavilion, General Electric, and Mr. Lincoln for the state of Illinois. He announced that there was another piece of real estate left at the World's Fair that he wanted to get. And we all stared at him. Here we were, only five of us, and here he was saying, 'I want to do a little boat ride for children.' And we thought, 'God, what's he talking about? Here we're doing Animatronic figures and he wants us to do a little boat ride?' Of course, there's a long story in how we did Small World, but we managed to open it nine months from the day Walt came in. There's never been an attraction ever designed, constructed, and installed in nine months!"

It wasn't easy. Alice Davis, wife of longtime Disney animator and Imagineer Marc Davis, was in charge of the costumes for the scores of dolls inhabiting Walt's Small World. "Walt always asked you to do something that was far beyond what you thought you were capable of doing, and he always made you surprise yourself by reaching that goal. He had a marvelous way of making you want to please him, and when you did you walked on air for a few days. We had less than one year to get the whole show together, and we had lots of problems with the dolls, like with the cancan

BELOW: *Walt enjoying It's a Small World*

Many, many years ago, I had been intrigued and amused by some goofy little wooden figures of Rolly Crump's that my brother-in-law, Bob Brown, owned. It was a real delight to meet Rolly when we were making this documentary. It was obvious that he had a great working relationship with my dad.

DIANE DISNEY MILLER

"What's-His-Name Crump"

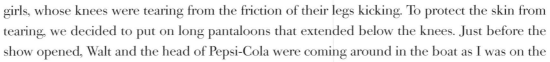

Walt sometimes had a little trouble with names. As Imagineer Rolly Crump tells the story, "When I was first hired, I went up to introduce myself to Walt. Shaking my hand, he said, 'Roland? Roland Crump?' And I said, 'Yes, sir.' And he said, 'Well, it's a pleasure having you on board.' And I said, 'It certainly is, Mr. Disney.' He said, 'No, it's Walt, and don't you forget that.' And I said, 'Okay, fine.' During my first weeks there Walt called me Roland. Then one day he he started to call me Owen. And I went along with it. (I think he called me Owen because there was a successful screenwriter named Owen Crump.) So I was Owen for a while. And then one day I became Orland—'Orland, I want you to do this.' In fact, a lot of guys I worked with still call me Orland. So I was Orland for quite a while. But the real coup de grâce came in a meeting when he referred to me as 'What's-his-name.' So I was what's-his-name that day, and then it went back to Orland, and, finally, by the time the year was out, I was Roland, and then eventually he started calling me Rolly."

Rolly and Walt

girls, whose knees were tearing from the friction of their legs kicking. To protect the skin from tearing, we decided to put on long pantaloons that extended below the knees. Just before the show opened, Walt and the head of Pepsi-Cola were coming around in the boat as I was on the

Cancan girls in pantaloons

bridge, leaving. Walt called out to me, 'Alice, how come you're putting long pantaloons on the cancan girls?' I knew he didn't want a long explanation, so I replied, 'Walt, you told me that you wanted a family show.' And with this, they both laughed, and everything was fine."

Of course, the World's Fair paid off in all the ways Walt had predicted. He proved that he could sell to an east coast audience; he brought new attractions back to Disneyland; and he got other companies to pay for his technological advancements and more.

But even if none of that had worked out, the experience would have had to have been called a success. As Sklar describes it: "The only show that drew more people was the General Motors pavilion, because they had so much greater capacity. With this exception, the Disney shows were the most popular at the World's Fair. The success vindicated his idea that people would flock to attractions that could communicate entertaining stories. We knew how to talk to people. We knew how to communicate with people. We knew how to get them excited."

The Disney family returns from Diane and Sharon's first trip to Europe, 1949.

"A JOY TO TRAVEL WITH"

SOME PEOPLE TRAVEL to get away from it all, but for Walt traveling was an adventure, an opportunity to experience new things and to talk to new people. "He studiedpeople," remembers artist and Imagineer John Hench. "When we would travel somewhere he watched people; he would really open up and observe everything."

"Walt was a very curious man," says his son-in-law Ron Miller. "He was curious about everything. Whenever he saw something he'd like to know a little bit more about, he would pursue it, ask questions. He was a great traveler, he loved seeing the country. He loved seeing history. He was a joy to travel with."

Walt frequently traveled with his brother-in-law, Bill Cottrell, who became the first president of WED. Cottrell recalled a visit to Radio City Music Hall in New York. The show was fine, but Walt was more interested in scrutinizing the machinery backstage.

Whenever Walt traveled, he gathered ideas for his work. His friend Ray Bradbury describes this tendency poetically: "When he went to museums in other countries, Walt was a jackdaw in the fields of the Lord. When he found a bright object, he'd think, 'Oh my God, that's good,' and carry it

ABOVE: *"He is great to travel with," said brother-in-law Bill Cottrell.*

LEFT: *Curious Walt*

161

✳ **One night we had dinner in Paris, and Daddy was so sure that he spoke beautiful French, and he was determined to order his dinner in French. . . . He ordered something like camel.**

SHARON

back to the studio." In the summer of 1949, for example, Walt took his family on a memorable trip to Europe, where he was working on *Treasure Island*. One afternoon, Walt returned to their Paris hotel room carrying boxes full of tiny Frenchwind-up toys. He got them going on the hotel room floor. "Look at that movement," he said enthusiastically, "with just a simple mechanism." Not so many years later, he was pioneering Audio-Animatronics. And when he visited Tivoli Gardens in Denmark he saw many things that came back into Disneyland.

Over the course of years, Walt also explored his personal history when he traveled. "For years I had been hearing about a Disney Street and a Disney Place in London," he wrote to his sister Ruth in 1965. "On this last trip we had a little extra time, and I decided one morning to go find them. Lilly went along, reluctantly, pooh-poohing the idea of looking up ancestors. We found the streets all right, and out of curiosity I asked our London office to see if they could find out how they came to be named Disney. The report came back that the streets were named Disney in 1860 or thereabouts, after a philanthropic gentleman of that surname." However, Lilly got a good laugh out of that report, because it went on to say that before they acquired the name of Disney, the streets had been known as Harrow's Dunghill.

Walt particularly enjoyed revisiting places that had been of importance to him as a young man. In 1948, when he went to the Chicago Railroad Fair with Ward Kimball, Walt took Kimball along on a nostalgic tour of Chicago. "I'd tell him that there was some jazz music playing," says Kimball, "And he would say, 'We can do that anytime. Let's go riding on the El. So we'd go where he delivered some mail when he

ABOVE: *Walt and Lilly on Disney Street in London*

RIGHT: *On a trip to Marceline, Walt and Roy recall the proper way to get over barbed wire.*

was working for the post office or something like that. Then we'd catch another train to see something else. We'd ride the elevated train half the night. He'd be looking out the window and reliving his childhood."

Walt's son-in-law Ron Miller remembers a similar incident from a trip to Paris, when the studio was filming the Fred MacMurray film *Bon Voyage.* "I was standing with Walt," says Ron, "and all of a sudden he started reminiscing, 'I remember this so well when I was a young man.' And he went over to a store down the street. I started to follow him, I don't know why, but I did. He looked in this store and he said, 'Ah, what fond memories.'"

On trips in the 1950s and early '60s Walt and Roy went to Marceline, where they enjoyed revisiting their childhood. Says Marceline resident Rush Johnson, "It was fun watching them cross the barbed wire fence. Being from the country, it's nothing to me, but it was fun to watch them climb over in their suits and ties and walk down to the cottonwood tree. They looked like they were hugging the tree, they were so happy."

A cruise through British Columbia waters in 1966 was a particularly memorable trip for Walt's family. It was the last trip the entire family would take together. Says Diane, "We had all my children from Chris down to little two-year-old Ronnie as well as Sharon, her husband Bob, and their little baby, Victoria, who was about six months old. On the trip we celebrated Tammy's birthday and ten days later my parents' wedding anniversary. It was an idyllic trip, cozy and fun, beautiful things to look at." Walt seemed to revel in his family that entire vacation. When he grew weary, he'd retire to the deck with books about city planning or universities; his mind was very much on Epcot and CalArts in those days. "Every time we would drop anchor, Bob Brown and I would get one of the crew members to lower the little motorized dinghy and we'd go salmon fishing," says Ron. "And I remember Walt kept wondering what we saw in going salmon fishing every darned time we dropped anchor. But it was just good sport. He was not a fisherman."

Walt's last trip, less than two months before he died, was to Williamsburg, Virginia, with Sharon and Bob. They had no idea he was ill, and he showed his usual fascination with all he saw. "We walked and walked," said Sharon. "He always wanted to know how things worked, how they made it profitable. He was always analyzing things. He wanted to know why they did things one way instead of another."

Walt would always take beans in cans with him, because he loved that and he couldn't get good chili and beans in London. He could get gourmet food but we'd have dinner in his suite in the hotel and later he'd get the cans of chili beans and we'd have the crackers and the whole bit.

Studio executive CARD WALKER

Card Walker

THE CITY OF THE FUTURE

THE FIRST 60 YEARS of Walt's life were dedicated to entertainment; whether in animation, live-action films, or Disneyland. But he was learning a great deal more than just how to make people laugh or cry. He was learning how to educate, how to use technology, how to deal with large crowds of people. And he was ready to start using all this information for something far more ambitious than any of his prior efforts—a city of tomorrow. He dubbed it the Experimental Prototype Community of Tomorrow: EPCOT.

"Walt wanted to try going beyond the park experience," says adviser and consultant Buzz Price. "He wanted to try improving the environment, the urban setting. He was full of ideas about what that place would be like. Epcot would not be just a park, but an urban experiment where you could try to improve the way people live, creating alternatives to our frantic, automobile existence."

"Walt was troubled by what he saw as the diminution of the neighborhood," says author Ray Bradbury about his friend Walt. "All you had to do, even 30 or 35 years ago, was to walk into Hollywood to see the destruction of the city. And he saw the coming of the mall. If the city fathers didn't know what cities were, people like Walt Disney were compelled to know."

With the help of Price, Walt settled on Florida as the place for his new project. Explains theme park executive Dick Nunis, "Florida came to the forefront very quickly for several reasons. One, it had a good tourist population: 17 million. Two, it had good transportation, and Walt loved the fact that I-4 went right through our property and the Sunshine Parkway was just to the north. Three, there was a lot of land at a reasonable price."

While Walt's plans included building a new theme park in Florida, it wasn't the idea of an East-Coast Disneyland that drove him in this direction. It was his new city that excited him the most. As he moved forward, in fact, he was prepared to leave a good deal of the studio's enterprises in the hands of others. Son-in-law Ron Miller had a number of conversations with Walt about this decision. "He was so excited about Epcot," Miller says. "Walt always looked for new challenges, and Epcot was his new and fresh challenge. He knew how huge the project was. And he once said to me, 'You know, I think I need about 15 years to conclude this project. I think we're in a position now where I can turn over the films to Bill Anderson, Jim Algar, Winston Hibler, Bill Walsh, and you. You do a good job and I have confidence in you, and I have to concentrate on Epcot.'"

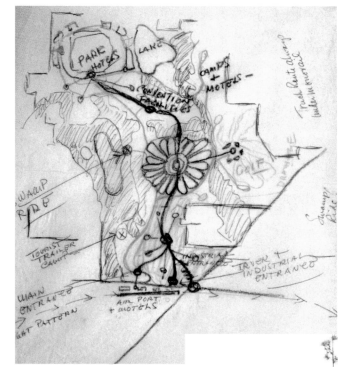

ABOVE: *Walt's own sketch for the Florida Project*

RIGHT: *Walt and Card Walker examine plans in Florida.*

Walt set about buying huge quantities of land in Florida—ultimately twice the total acreage of Manhattan Island. He had to make these purchases in secrecy to prevent the price of the land from skyrocketing. Says Dick Nunis, "In the early days the code name was Project X. When any of us would travel to Florida we never bought a ticket that would take us directly to Florida. We would go through another city to get into Florida so no one could track us back to California."

Card Walker was with Walt on a number of these trips. He remembers, "One night we were having dinner in a small restaurant and this waitress spotted Walt and came over to the table, saying, 'I think I know who you are. You're Walt Disney.' At first he denied it— 'Oh, no, I'm not Walt Disney'—but finally Walt said, 'Promise me you won't tell anybody who I am.' I think she wanted his autograph."

Naturally, businessmen in the Orlando area noticed that somebody was buying up land, and a guessing game ensued about the identity of the purchaser. Inevitably, the story got out. According to Nunis, "Walt had some members of the press at the studio for lunch. A young journalist from the *Orlando Sentinel* asked Walt lots of questions about Florida. She went back to her office and said, 'Walt Disney knew too much about Florida, and particularly central Florida. I think Disney is the one who's putting together the project down here.' At first no one believed her, but then the story broke and land prices went up immediately."

There's no way to know exactly how Epcot would have turned out if Walt had lived longer, because of his well-known pattern for changing and improving ideas as they developed. But a number of sketches survive that give some notion of his plans. Author and historian Paul Anderson has carefully studied this topic. "Walt developed a plan for Epcot that was based on radial design. (One of his Epcot planners once quipped that Walt thought that everything could

"They think you can walk on water"

Marty Sklar

✳ **Walt's first employee in Florida was a gentleman named Joe Potter. At the end of a long day of discussion, Joe said, "Walt, you know I've been in Florida for a few months now, and those people there think you can do anything. They think you can walk on water." Walt didn't say anything. He got up, walked through the door, and closed the door behind him. We could hear his footsteps going down the hall. All of a sudden we could hear the footsteps coming back. Walt opened the door and stuck his head in, saying, "I've tried that," and closed the door and left.**

MARTY SKLAR

be solved by radial design.) At the very center of the radial was a 50-acre domed-in city, the dynamic center of the city. Here's where we'd find the restaurants, the entertainment, the shops, and a 30-story, futuristic, cosmopolitan hotel.

A high-rise hotel was planned for Epcot's center.

"At the very heart of the central city we find the transportation lobby. This is where the two forms of transportation within Epcot would meet. You had the people-mover, which was a continuing service of vehicles transporting people from the city center out to the low- and high-density residential areas. And you also had the monorail, the high-speed transportation system, that took people to the entrance complex, to the airport, to the theme park. Walt once said that in Epcot the pedestrian will be king, so the plans indicate that the transportation, like the monorail or the people-mover, would be elevated one level above the walkways.

"Surrounding the dynamic city center you have the high-occupancy residential area of apartment buildings. Circling this area is a broad, expansive greenbelt, where you would find parks, churches, schools. And then radiating out from that, almost like spokes on a wheel, are the low-occupancy residential areas, the houses. These houses faced inward to a greenbelt that contained walkways, rivers, and lakes, and an elevated people-mover station to take residents into the city center. It was really a brilliant design."

Walt was eager for Epcot to be a place where America's giant corporations could try out their latest innovations on a willing populace. Marty Sklar was a recent college graduate when he started to work with Walt, at the time Disneyland opened. Less than a decade later, he was part of the inner circle working on Epcot. He recalls, "Every time Walt visited the laboratories of the great corporations—the Sarnoff labs at RCA, General Electric labs, and IBM— they would trot out all the great things they were working on for the future. He would ask them when he would be able to buy this technology, and quite often they admitted to not knowing if the public would ever be interested. So I think

this became the genesis of much of his thinking for Epcot. Walt wanted to be a middleman between the public and these big corporations, introducing technologies in a way that demonstrated how the innovations could be part of people's lives. One day he told me about how the noise from trash trucks woke him up the night before. 'Isn't there a better way to collect trash?' he asked. Ultimately that ended up with our finding a Swedish trash-collection system, which we implemented at Walt Disney World. Walt was constantly finding those kinds of things and bringing

TOP: *The Transportation Center shows the high-speed monorail and slower people-mover*

ABOVE: *City plans were based on a radial design.*

LEFT: *Residential areas surrounded the city's center.*

've always had a feeling that any time you can experiment you ought to do it. You'll never know what will come out of it. . . . When my boys come to me with an idea that sounds plausible, I try to go with them on the experiment. Because you'll never know what will happen.

WALT DISNEY

ABOVE AND RIGHT: *A 3-D model of Epcot was created for the 1998 CD-ROM* Walt Disney: An Intimate History of the Man and His Magic.

them to the public in a way that they could see, understand, touch, and live in."

Adds Imagineer John Hench, "Walt believed that the experience was most important. People could always read about ideas or see photographs of new concepts. They would find it more compelling if they went through it themselves. Once people experienced something first-hand they could go home to their own communities and make changes."

It's unlikely that Walt really considered Epcot a place for people to live over long periods of time. According to Paul Anderson, "The population of the city was really going to be sort of long-term transient. If you lived in Epcot you would need to work there, be involved in it, and participate in Epcot." Says designer Bob Gurr, "Walt was going to provide the playground where he could invite all kinds of companies to come with their products and ideas. This meant that people from different companies could be living there almost as if they were on sabbatical. We discussed at great length how you handle a community that didn't have any citizens living

Books behind Walt's desk reveal his interest in city planning.

there, how you'd handle issues like voting, for example. Walt always pointed out living in Epcot could only be on a temporary basis, say for nine months at a time, and then people would return to their regular communities. Walt figured this is how a modern community of tomorrow would evolve." Walt's fascination with this dream led him to exhaustive study. He was seldom without a book about city planning. Two of the books he studied were *Garden Cities of To-Morrow*, by Ebenezer Howard, who is considered to be the father of the city planning movement, and *The Heart of Our Cities*, by Victor Gruen.

According to Gurr, a typical workday, "was at a table scattered with drawings. Walt was at the table, sketching away with a big pencil while the rest of us were sitting around, ideas going back and forth, right and left. I vividly remember sitting next to Walt on a plane when he pointed to the center of Epcot, an oval-shaped area. Walt said, 'When this Epcot gets up and running, and we have all the participants there, this spot with a little bench is where Lilly and I are going to sit and watch.' I thought this was pretty interesting. He could see the big picture, but he could also have in mind this little detail and where his part was going to be within that little detail. And this was all done with a wave of a pencil and drawings."

Roy and Edna Disney at the opening of Walt Disney World, October 1, 1971

Walt didn't live long enough to bring any of these dreams to fruition. In fact, he passed on before ground was even broken. John Hench: "Roy Disney told me about his last visit to Walt in the hospital, when Walt was talking very excitedly about the Florida project, which Walt was envisioning on the ceiling of the hospital room. He was explaining to Roy the reason for building the theme park at the end of the road—the north/south road—and how important it was to have a kind of Disneyland located nearby because Disneyland had a reputation and an identity. He wanted people to see something familiar in Florida so that they could go on from there."

After Walt died, there was some question about whether or not to proceed with the Florida project. Roy Disney consulted with other family members and decided to move forward on his little brother's last dream. Says Roy Disney's son, Roy E. Disney, "My dad was trying to retire when Walt died. He was 73 and literally had tickets in hand for the steamer that would take him and my mother around the world. He sold the tickets and for about the last two years of the Florida project we'd kid him: 'Grandpa, you're just going to curl up your toes when this is over, aren't you?' We never expected that he would die five years later, just a few months after the opening of Walt Disney World."

RIGHT: *(from left) Joanna, Chris, Tamara, Jennifer, and Walter (in foreground)*

FAR RIGHT: *Walt and Lilly with (from left) Tamara, Walter, Joanna, and Jennifer*

LOVE AND LAUGHTER

WALT WAS A DOTING GRANDFATHER. He opened up his whole life to his grandchildren. The worlds he had created for himself—his home life with Lilly, the studio, and especially Disneyland—became the dazzling backdrops to childhood adventures that touch his grandchildren's hearts even today.

BELOW: *Walt, Diane and Ron Miller, and grandchildren Tamara (left), Joanna, and Chris, on the Mine Train through Nature's Wonderland*

BOTTOM: *Walt adjusts Joanna.*

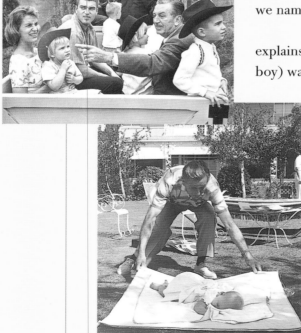

Walt's daughters, Diane and Sharon, had ten children between them, seven of whom were already born by the time Walt passed on. Diane and Sharon both remembered their father's impatience for grandchildren. "He liked to say that he identified with the king in *Cinderella*, for he, too, was looking forward to the day when he would have grandchildren," says Diane. "I must have taken his message seriously. Every time I was expecting a baby, my dad was thrilled."

According to Ron, Diane's husband, "Walt was a little disappointed that we named our first child Christopher, not Walt."

Diane resolved to make up for that with her next male child. But, as she explains, "three little granddaughters followed Chris. The day our fifth child (a boy) was born, Dad came to the hospital no more than an hour after the delivery. I heard his characteristic cough in the hall, and I called out, 'Daddy, Daddy, I'm in here.' He came in and I said, 'Daddy, his name is Walter Elias Disney Miller.'

"'You're going to put the Elias in, too?' he said with a big grin. He was really happy."

Artist Sam McKim ran into Walt the next day. "When Walt came into the studio he passed around a big box of cigars. On each cigar it said *Walter Elias Disney Miller*. Walt was beaming. He was very proud that a grandson was going to carry his name."

Walt's demanding work schedule didn't prevent him and Lilly from babysitting for their growing family. "At least one weekend a month," recalls Joanna, Diane's second child, "we'd go spend a night or a couple of nights at Granny and Grandpa's. It was always so much fun. We'd play on the lawn and around the great big pool. We'd stack up the patio furniture to make jets and rockets. And Grandpa would often be sitting there on the lawn, reading scripts, enjoying the glow of all the activity around him."

The grandchildren also spent time with Walt and Lilly at their second home in Palm Springs. Diane's fourth child, Jennifer, fondly recalls playing with the wax pencils in Walt's home office there and the "atmosphere of love and laughter" where no door was shut and everything was possible. A favorite memory involves driving with Walt on the roads near the house. At every speed bump "my grandfather would make this terrific sound—'Brrrumpph.'"

Walt's grandchildren remember hearing harsh words from him only in response to their own squabbles. One incident is still sharp in Jennifer's mind: "He must have been working, and we were really fighting and making a lot of noise. We heard him yell from the other side of the yard, and we were silenced. I just remember what a shock it was. I had never heard him yell at us before."

This bird cage entranced Walt's grandchildren.

Naturally, Walt's house offered some particularly special attractions for the children. In the home theater they watched Walt's old cartoons as well as *Fantasia*, *Mary Poppins*, and other Disney classics over and over. "I actually didn't see a movie in a public theater until I was about 11 or 12," says Joanna. The fully equipped soda fountain was also a big draw. "We'd play with that, too, and not just on movie days. He had all the syrups, and you could make yourself sodas or root-beer floats."

When Walt and Lilly babysat Diane and Ron's children, Walt would drive the children to school in the morning. A studio driver would then pick them up at school and bring them to his office. There, the children would do their homework and amuse themselves while Walt finished his work day, and then he'd drive them home.

Sam McKim recalls an encounter with Walt at a studio concession stand: "I walked up to pay the cashier and there was Walt at my elbow. He was shaking and squeezing these little raisin boxes to see how full and fresh they were. He looked over at me and said, 'You know, Sam, I have some grandkids coming up to visit me this afternoon and I always like to have something in my pockets for them.'"

"He'd bring us into his office, full of all his wonderful little things," recalls granddaughter Tamara, "and make us do our homework. We loved the little gilded wind-up bird cages. They contained miniature Audio-Animatronics birds that held our attention for countless hours. And there were miniature books and all sorts of things that little kids could put their fingers on. Afterwards, we were allowed to go view a movie. If there was spare time, we could run around the sets and live out our own little fantasies."

Chris admits that Walt's studio office wasn't an ideal environment for schoolwork: "We'd try to get our homework done, but we would be

Walt comes down to grandson Walter's level.

My brother Walter, who was then about three, was holding a camera. And as Walter took pictures, he held the camera further down, down, down. And Grandpa was crouching lower and lower to let Walter get a shot of him.

JOANNA MILLER RUNEARE

fiddling around most of the time with the stuff at hand." Sometimes Walt joined the children in their diversions. "He would have us close our eyes and take one of his grease pencils and scribble on a piece of paper. Then Grandpa would take the scribbles and turn it into a silly animal or some sort of who-knows-what."

And then there were overnights with Walt and Lilly at the little apartment over the firehouse in Disneyland. "It was like waking up in the morning and having your dream continue," says Chris. "You'd look outside just after dawn and see the empty streets of Disneyland. Maybe a fellow or two pushing a broom, someone preparing for the onslaught of the crowd. It was just a remarkably quiet, tranquil moment. It was like time standing still to view Disneyland and see absolutely nothing happening where usually there's an outrageous amount of activity."

Walt would take his grandchildren into the park after hours or in the early mornings. "That was really exciting," says Chris. "I remember Grandpa once taking us into the submarine ride while it was still being built. That was rather unique—walking among the colorful coral reefs and kelp beds without having to worry about getting wet."

Sometimes, Walt wanted to show off his grandchildren. According to Chris, "There were at least two occasions when my grandpa recruited me and my oldest sister, Joanna, to accompany him on a Disneyland Main Street parade. It was terrifying, frankly. He'd sit in the car next to us, with his arm around us for reassurance, but I was petrified, driving down the street staring at all these adoring people who were probably looking at my grandfather but seemed to be staring directly at me."

Walt was exceedingly generous to all children, but especially to his grand-children. "When I was about eight years old my grandfather gave me a red Disneyland Autopia car," recalls Chris. "It was a gas-powered miniature automobile. And he pretty much let me loose on the Disney studio lot with it. This was about as much fun as you could have. The Disney studio was like an enormous, life-size Autopia for us."

"Every Christmas was wonderful," adds Tamara. "It was quite a production. My mother tried hard not to spoil us. But my grandfather had boxes and boxes of wrapped presents—anything you can imagine. I think the one gift that had the most impact on me was a walking Mary Poppins doll. At my age, the doll was almost life-size to me. Since we all had spent so much time on the set, Mary Poppins was really a part of our family. To receive a doll that would actually walk when you led her by the hand was wonderful."

Walt's public stature and fame always came as a surprise to his young grandchildren. "From my point of view, my grandfather was doing what all grandfathers do," Chris says. To Joanna, "He was just a grandpa. Just like everyone has a grandpa."

TOP: *The fire station apartment*

CENTER: *Walt with Chris, Joanna, and Tamara*

ABOVE: *Joanna and Chris in the "little red car" with their grandpa*

✳ **In conversation, there was always eye-to-eye contact. There was always a directness with him and the feeling that, no matter how trivial, he would listen to anything a child had to say.**

TAMARA MILLER SHEER

STILL DREAMING

ONE OF THE MOST REMARKABLE aspects of Walt's final years was the hectic pace of his workday. Entering his 60s and approaching an age when many begin thinking of retirement, Walt worked as if he were just getting started.

"A typical day in the 1960s would start around 8:30, when Walt arrived," recalls his secretary, Lucille Martin. "He would look at his mail—it would be open on his desk—and answer letters and then read scripts (he had a stack of scripts on the table beside his desk). Meetings would be scheduled throughout the day, and in his outbox would be a stack of photographs to autograph for any of his guests. He would break for lunch about 12:00 or 12:30, and he usually had guests for lunch.

"To remind him not to spend too much time chatting with his guests before heading for the commissary, it was a little ritual of mine to ring a big ship's bell on his desk when it was time to leave for lunch. After lunch, he would always look at film dailies and have story meetings. So he was out of the office for several hours during the day. When he'd come back in the afternoon, it was to more mail, more letters, more phone calls.

"Then, at the end of his workday, he would ask us to call Hazel George, the nurse, and she would come up and give him a massage. Afterwards, he would always shower and change clothes and be fresh to go home to Mrs. Disney."

The list of Walt's projects during this period is staggering. There really seemed to be no boundaries to his interests or energy, and one project often inspired another. In addition to Epcot, his city of tomorrow, Walt worked on the 1960 Olympics in Squaw Valley, California; the 1964-1965 New York World's Fair; many ongoing film productions, including *Mary Poppins* and *The Jungle Book*; and a number of other undertakings, some of which have faded from public memory with the passage of time.

One small (by Disney standards) project with a particularly personal appeal for Walt was based in Marceline, Missouri, where he had lived as a young boy. Here, Walt intended to re-create the American farm as it was at the beginning of the 20th century. It was an idealized vision that was to

Lilly and Walt at the 1961 Olympic Winter Games in Squaw Valley, California

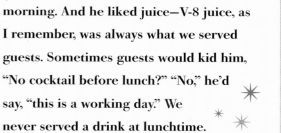
He always had a cup of coffee in the morning. And he liked juice—V-8 juice, as I remember, was always what we served guests. Sometimes guests would kid him, "No cocktail before lunch?" "No," he'd say, "this is a working day." We never served a drink at lunchtime.

Walt's secretary, LUCILLE MARTIN

Walt's scripts were spread out on a counter behind his desk.

ABOVE: *Walt and Roy in front of one of their childhood homes in Marceline, Missouri*

BELOW: *One of Walt's unfulfilled plans involved a ski resort at Mineral King.*

include hayrides, baby farm animals, period farm buildings and lodgings (but with modern conveniences like indoor plumbing), and a swimming pool made to look like a pond. Walt bought large tracts of land in Marceline, including his family's old farm—and planned to market it as a tourist destination. Rush Johnson, a Marceline resident, was involved in the project's conception and recalls Walt's confidence in its appeal. He explains, "Walt said, 'Rush, when I set my rear end on that table on Sunday night and introduce "Disney's Wonderful World of Color," I'll say, "Folks, by the way, when you're on vacation in the Midwest, go by my hometown and visit. You'll be really surprised at what you see."' Then he said, 'What are you gonna do with all the people when they get here, Rush?'"

Walt never really got the Marceline project off the ground, and, after he died, enthusiasm for the venture faded. Now, nearly 40 years later, Marceline officials are once again working to create historical attractions in their community.

Another project on Walt's mind during this period was called Mineral King. Explains Disney historian, Paul Anderson, "In 1958, when he was making *Third Man on the Mountain* in Switzerland, his interest in winter sports was rejuvenated. He spent that trip in Switzerland questioning everybody at the ski resort—the lift operators, the resort owners, the restaurant people, the hotel people—learning anything and everything he could about how ski resorts were run. Nothing really came of this until 1965, when the United States Forest Service put Mineral King Valley in the Sierras out for bid for development of a winter ski resort.

"Walt really wanted to do with the ski resort what he had done for the theme park—to make it something special for the whole family. He was very concerned to offer not just skiing but also activities in all price ranges for the whole family. He had plans for cave exploring, canoeing, wilderness lectures by Donald Duck, dances on top of the mountain, and even an Audio-Animatronics show that eventually became the Country Bear Jamboree attraction in Walt Disney World."

Typically, when Walt told people about his concept, they were immediately brought on board. Recalls artist Floyd Norman, "I was lucky enough to hear Walt make the pitch for Mineral King, and I thought it was a fabulous idea. He always made a project seem so great and exciting that you couldn't wait to get started on it. You really wanted his dream to come true. This pitch was filled with that kind of enthusiasm and the feeling that he really believed he could make it work. And you believed it, too."

174

Still, Walt's effort to get his bid accepted was an uphill battle, and victory or defeat appeared to rest on political connections. But with the involvement of Senator Robert F. Kennedy—and his insistence that the decision be based exclusively on merit—Walt won out. "In December of 1965," relates Anderson, "Walt and Roy got an early Christmas present—the award of the Mineral King ski proposal. Unfortunately, following Walt's passing, the Sierra Club and its political allies, not fans of Disney from an American cultural standpoint to begin with, were able to shut the project down with their opposition to a proposed road through a national park."

ABOVE: *Walt reviews plans for CalArts.*

Walt's enduring successes naturally overshadow his failures. One such success is the California Institute of the Arts, or CalArts. This was an idea to which Walt was deeply committed. It dates to the late 1930s, when Walt first explored ways to provide better training for his artists. Ambitious but short of funds, Walt appealed to Mrs. Chouinard of the Chouinard Art Institute, who generously agreed to provide art instruction to the Disney animators on the understanding that payment would be made in the future. The arrangement was a great success for Disney, and, with the studio's success, the Chouinard Art Institute was repaid in full. In the 1960s, however, the Chouinard Art Institute ran into financial troubles. Walt helped out, but an idea began to form that was far more grand than simply keeping Chouinard going.

He had been thinking of a new way to teach the arts—a multidisciplinary approach that would combine dance, music, art, theater, and film. Recalls animation great Chuck Jones (whom Walt selected to be on CalArts' first

Mrs. Richard Von Hagen
and
Mr. Walt Disney
on behalf of the
Board of Trustees of
The California Institute
of the Arts
cordially invite you to attend
the World Premiere of
"MARY POPPINS"
starring
Julie Andrews
and
Dick Van Dyke
and a presentation of
"THE CAL ARTS STORY"

GRAUMAN'S CHINESE
THEATRE
6925 Hollywood Blvd.
Thursday, August 27, 1964
8:30 P. M.

R. S. V. P.   BLACK TIE

One Job Worth Having

Chuck Jones

Chuck Jones became famous for his work at Warner Brothers. But he spent a brief time working for Walt Disney. Walt respected his work sufficiently to ask him to serve as a member of the board of CalArts. Jones tells the story of his last conversation with Walt during his brief tenure as his employee:

"He asked me to come in and talk to him, which I did, and he said, 'Well, why are you leaving? Don't you enjoy it here?' I said, 'Yes.' But I added, 'Actually, there's only one job here worth having, and that's yours.' And he said, 'That's true, all right. . . . Unfortunately, it's filled.'"

Alice and Marc Davis

board of directors), "Walt thought that a great art college would be one where people from the various branches would be able to observe other people at work. He said it would be a great thing if ananimator could happen by a musician playing a fiddle. He could stand there and watch the musician for a while—study his positions, the way he puts the handkerchief over his shoulder and so on—and sketch him playing. And the musician could learn whatever it is the animator is trying to find out about musical instruments."

Walt envisioned an atmosphere of constant overlap and collaboration between dancers, artists, animators, musicians, and filmmakers. Recalls Alice Davis, skilled costume designer and wife of Imagineer and animator Marc Davis, "Walt wanted to have closed-circuit television in the school, so the students who were studying fine arts or illustration could watch and draw the dance students as they performed. He was going to have an art gallery where students could put up their work for sale to help pay their tuition or pay their rent. He'd have the costume design students and the garment students all working together and learning their trade while they were at school. He had great plans of Picasso spending the summer at the school and giving classes for the students, and he also wanted to come and teach himself."

To put his idea into motion, Walt formed a small board. One of its first acts was the merger of the Chouinard Art Institute and the Los Angeles Conservatory of Music. Buzz Price, a longtime Disney consultant and a founding CalArts board member, recalls the first steps: "Walt never missed a board meeting. We had them every month. And he carefully added people who would help him get it done. Slowly but surely we began to evolve a solid support structure of people who were interested in seeing it happen. But it was a long struggle to prove his point."

Walt's commitment to CalArts was not just in providing ideas. In his will, he arranged to have fully half his estate go to the new institution.

WALT DISNEY... 1901-1966

BASSET
SCRIPPS-HOWARD
NEWSPAPERS

WALT'S DEATH

WALT'S DEATH, ON DECEMBER 15, 1966, shocked the world. To millions of fans, a world without Walt Disney was unimaginable. Only a couple of months earlier, even his immediate family had no idea that they were going to lose him so soon. In the beginning of his last year, he served as the grand marshal of the Tournament of Roses parade, and the months that followed were as jammed with activity as ever. Plans for CalArts and Mineral King, *The Jungle Book*, *The Happiest Millionaire*, Epcot, and new Disneyland attractions continued to unfold.

At the end of October, the Miller family declined an invitation to join Walt, Lilly, Sharon, and Bob Brown on a trip to Williamsburg. As Diane remembers, "We said 'No. We can't go. It's Halloween. The kids love Halloween and they wouldn't miss it for anything, not even for a trip with Grandpa.' It seems short-sighted now."

Diane tells the story of the last few months of Walt's life:

"He was going to have surgery on the back of his neck. That was it. They were going to fix a problem caused by an old polo injury. And in routine, pre-surgery X-rays, they found

something on his lung. I first learned of it when my mother came to my door one morning in our home in Encino. Usually she'd call; we'd talk on the phone every day of my life. And here she was at my kitchen door. She said, 'They took an X-ray of your father's lung, and they found a lump the size of a walnut.' I don't remember what was said after that, but the implications were pretty clear. The night before his surgery, Dad had driven up to our house and visited for a while and then he drove down the driveway and stopped at the level area at the bottom of the hill. Ron remembers seeing him sitting there in his car for some time, just watching.

"On the day of the operation, we were all sitting in the room when the surgeon came in after the surgery and said, 'Well, it was just as I suspected. The tumor had metastasized—I give him six months to two years.' Of course, it was like dropping a bomb in the room. Mother was really in a state of denial, and I was shocked. He was in the hospital for some time and had cobalt treatments until he got too weak for the cobalt. He came out briefly and Mother took him to Palm Springs. Then I got a call from her. She said, 'We can't stay down here. He's in too much pain; I can't take care of him.' So they came home, and he went right back into the hospital and he never came out.

"To me, the most poignant story from this time was his last visit to the studio lot the day before they left for Palm Springs. I picture him going around the lot and looking at this place that he had built—seeing the people that he'd brought along and with whom he'd done all these amazing things, and knowing he had to leave it all behind.

"Ironically, he celebrated his birthday—the fifth of December—in the hospital. It was getting close to Christmas. I wanted to bring in a tree, and I thought they wouldn't let me. The last day of his life I didn't go to the hospital. I decided to go Christmas shopping. I guess I was playing a little game of my own. I would say to the salesman, 'My father has been ill and he's lost a lot of weight. I need a nice cashmere sweater. . . . ' And I bought some things and I went home and my mother called and she said, 'Oh, Walt was so wonderful today. He was so strong, I know he's going to get better. When he pulled me down to kiss me, his arm was so strong around me, I felt such strength in his arm and his hands.'

"Next morning we got a call to say Walt's had a turn for the worse. And I knew what that meant. I got in the car and went down to Mother but she wasn't quite dressed. It seemed to take her forever. Everything was very slow and methodical. Even the earrings. I remember thinking, you don't need earrings today. But everything was so slow and deliberate, like, 'If I delay this for as long as I can, maybe it will never happen.'

"When we got to the hospital, I wanted to dash up there, but we had to go very slowly, slowly. As we got off the elevator on the floor and walked down the corridor, I turned and saw Ron go striding right into Dad's room and then come out with his arms up as though someone had pushed him back.

Walt was the grand marshal for the Tournament of Roses *parade, January 1, 1966.*

"When we went into the room, Dad's hands were on his chest and he was gone. Uncle Roy was standing at the foot of his bed, massaging one of Dad's feet. Just kind of caressing it. And he was talking to him. It sounded something like, 'Well, kid, this is the end I guess.' You know, that sort of thing. And I saw his love as I'd never seen it before."

Today, some 35 years after Walt's passing, his close associates still tear up when they talk about losing their boss, mentor, and friend.

Actor Buddy Ebsen: "I was driving to work from my home in Newport Beach and the radio was going. And they announced Walt's passing. Then they cut-in Julie London's voice and she sang the Mickey Mouse Club song. She did it very tenderly and with great sympathy. 'M-I-C-K-E-Y M-O-U-S-E.' I had to pull off the road because my tears were blinding my ability to drive."

Songwriter Robert Sherman: "He was up in the third floor of the animation building after a run-through of *The Happiest Millionaire*. He usually held court in the hallway afterwards for the people involved with the picture. And he started talking to them, telling them what he liked and what they should change, and then, when they were through, he turned to us and with a big smile, he said, 'Keep up the good work, boys.' And he walked to his office. That was the last we ever saw of him."

Artist Peter Ellenshaw: "I saw him coming down the long corridor. He was walking and limping, and I said, 'Gosh, you look as though you're in pain, Walt.' He said, 'No it's nothing. An old polo injury. I've got to go and have my back fixed.' Then, of course, next thing I hear, he's in the hospital, and I ask his secretary if I can go to see him. She said, 'No. No one's allowed.' So I did a painting of a smoke tree—I knew he loved smoke trees—and I said, 'I would like to take this over to him.' She said, 'No, you can't. I'll take it over.' So she took it over and gave it to him. That was my farewell gift to Walt. Months later, I would wake up crying and thinking, 'I've lost Walt.' "

A corner of Walt's office

Disneyland writer Jack Lindquist: "I never cried when my dad died. I did when Walt died."

Secretary Lucille Martin: "I never dreamed that Walt Disney would die. I didn't think they'd let him. When it happened it was just unbelievable. They closed the studio and we were supposed to go home but we couldn't go home. It was just hard to believe. It took us about a year to answer all the letters of condolence that were sent in from all over the world. There were just stacks and stacks of them. We thought we'd never answer them all. We even had temps in, assisting us. Mrs. Disney signed most of the letters; Diane also signed letters, and Sharon signed letters that came in from their friends. Answering all those letters took almost a whole year."

Friend Ray Bradbury: "The day of his memorial service, my wife answered the phone. It was CBS Radio calling. They wanted to speak with me. My wife was able to say 'Ray's not here. He's on his way to Disneyland with the children.' And this was planned months ahead. It had nothing to do with the funeral. When I came home and heard that she had been able to say that on the phone, I cried. I was so glad I had done the right thing without knowing it."

Animator Ollie Johnston: "I cried in my wife's lap."

Artist X Atencio: "The day he died, John Hench came down to my office and we sat in there and talked about it. It was so somber around there it was like a morgue. So John and I talked about Walt, until they said, 'We're closing the studio.' It was the 15th of December, and that was traditionally the day I'd go out and buy my Christmas tree. So I went home and said, 'Well, I'll take advantage of being off for the afternoon and go buy a Christmas tree.' So I did. I got home, and it was dark. And I started to cry, and I cried like a baby. It sort of hit me, because I was all by myself."

Composer Buddy Baker: "I used to have dreams of meeting him down at Smoke Tree in Palm Springs for at least five or six years after he passed on. I think all of us at the studio felt that he was still there, because I know in some of the meetings someone would say, 'Well, Walt wants this,' and Walt was long gone. To the day when I left the studio, I always felt Walt was still there."

PART 5

WALT'S LEGACY

Although Walt Disney died in 1966, his legacy lives on in many ways, some more obvious than others. On a personal level, he inspired those close to him as well as the millions of fans who remember him and who continue to feel his influence. He was the pioneer of the theme park, feature-length animated films, and nature films. He virtually invented the form of motion picture known as "family entertainment." Anyone who takes pleasure in any of these creations—whether it is a product of the Disney company or not—owes a debt to Walt.

Beyond his creations, Walt has affected millions of people in a very personal way. Recently, for example, Ralph Castaneda, Jr. wrote to the Walt Disney Family Museum, a website dedicated to Walt's life and works, "One of the things I've learned from Walt that I use in my everyday work and life is that nothing is impossible. My favorite quote from Walt is 'Actually, it's kind of fun to do the impossible.' I try to remind myself and others of this every day."

When Walt was a boy, he took art classes in Chicago. At the time, he was just another child eager to learn how to draw better. About 80 years later, Timothy Lennon, conservator of paintings at the Chicago Art Institute, wrote to Walt's daughter Diane, "From my earliest recollections, the films your father produced have been among my most wonderful and most indelible impressions. The animated features and the live-action films provided me with some of my most delightful childhood memories. It has been a further delight to take my own children to these same films, as well as to the parks, and to see and share in their enjoyment. . . . May I simply say that he has given more pleasure to more people than most artists of this century, and his place in the history of the arts is high and secure."

THOUGH THE NUMBER of Disney Company employees who knew Walt personally continues to diminish each year, his influence is still felt by many of today's cast members (as the park's employees are still called). As Joseph Titizian, a cast member at Disneyland, recently wrote to the Walt Disney Family Museum, "Even though Walt hasn't physically been in Anaheim for nearly 35 years, we all work with the feeling that his spirit is here and we are still his hosts or ambassadors to the world. We welcome guests to his park . . . the place where he spent so much time and energy, the place where he could personally invite and entertain the world. Walt lives on in our hearts and minds today, even for those of us who were born after his death."

Many artists, historians, scholars, and critics have reflected on the meaning of Walt's ongoing contributions to the world. Here are a handful who have shared their thoughts:

Paul Goldberger, internationally known architecture critic for *The New Yorker* agrees with the late architect and architectural scholar, Charles Moore, who suggested that Disneyland was one of the most important 20th-century constructions in the western hemisphere. Goldberger regards Disneyland as a model for a new kind of urbanism.

"Walt Disney realized before anybody else that, while much was gained in the sort of new suburban automobile-landscape of southern California, something critical was lost. That was the experience of urbanism—being in a public place, where you walk around, see other people, and enjoy this wonderful combination of security and surprise. Real cities might still have had surprise, but they no longer had security. And the suburbs may have had security, but no surprise. That whole element of a traditional village had just disappeared, with people going in their cars on freeways and sitting in little tracts, and not connecting in the way they once did.

"The shopping mall, town square, and entertainment zone were combined for the first time in Disneyland. This idea that you could combine a return to that experience with entertainment was pretty dazzling. How much of that success was because Walt Disney understood these things and how much was just intuitive is an open question.

"In the 46 years since Disneyland opened, we've seen the real city and the theme park become more and more alike. Cities are less necessary economically because we don't need them to do business the way we once did. By and large, cities have survived by becoming places of entertainment, which means that real cities have become more like Disneyland. I can't say this never would have happened without Disneyland, but I do see a line of descent starting with Walt Disney and going to the cities we find today."

News anchor **Walter Cronkite**, long known as "America's most trusted man," argues that Walt's creation of the feature-length animated film replaced centuries-old fairy tales in the pantheon of childhood.

"Naturally, I think of Walt Disney as a moviemaker, as well as the genius who invented the theme park, though they're both probably of equal importance. He developed the full-length animated motion picture to a point where, in this visual age, it has supplanted the old *Aesop's Fables* as a staple of childhood. The films tell fairy tales with magnificent color animation that makes them come alive and has continued to feed the imaginations of children and adults. Anyone who has ever seen these films keeps them in mind and wants to see them repeated, even as we reread the classics like Hans Christian Andersen. For me, the Mickey Mouse scene in *Fantasia*, where he acts as the Sorcerer's Apprentice and performs with the brooms, comes immediately to mind as a visual fairy tale. Walt Disney was also convinced that integrity and cleanliness of approach were necessary. None of his material could be considered dangerous to children in any way, even with the small degree of violence that appeared in them. It was of the classical fairy-tale type."

Walter Cronkite

Maurice Sendak may well be the most creative author and illustrator of children's books of the past century. His books *Where the Wild Things Are* and *In the Night Kitchen* are now classics of children's literature. He was first inspired by Disney cartoons.

"There was always a double feature—and in between each feature was a cartoon, most likely a Disney cartoon, with the emblematic opening of Mickey's humongously large head, with emanating rays, as though he was the Sun God. The sight of that tremendous head—I'm 72 now—is as vivid to me now as it was then. Its rendering, the simple colors, the black-and-white and the red tongue and yellow rays of sunlight had an extraordinary effect on me, even though I was hardly aware of graphics when I was a kid. I suspect this was the beginning of a creative process

Maurice Sendak

being conjured up inside me. And bringing to consciousness that color, shape, and line would be the most important thing in life.

"Then there was the visit to Radio City Music Hall to see *Snow White*. I remember her skirt, I remember her waist, and the puff sleeves all in soft, graded colors. And the seven dwarfs were in subtle gray-greens, gray-browns, a palette that was captivating. It's still in my work. It has been imprinted and integrated. You can find, in probably all my work, the muted palette that came from *Snow White*. I just remember the sheer beauty of the compositions. That was the best of it."

John Canemaker is an animator, author, and currently director of the animation program at New York University's Tisch School of the Arts. As one of America's most respected animation historians, he believes Walt's legacy in this field is second to none. But he also feels there's reason to lament the fact that Walt wasn't able to carry the form even further.

"It's hard to imagine the world of animation without Walt Disney. His contribution was extraordinary, actually changing the whole direction of animation in a way that probably would not have occurred without him. He was a visionary. When he saw something he liked, he just—in his words—'plussed it.' Of greatest importance, he extended the emotional borders of animation. He made animation that could compete on a social and psychological level with that of live action, possibly because he wanted to be a live-action director when he first came to Hollywood. Creative powerhouse that he was, Walt Disney transformed a lesser thing and made it into a fantastic primary thing. If he couldn't be a live-action director, he'd apply live-action principles and aesthetics to this simple, often crude art form, taking it into another level, another direction.

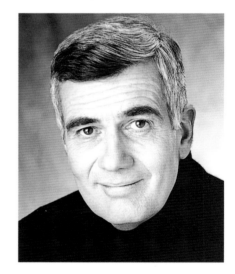

John Canemaker

"Animation takes two paths as I see it: it either announces that it is an abstraction, a cartoon, or the path takes Walt Disney's trick of saying this isn't a cartoon at all. It's real. It will make you cry as well as laugh. Both paths are valid, and both create wonderful animation. It's just that Disney did more to push the path toward believability than anybody had done until that point, and perhaps no one could have done it more powerfully and more quickly than he did.

"At the same time, he kept emphasizing that animation was a different art form. While he did apply to animation certain things from live action, he kept emphasizing in the 1930s that they should develop in animation what was unique to the medium. The fact is, much feature animation hasn't gone beyond the blueprint of *Snow White*. *Fantasia* was a way to get beyond that, and the *Silly Symphonies* were just exploring, exploring. The question is, where was he going with it?

"I believe Walt lost his consuming interest in animation as a result of the strike in 1941. That was a body blow. Maybe his diversifying after the war into other fields, including live-action films, wouldn't have occurred otherwise. Just look at the things that were never finished, like *Destino*, using [surrealist painter Salvador] Dalí's work. The great painters and poets and playwrights, musicians, and songwriters—like Stokowski and Dalí—were all coming to him. But that was discontinued, and we still haven't gotten it back."

Frank Gehry is one of the world's great architects and the designer of Disney Hall—a concert hall currently under construction in Los Angeles. Gehry looks to Walt Disney as a personal model of a man who never let the naysayers get in his way.

"People who are involved in creativity, like I am, often find ourselves pushed around by a world that doesn't understand us, because the ideas are new. And they reject you. There's a tenacity, a belief in yourself, that is required to make it through. And Walt epitomized that. He epitomized the idea that one person can make a difference. Those of us who try to do that need a few role models, and he is at the top of my list. When I'm down and low, I think of him. He was just an ordinary guy, an ordinary bloke. He wasn't a Ph.D. in history. He was just a guy from Missouri who believed in his stuff and never gave up. To me, he represented someone who, against a lot of odds, made a place in the world that was his, forever."

Leonard Maltin has written extensively about Walt's films and cartoons. His authoritative book, *The Disney Films*, has just been re-released. Maltin takes note of Walt's contribution to the world in creating the model for family entertainment.

"After making *Snow White and the Seven Dwarfs*, Walt was asked in an interview whether it was a children's film. Walt said no. The idea was to make a film that children and their parents would enjoy. He virtually defined the term *family film*, establishing a goal some have reached for ever since. This is a credo some others have foolishly forgotten, which is silly because the master laid out the plan for them years ago.

"Walt also established a studio that was based on continuity. In that sense, the company still bearing his name is unique in Hollywood. There is

Leonard Maltin

no other entertainment company that continually draws on its past the way Disney does—in literal as well as figurative ways. Today's animators still call up vintage animation drawings to study how some of the old masters at the studio accomplished what they did. Warner Brothers still does things with Bugs Bunny, but the staff is completely different. They don't have the library or archive that Disney does to draw on. There is no equivalent.

"And, of course, Walt left behind films that can still serve as a yardstick for others who want to do it right. You couldn't ask for a better role model than *Mary Poppins* when it comes to great entertainment."

John Lasseter is the creative force behind the Pixar films *Toy Story, Toy Story 2*, and *A Bug's Life*. Any number of his fans have said that Lasseter is the closest thing to Walt Disney in Hollywood today. Appropriately, Lasseter gives Walt full credit as the prime inspiration in his work.

"My mother was a high school art teacher for about 38 years, and art was all around our house, but my thing was cartoons. I used to watch cartoons on TV all the time, but my favorite thing was going to the movies whenever a Disney film came out. The Disney animated films were always special because I found the characters and the stories so engaging. You stop thinking about them as animated films or cartoons. They were stories that moved you. That's what has always inspired me about those films.

"When I was in high school I discovered a book in the library called *The Art of Animation*, by Bob Thomas. It told how they made films at the Disney studio. At that moment it dawned on me that you could do this for a living—make cartoons and make money. I said, 'OK, that's what I want to do.'

"Every Sunday night we watched Walt on television. He was such a memorable figure and seemed to embody what all the films were about. So whenever I saw a Disney animated film, in the back of my head there was always Walt.

"Because I went to the California Institute of the Arts and was taught by some great old Disney animators and artists, I started hearing the stories of Walt and realized that he was really involved in the making of all these films. It was not just his name above the title, he was in these films. I was always inspired by his drive for the story and the characters.

"I heard that Walt always believed you could take new technology to keep pushing the art form, but always in the service of the story. The story was everything. As an audience member, you walk into a theater with your popcorn and Coke, the lights dim, and within a few minutes you should be into the story. You forget about when your homework is due or whether your checkbook is balanced. You're being entertained. You want to be swept away in this world of fantasy. And that's what Walt always did so well. You didn't realize you were looking at incredible technology and incredible artistry. That's something I carry through in my work. At Pixar Animation Studios—art challenges technology. We come up with a story idea first, then we say we don't know how to do it. Well, let's figure out a way to do it using the new technology. But it's always in service of the story."

A longtime broadcaster, **Bruce DuMont** is president and founder of the Museum of Broadcast Communications in Chicago. He believes that, in addition to the wide array of quality programming Walt created for TV, he also pioneered in building an entertainment company through a variety of media.

"What companies are doing today, building upon media platforms they have in place, is what Walt Disney did in the '50s and '60s when there was this creative merger between Walt Disney and Leonard Goldenson at ABC. Walt realized he had a brand name at the motion-picture box office, which was indelibly etched in the culture. Then, along came this new thing called television, and he realized that it would be a phenomenal delivery system for his motion picture business. He also realized that the brand name could be expanded into theme parks. With the television broadcast going into millions of homes, it solidified the association with family entertainment and became the vehicle to promote the theme parks, too. I think that may make him the father of commercial synergy."

Ray Bradbury

In 1964, author **Ray Bradbury** met Walt Disney by chance at Saks Fifth Avenue in New York. They had lunch the next day and became regular companions thereafter. They shared a fascination with the future and a faith that people would behave well if they were given the proper information.

"I look upon myself as a defender of the faith. When Disneyland opened, New York intellectuals made fun of it. I made my first trip there after it had been open about eight months, and I clearly saw what makes it so extraordinary: Disneyland liberates men to their better selves. It's true. The great thing is to walk around and see smiling people. Smiles, given away. They'd like very much not to smile, but they can't help it. And in the middle of the night you wake up and you feel something tugging at the corners of you mouth. And you put your hand up and, by God, there's a smile there.

"What was Walt Disney's biggest asset? I think the totality of Walt Disney. His gift of himself to the world. Because when you drop him in a glass of water, like a Japanese flower he just expands in all directions. It's the expanse of Disney that's moved out into the world in so many different ways and has done nothing but good. You can't point to anything that's ever come about that you can consider evil. It's the total man that's a gift to our time.

"A lot of people question me about the myth that Walt Disney was frozen after he died. And I say, Walt didn't have to be frozen because he's gonna be around forever. When you walk around the studio, they talk about him as though he were still alive."